BEST *of the* BEST
COOKBOOK

the BEST RECIPES *from the* 25 BEST COOKBOOKS *of the* YEAR

RECIPES

FROM THE EDITORS OF

FOOD&**WINE**

FOOD & WINE BEST OF THE BEST VOL. 12
EDITOR **Kate Heddings**
DESIGNER **Patricia Sanchez, Nice Kern, LLC**
SENIOR EDITOR **Zoe Singer**
ASSOCIATE FOOD EDITOR **Melissa Rubel**
COPY EDITOR **Lisa Leventer**
PHOTO EDITOR **Anthony LaSala**
PRODUCTION MANAGER **Matt Carson**

FOOD & WINE MAGAZINE
S.V.P./EDITOR IN CHIEF **Dana Cowin**
CREATIVE DIRECTOR **Stephen Scoble**
MANAGING EDITOR **Mary Ellen Ward**
EXECUTIVE EDITOR **Pamela Kaufman**
EXECUTIVE FOOD EDITOR **Tina Ujlaki**
ART DIRECTOR **Courtney Waddell Eckersley**

AMERICAN EXPRESS PUBLISHING CORPORATION
PRESIDENT/C.E.O. **Ed Kelly**
S.V.P./CHIEF MARKETING OFFICER **Mark V. Stanich**
C.F.O./S.V.P., CORPORATE DEVELOPMENT & OPERATIONS **Paul B. Francis**
V.P./GENERAL MANAGERS **Frank Bland, Keith Strohmeier**
V.P., BOOKS & PRODUCTS/PUBLISHER **Marshall Corey**
DIRECTOR, BOOK PROGRAMS **Bruce Spanier**
SENIOR MARKETING MANAGER, BRANDED BOOKS **Eric Lucie**
ASSISTANT MARKETING MANAGER **Lizabeth Clark**
DIRECTOR OF FULFILLMENT & PREMIUM VALUE **Phil Black**
MANAGER OF CUSTOMER EXPERIENCE & PRODUCT DEVELOPMENT **Charles Graver**
DIRECTOR OF FINANCE **Thomas Noonan**
ASSOCIATE BUSINESS MANAGER **Desiree Bernardez**
OPERATIONS DIRECTOR (PREPRESS) **Rosalie Abatemarco Samat**
OPERATIONS DIRECTOR (MANUFACTURING) **Anthony White**

FRONT COVER
PHOTOGRAPHER **David Prince**
PROP STYLIST **Alistair Turnbull**

BACK COVER
PHOTOGRAPHERS (LEFT TO RIGHT) **Maren Caruso; Tina Rupp; Tim Turner**

INSIDE FLAP
PORTRAITS PHOTOGRAPHER **Andrew French**

ISBN 10: 1-60320-055-X
ISBN 13: 978-1-60320-055-4
ISSN 1524-2862

Published by American Express Publishing Corporation
1120 Avenue of the Americas, New York, New York 10036

Manufactured in the United States of America

BEST *of the* BEST
COOKBOOK
the BEST RECIPES *from the* 25 BEST COOKBOOKS *of the* YEAR
RECIPES

FOOD&WINE
BOOKS

American Express Publishing Corporation, New York

CONTENTS

Best of the Best Exclusives Recipe titles in **bold** are brand-new dishes appearing exclusively in *Best of the Best Cookbook Recipes.*

Best of the Best Exclusives Recipe titles in **bold** are brand-new dishes appearing exclusively in *Best of the Best Cookbook Recipes.*

RECEIPES

FOREWORD

Over the course of a year, the Test Kitchen at FOOD & WINE Magazine must go through 60 chickens, 40 pounds of potatoes and 15 pounds of sugar to evaluate all the contenders for *Best of the Best Cookbook Recipes*. Ultimately, we assess 200 new cookbooks to find the year's 25 finest; we look for the best recipes—ones that are doable, original and delicious—but we also search for books that have a unique point of view and represent the breadth of what's available.

Our list inevitably includes Italian cookbooks; this year, though, the number of Italian standouts was extraordinary. Superchef Mario Batali explores Italian grilling in his sixth book, while TV talent Giada De Laurentiis gives her fans dozens of incredibly easy, tasty and smart recipes in her fourth book. And from two authors new to the cookbook world, New York City chef Andrew Carmellini and San Francisco chef Nate Appleman, come excellent, impassioned cookbooks. Carmellini's garlicky chicken *alla griglia* and Appleman's tender braised short ribs are not to be missed.

Chefs continue to keep their recipes simple in their cookbooks, but now many of them have looked to their roots for inspiration. Miami chef Michelle Bernstein explores her Jewish-Latin background in recipes like her multi-culti chicken soup with egg noodles, dill, chiles and chayote. And Manhattan chef Sara Jenkins references a childhood spent traveling the Mediterranean in classic and creative recipes like crème caramel flavored with cardamom.

We've seen lots of retro cookbooks in the past few years, and that trend is still going strong. Sheila and Marilynn Brass, the authors of *Heirloom Baking,* published a wonderful follow-up called *Heirloom Cooking,* with dozens of delightfully old-fashioned recipes like Swedish meatballs in a sour cream sauce. And from Beatrice Ojakangas, *The Best Casserole Cookbook Ever* brings '50s classics back to the dinner table. We thoroughly enjoyed her creamy chicken Alfredo with pasta.

In this book we've reprinted the recipes exactly as they appear in their original volumes, and we've added some cooking tips and notes highlighting what we love most about each dish. Additionally, almost every author in the book has given us a never-before-published exclusive recipe. We urge you to try Bobby Flay's juicy beef skewers with his homemade sweet-and-tangy piquillo pepper steak sauce and Flo Braker's ethereal coconut cream pie in an unusual crust made from zwieback toasts.

Whether you're the kind of cook who loves the idea of adding chiles and chayote to a chicken soup or the type who prefers comfort-food classics like chicken Alfredo, we hope you'll find lots to love in this book.

Dana Cowin
Editor in Chief
FOOD & WINE Magazine

Kate Heddings
Editor
FOOD & WINE Cookbooks

SHORT RIBS ALLA GENOVESE, P. 14

A16: FOOD + WINE

by NATE APPLEMAN *and* SHELLEY LINDGREN *with* KATE LEAHY

a16 is a five-year-old Italian spot in San Francisco as well as a highway in southern Italy connecting Naples and Apulia. Before launching their restaurant, the A16 team traveled this road through the Campania countryside over and over again; the bold, rustic food and wine they discovered on those trips inspired their popular restaurant, and their lovely book. With its "less is more" approach, A16's cuisine is extremely simple for the home cook to re-create. Nate Appleman, A16's chef, expresses this clearly: "Whenever I tinker with a recipe, I find myself removing ingredients, rather than adding them." The result: short ingredient lists, clear directions and superb southern Italian food.

Published by Ten Speed Press, $35

by NATE APPLEMAN *and* SHELLEY LINDGREN *with* KATE LEAHY

Braising (long, slow cooking) makes tough cuts like short ribs very tender. Salting the ribs a day ahead of time, as Appleman does here, produces meat that's even more tender and also perfectly seasoned.

SHORT RIBS *alla* GENOVESE

SERVES 6

5 pounds short ribs (about 6 ribs total)
Kosher salt
¼ cup extra-virgin olive oil, plus more for finishing
1½ cups dry red wine
½ carrot, peeled and finely chopped
1 celery stalk, finely chopped
1 salt-packed anchovy, rinsed, filleted, and soaked and then minced
2 cloves garlic, peeled but left whole
5 black peppercorns
4 red onions, thinly sliced
3 tablespoons red wine vinegar
1 sprig rosemary

When buying short ribs, look for thicker, meatier cuts that come from the chuck end. We braise 2- to 4-rib slabs, but you also can use individual ribs cut from the slab. If you use boneless short ribs, decrease the braising time to about 1¾ hours. Avoid short ribs cross-cut for Asian preparations (they are a thinner, more sinewy, less meaty cut). Season the short ribs with salt at least a day before you prepare the dish.

Trim some of the fat from the short ribs, leaving the tough outer sinew and silver skin intact. Season the ribs evenly with about 2 tablespoons salt. Cover and refrigerate at least overnight or up to 3 days.

Preheat the oven to 275°F.

In a large Dutch oven or other heavy-bottomed pot, heat 2 tablespoons of the olive oil over medium-high heat. Working in 2 batches (so as not to crowd the pot), add the ribs and brown evenly on all sides. Transfer to a plate and set aside. Pour out the fat and check the pot for burned bits of meat. If the pan looks scorched, deglaze it with ¼ cup of water, dislodging any browned bits from the bottom. Strain the liquid through a fine-mesh sieve and taste it. If it tastes appealing, reserve it to add to the braising liquid. If not, discard it. Reserve the pot for the sauce.

Meanwhile, in a small pot, reduce the wine over medium-high heat to about ½ cup. Set aside.

To make the sauce, add the remaining 2 tablespoons olive oil to the reserved pot and heat over medium-low heat. Stir in the carrot and celery and sweat slowly, stirring occasionally, for about 5 minutes, or until the vegetables begin to soften; lower the heat if needed to prevent the vegetables from burning or browning too quickly. Stir in the anchovy, garlic, and peppercorns and continue to cook for 3 minutes, or until the garlic begins to soften. Add the onions with a pinch of salt (the short ribs have been seasoned, so go light with seasoning the vegetables) and cook, stirring occasionally, for about 5 minutes, or until the onions are soft and translucent. Stir in the vinegar and the reduced wine and remove the pot from the heat.

Return the short ribs to the pot with the rosemary sprig and cover tightly with aluminum foil or a lid. Transfer to the oven and braise for about 2½ hours, or until the short ribs are tender when pierced with a fork.

To serve, remove the rosemary sprig and transfer the ribs to a large, rimmed serving platter. Ladle the sauce on top, and drizzle with olive oil to finish. Serve immediately.

These ribs will be even better if cooled down completely, then refrigerated and served the following day. Before reheating, scrape off and discard some of the fat that has risen to the surface. To reheat, preheat the oven to 400°F. Remove the ribs from the braising liquid, bring to room temperature, place on a rimmed baking sheet, and roast in the oven for about 25 minutes, or until the outside sizzles and the inside is heated through. Heat the sauce in a medium pot over medium heat, and remove the sprig of rosemary. Place the ribs on a rimmed serving platter, ladle the sauce on top, and finish with a drizzle of olive oil.

PAIR WITH Negroamaro (Puglia)

by NATE APPLEMAN *and* SHELLEY LINDGREN *with* KATE LEAHY

Good Italian oil-packed tuna is an excellent option for this delightful salad. Try to use perfectly ripe tomatoes; their juices will help flavor the liquid that pools in the plate and soaks into the toasted bread.

TUNA CONSERVA *with* TOMATOES, CUCUMBERS, CAPERS *and* BREAD

SERVES 6

½ pound country bread or baked pizza dough

¾ cup extra-virgin olive oil

2 Persian cucumbers or 1 English (hothouse) cucumber

1 pound tomatoes, cored and quartered

1 tablespoon salt-packed capers, soaked and chopped

5 basil leaves, coarsely torn

Kosher salt

1 tablespoon red wine vinegar

¾ cup Tuna Conserva (recipe follows) or high-quality olive oil–packed tuna, drained

Not to be confused with thick Sicilian caponata made with eggplant, Neapolitan caponata originated with local sailors who tossed tomatoes and a dash of seawater with the ship's store of hardtack. We have added cucumbers and capers to this simple tomato and bread salad, using baked leftover pizza dough torn into bite-sized chunks, and accented the flavors with tuna. Toasted crusty bread also makes a fine salad, but it's worth keeping this recipe in mind when you have extra dough after a pizza-making frenzy.

Preheat the oven to 350°F.

Tear the bread into large bite-sized pieces. In a large bowl, toss the bread with about ½ cup of the olive oil, coating the bread evenly. Spread the pieces in a single layer on a rimmed baking sheet and toast for about 10 minutes, or just enough for the bread to turn slightly golden but not as crunchy as croutons. Remove from the oven and let cool.

Slice off a piece of cucumber and taste it. If the skin is bitter, peel the cucumbers. Otherwise, keep the peel. Halve the cucumbers lengthwise and remove the seeds with a spoon. Cut into chunks about the same size as the tomatoes.

Place the tomatoes and cucumbers in a large bowl, add the capers and basil, and season with a pinch of salt. Drizzle the remaining ¼ cup olive oil and the vinegar over the mixture and toss thoroughly. Add the tuna and bread and toss again just until incorporated.

Arrange the salad on a platter and serve immediately.

PAIR WITH Fiano di Avellino (Campania)

by NATE APPLEMAN *and* SHELLEY LINDGREN *with* KATE LEAHY

TUNA CONSERVA

**MAKES ABOUT 2 CUPS FLAKED
PRESERVED TUNA**

1-pound piece ahi tuna fillet
Kosher salt
½ fennel bulb, halved
½ red onion
1 celery stalk, halved
3 cloves garlic
1 lemon, halved
1 bay leaf
1 tablespoon black
    peppercorns
Generous amount of
    extra-virgin olive oil

While Naples and Bari have ready access to fresh seafood, many of the towns along the A16 autostrada are hill towns, where a regular supply of fresh seafood was once hard to come by. Resourceful home cooks solved the problem by preserving tuna in olive oil, a versatile and delicious preparation—so versatile, in fact, that it never leaves the A16 menu.

Look for ahi (yellowfin) tuna and ask the fishmonger to cut the piece with the grain. Thick pieces cut against the grain tend to flake apart as they poach. Ideally you want a piece 1½ to 2 inches thick. If the piece you buy is thin on one end and thick on the other, divide it in two and pull the thinner piece out of the poaching water the moment it is done, leaving the thicker piece in the pan.

Some recipes for tuna conserva *call for poaching the fish slowly in olive oil, but we poach our tuna in water for two reasons. First, you have more control because you can monitor the temperature of the tuna more effectively, pulling it out of the water before it overcooks. (The carryover cooking time for fish cooked in oil—how long the fish continues to cook once it is removed from the oil—is longer than for water.) Second, the olive oil retains its flavor because it is never heated.*

Season the tuna generously on all sides with salt. Cover and refrigerate for at least 2 hours but no more than 1 day.

In a medium pot, combine the fennel, onion, celery, garlic, lemon, bay leaf, and peppercorns and add water to cover by 2 inches. Bring to a simmer over medium heat, then carefully lower the tuna into the water. Adjust the heat to a gentle simmer and poach the tuna for about 8 minutes (or up to 15 minutes if using a very thick portion), or until medium-well done. It will firm up and change from red to brownish gray on the outside and to just slightly pink on the inside. Be careful not to let the water boil or the tuna will become tough. You can check on the progress by piercing the middle of the fillet with a knife and peeking at its color.

With a wire skimmer, carefully remove the tuna from the poaching liquid and place it on a plate. Discard the poaching liquid. Check the tuna for dark blood spots and skin and trim them off. Cover the tuna with a clean, damp kitchen towel and let cool to room temperature. Once the tuna is room temperature, taste a small piece. If it tastes bland, season it with more salt. Place the tuna in a container with a tight-fitting lid and add olive oil to cover completely—the smaller the container, the less oil you will need. Cover the container and refrigerate.

To use the tuna in the preceding recipe, remove a chunk from the container and scrape off the excess oil. Flake the tuna with a fork and then let it come to room temperature. Make sure the balance of the tuna is covered with oil before returning it to the refrigerator. It will keep for up to 2 weeks.

by NATE APPLEMAN *and* SHELLEY LINDGREN *with* KATE LEAHY

Appleman quickly fries salt-packed capers in olive oil until they're puffed and crispy; they're amazing with the creamy potatoes here.

ROASTED POTATOES *and* CAULIFLOWER *with* RED ONION, CAPERS *and* CHILES

SERVES 6

1 pound Yukon Gold potatoes, similar in size, cut into 1-inch pieces
Kosher salt
½ cup extra-virgin olive oil
1 head cauliflower (about 2 pounds)
⅓ cup salt-packed capers, soaked (see Editor's Note)
½ teaspoon dried chile flakes
1 red onion, sliced
3 tablespoons red wine vinegar

In this embellished version of the classic roasted potato contorno, *cauliflower florets add a crispy, sweet element to the potatoes' buttery flavor. You also can serve the dish at room temperature with a few diced pickled peppers.*

Preheat the oven to 450°F.

In a large bowl, combine the potatoes with about 1 teaspoon salt and 2 tablespoons of the olive oil and toss to coat the potatoes evenly. Transfer the potatoes to a rimmed baking sheet, spreading them in an even layer. Reserve the bowl for seasoning the cauliflower. Roast the potatoes, rotating the pan front to back about halfway through cooking, for about 40 minutes, or until cooked through and golden.

Meanwhile, remove the core of the cauliflower and separate the head into florets. Cut the largest florets in half, so that all of the florets are uniform in size. Transfer to the same bowl used to season the potatoes, add about 1 teaspoon salt and ¼ cup of the olive oil, and toss to coat the florets evenly. The florets must be generously coated with olive oil to brown evenly.

Heat a large ovenproof sauté pan over high heat. Give the cauliflower a final toss in the bowl and then transfer to the sauté pan. Using a rubber spatula, scrape any oil remaining in the bowl into the pan. Cook the florets, stirring occasionally, for about 7 minutes, or until they begin to turn golden brown on the outside but remain firm on the inside. Transfer the sauté pan to the oven and roast the florets, stirring them a few times to ensure even cooking, for about 20 minutes, or until browned but not completely soft.

EDITOR'S NOTE
Salt-packed capers (which Appleman prefers to brined) should be soaked in a few changes of cool water for 30 minutes before using. Drain them well and pat dry before frying to create crispy little "blossoms." You can use these as a garnish whenever you want to add a little salt and crunch to a dish.

While the potatoes and cauliflower roast, heat the remaining 2 tablespoons olive oil in a small pot over medium heat. Pat the capers dry with a paper towel and carefully add them to the oil (they may splatter). Fry the capers for about 2 minutes, or until they bloom and become crispy. Stir in the chile flakes and onion and cook for 3 minutes longer, or until the onion softens. Stir in the vinegar and remove from the heat.

When the potatoes and cauliflower are ready, remove from the oven and let cool slightly before combining. Then combine them in a large bowl, add the onion mixture, and toss gently until all of the ingredients are evenly distributed. Taste for seasoning and add more salt and vinegar if needed to balance the flavors. Serve hot or at room temperature.

by NATE APPLEMAN *and* SHELLEY LINDGREN *with* KATE LEAHY

Make this little chicken once and you'll never want to buy a bigger bird: It cooks quickly and evenly, so the meat is always succulent.

ROASTED YOUNG CHICKEN *with* RADISHES *and* SALSA VERDE

SERVES 6

- 3 tablespoons dried oregano
- 1 teaspoon aniseeds
- 1 teaspoon dried chile flakes
- 6 (1-pound) young chickens or 12 (8-ounce) quail, patted dry

Kosher salt

- 1 cup loosely packed fresh flat-leaf parsley leaves
- ½ teaspoon salt-packed capers, soaked
- ½ cup fresh bread crumbs, toasted
- ½ clove garlic, coarsely chopped
- ½ cup extra-virgin olive oil
- 2 tablespoons freshly squeezed lemon juice
- 1 bunch red radishes, trimmed

Known in France as poussins, *young one-pound chickens are traditionally eaten in the spring. When we can get these tasty little birds, we serve them roasted with salsa verde and a refreshing radish salad. When we cannot get them, we use quail, which are about half the size of young chickens. The simple spice rub works equally well with a regular chicken, a Cornish hen, or a pheasant. When preparing any of these birds, season them a day or two before you cook them, first with salt, then with the spice rub. If using quail for this recipe, roast the quail for 5 minutes, rotate the baking sheets front to back, and roast for about 5 minutes more, or until the juices run clear when a thigh is pierced with a fork.*

In a spice grinder or in a mortar with a pestle, grind together the oregano, aniseeds, and ½ teaspoon of the chile flakes to a powder. Season the chickens' skin and cavities with about 2 tablespoons salt, followed by the spice rub. Cover and refrigerate at least overnight or up to 2 days.

Preheat the oven to 500°F. Bring the chickens to room temperature.

Meanwhile, make the salsa verde. In a food processor or mortar, combine the parsley, capers, bread crumbs, garlic, and the remaining ½ teaspoon chile flakes. Pulse a few times, or crush with a pestle, until coarsely blended. With the processor running, or while you continue to crush the mixture with a pestle, drizzle in the olive oil. Stir in the lemon juice and a pinch of salt. Taste for seasoning and add more lemon juice and salt if needed.

continued on p. 24

by NATE APPLEMAN *and* SHELLEY LINDGREN *with* KATE LEAHY

EDITOR'S NOTE
The bright, herby salsa verde in this recipe would be terrific even with a store-bought rotisserie bird. Or make an Italian-style chicken salad by tossing chopped leftover chicken with the salsa verde; serve over dressed salad greens.

Using a mandoline or a sharp knife, carefully slice the radishes into thin slices. Toss the radishes with a pinch of salt and a couple of tablespoons of the salsa verde.

Roast the chickens on 2 rimmed baking sheets, rotating the pans front to back about halfway through cooking, for about 20 minutes, or until the birds are golden brown and the juices run clear when a thigh is pierced with a fork.

Serve the chickens on a warmed platter and spoon the radishes around the sides. Drizzle some of the salsa verde over the top of the birds. Pass the remaining sauce at the table.

PAIR WITH Carricante (Sicily)

BEST OF THE BEST EXCLUSIVE

Combining three types of pecorino gives these cheese crisps (*frico*) so much depth of flavor. Appleman serves them at his San Francisco restaurant SPQR with the sweet-and-sour sauce *agrodolce.*

GRIDDLED PECORINO
with WALNUT AGRODOLCE

SERVES 4 AS A FIRST COURSE

- 2 tablespoons golden raisins
- 3 tablespoons extra-virgin olive oil
- ½ small onion, finely chopped
- 1 bay leaf
- ½ cup dry white wine
- 1 cup walnuts, coarsely chopped
- 1 tablespoon plus 1 teaspoon red wine vinegar

Kosher salt
- 4 ounces Pecorino Romano, shredded
- 4 ounces Pecorino Toscano *fresco* or other young pecorino cheese, shredded
- 4 ounces Pecorino Toscano *stagionato* or other aged pecorino cheese, shredded

EDITOR'S NOTE

In Italy, *pecorino* refers to any sheep's-milk cheese. Pecorino Romano is a hard, slightly briny grating cheese; Pecorino Toscano *fresco* is semisoft, with a milky taste; and Pecorino Toscano *stagionato* has a nutty, herbaceous flavor and semifirm texture. Buy these varieties at a good cheese store or from zabars.com.

1 In a small bowl, cover the raisins with hot water and let stand until plumped, about 10 minutes. Drain the raisins.

2 Meanwhile, in a medium skillet, heat the olive oil. Add the onion and bay leaf and cook over moderately high heat until the onion begins to turn golden, about 5 minutes. Add the wine and cook until evaporated, about 4 minutes. Add the raisins, walnuts and 2 teaspoons of the vinegar and cook over low heat until the pan is dry, about 6 minutes; discard the bay leaf.

3 Scrape half of the walnut mixture into a food processor and puree until smooth. Scrape the puree back into the skillet. Stir in the remaining 2 teaspoons of vinegar and season the walnut *agrodolce* with salt. Keep warm.

4 In a medium bowl, toss the three cheeses together. Heat a cast-iron or nonstick griddle over moderate heat. Sprinkle the cheese in four 3-inch rounds on the hot griddle and cook until bubbling on top and light golden on the bottom, about 2 minutes. Flip the cheese rounds and cook until light golden, about 2 minutes. Transfer to warmed plates, top with the walnut *agrodolce* and serve at once.

MAKE AHEAD The walnut *agrodolce* can be refrigerated for up to 2 days. Reheat before serving.

GRILLED LAMB CHOPS
SCOTTADITA, P. 28

ITALIAN GRILL

by MARIO BATALI *with* JUDITH SUTTON

many chefs can't write recipes that work in home kitchens. Star chef Mario Batali can, flawlessly, which is why all his cookbooks, including this one (his sixth), are so good. He explores the world of Italian grilling in his own inimitable way: "What you will find here is my take on the Italian grill, just as I have always passed the world of Italian cooking through my rose-colored glasses, through my own culinary prism." By that he means reimagining classic Italian dishes so they can be cooked over fire. For instance, instead of the usual method of braising pork braciole (stuffed rolls), Batali grills his until they're perfectly charred and succulent. His recipes are exciting and very doable.

Published by Ecco, $29.95

When he's cooking lamb chops, Batali pats them with a coarse mix of lemon zest, mint, sugar and salt—an inspired combination.

GRILLED LAMB CHOPS SCOTTADITA

SERVES 6

Grated zest of 3 lemons
¼ cup coarsely chopped
    fresh mint, plus 4 whole
    sprigs for garnish
1 tablespoon sugar
Kosher salt and freshly ground
    black pepper
24 lamb rib chops
    (about 3½ pounds)
1 cup goat's-milk yogurt,
    such as Coach Farm
1 tablespoon cumin seeds,
    toasted and finely ground
    in a spice grinder

Loosely translated, scottadita *means "burn your fingers," a reflection of the fact that these little chops are so irresistible you can't wait to start eating them. We usually cook them rare or medium-rare, but don't worry if you get distracted while you're tending them on the grill—even well-done, they are delicious. Scottadita is a classic Roman dish; the cumin yogurt adds a little bit of a North African touch, a nice foil for the mint-scented chops.*

Combine two-thirds of the lemon zest (reserve the rest for garnish), the chopped mint, sugar, and 1 teaspoon each salt and pepper in a food processor and process until the mixture has the texture of coarse sand.

Rub each chop well on both sides with a little of the mint mixture. Place on a baking sheet or platter, cover, and set aside at room temperature.

Preheat a gas grill or prepare a fire in a charcoal grill.

Combine the yogurt and cumin in a small bowl, blending well. Season with salt and pepper and transfer to a small serving bowl. Set aside.

Grill the chops, turning once, until medium-rare, about 2 minutes on each side. Pile the chops on a serving platter and garnish with the reserved lemon zest and the mint sprigs. Set out the cumin yogurt next to the platter, and serve immediately.

Scallions are an underutilized ingredient; turning them into a side dish is so smart. The ends get deliciously burnt and crisp on the grill.

SCALLIONS *with* ALMOND PESTO

SERVES 6

4 bunches scallions, trimmed
    (leave about 3 inches
    of the dark green parts)
About ½ cup Almond Pesto
    (recipe follows)
2 lemons, cut into wedges
Coarse sea salt

Grilled scallions are great, but they are often treated as a mere garnish. These are very reminiscent of a Catalonian dish of overwintered leeks called calcots. *The Almond Pesto is a variation on the* romesco *sauce traditionally served with* calcots.

Preheat a gas grill or prepare a fire in a charcoal grill.

Lay the scallions over the hottest part of the grill and cook for 2 to 3 minutes, or until lightly charred on the first side. Turn and cook for 2 to 3 minutes more, until lightly charred on the second side. Transfer to a platter.

Spoon the pesto generously over the white parts of the scallions and serve hot, with the lemon wedges and coarse sea salt.

ALMOND PESTO

MAKES ABOUT 1 CUP

2 garlic cloves
1 cup packed fresh Italian
    parsley leaves
2 teaspoons fresh thyme leaves,
    preferably lemon thyme
⅓ cup toasted unblanched
    almonds
Generous pinch of kosher salt
½ cup plus 2 tablespoons
    extra-virgin olive oil
¼ cup freshly grated
    Parmigiano-Reggiano

With the motor running, drop the garlic into a food processor to chop it. Add the parsley, thyme, almonds, and salt and pulse until the herbs and nuts are coarsely chopped, then process until finely chopped. With the motor running, gradually drizzle in the oil. Transfer to a small bowl and stir in the Parmigiano.

These rolls are all about big flavor—orange, salami, pecorino, mint. They're great because you can prepare them a day before grilling.

PORK SHOULDER BRACIOLE

SERVES 6

1½   cups toasted bread crumbs
4   ounces thinly sliced salami, cut into ¼-inch-wide matchsticks
½   cup freshly grated Pecorino Romano
1   bunch mint, leaves only, finely chopped
½   cup finely chopped fresh Italian parsley
Grated zest of 3 oranges
½   cup plus 2 tablespoons olive oil
Twelve ½-inch-thick slices boneless pork shoulder (about 2½ pounds)
Kosher salt and freshly ground black pepper
2   oranges, cut into wedges

Another variation on braciole, the stuffed rolls of beef, or veal, or pork Italians like so much. The orange wedges provide the sweetness that goes so well with beautiful grilled pork. Buy the best salami you can find for this—such as my dad's (see www.salumicuredmeats.com).

Combine the bread crumbs, salami, pecorino, mint, parsley, and orange zest in a large bowl and mix well. Add ½ cup of the olive oil and mix well with your hands or a spoon. Set aside.

Cut twenty-four 10-inch-long pieces of kitchen twine. Using a meat mallet, pound the pork pieces very thin. Season on both sides with salt and pepper. Spread a thin layer of stuffing (about ⅓ cup) on each slice of meat. Starting from a long side, roll each one up like a jelly roll and tie with 2 pieces of the twine, making a little packet. Place on a plate and refrigerate until ready to cook.

Preheat a gas grill or prepare a fire in a charcoal grill.

Brush the rolls lightly with the remaining 2 tablespoons olive oil and season with salt and pepper. Place the rolls over medium-high heat and cook, turning occasionally, until deeply marked with grill marks on all sides, about 15 minutes. Turn off one burner if using a gas grill, and move the rolls to the cooler part of the grill; or move them to the cooler perimeter of a charcoal grill. Cover the grill and cook, turning occasionally, for 20 to 25 minutes, or until the internal temperature is 185° to 190°F.

Transfer the rolls to a platter and serve with the orange wedges.

EDITOR'S NOTE
This recipe calls for slicing boneless pork shoulder, then pounding the pieces. Ask your butcher to cut the pork shoulder for you, or use pork cutlets; pound them lightly ⅛ inch thick before stuffing.

If you've got meaty scallops and beautiful heirloom tomatoes, you'd be foolish not to try this dead-simple, six-ingredient recipe. Large, crunchy flakes of Maldon sea salt bring out all the flavors.

SEA SCALLOPS *alla* CAPRESE

SERVES 6

- 2 pounds mixed great heirloom tomatoes
- 24 fresh basil leaves
- 3 medium red onions, cut into 1-inch-thick slices (see Editor's Note on p. 34)
- Kosher salt and freshly ground black pepper
- 5 to 6 tablespoons extra-virgin olive oil
- 12 giant diver scallops (about 2 ounces each)
- Maldon salt or other coarse sea salt
- 1 lemon, cut in half

EDITOR'S NOTE

Batali cooks these scallops on a piastra, which is a flat stone or metal surface heated on the grill until superhot. You can use a flat cast-iron griddle or a large cast-iron pan if you don't own a piastra. Let the surface heat for 10 to 15 minutes, covered, before grilling.

Scoring the scallops before grilling makes them open up like a flower. The trick here is to cook the scallops 90 percent on the first side, until very well seared, then just give them a quick finish on the other side.

Preheat a gas grill or prepare a fire in a charcoal grill. Place a piastra on the grill to preheat.

Slice the tomatoes creatively (leave very small ones whole, or halve them) and lay out on a platter. Tear the basil leaves over the tomatoes, strewing them about. Set aside.

Season the onion slices on both sides with salt and pepper. Place them on the hot dry piastra and cook, unmoved, for 7 to 10 minutes, until well charred on the first side. Using tongs, carefully turn the slices over and cook for 7 to 10 minutes on the second side, until well charred and softened. Transfer to a plate and let cool slightly, then separate the onion slices into smaller rings and scatter them over the tomatoes. Drizzle the whole mess with 3 to 4 tablespoons of the olive oil.

continued on p. 34

EDITOR'S NOTE
Run a skewer through each onion slice before grilling: This holds the pieces together and makes them easier to turn. Use metal skewers or bamboo skewers that have been soaked in water.

While the onions cook, carve a checkerboard pattern about ¼ inch deep into one side of each scallop. Season the scallops all over with salt and pepper, toss them in a bowl with the remaining 2 tablespoons oil, and stir gently to coat.

Place the scallops on the dry clean piastra, design side down, and cook for 5 to 7 minutes, unmoved, until almost cooked—they should be opaque almost all the way through. Flip them over and sear for just 30 seconds, then remove and arrange on the tomato salad.

Sprinkle the scallops and tomatoes with Maldon salt, squeeze the lemon halves over them, and serve.

BEST OF THE BEST EXCLUSIVE

To create this intensely chickeny sauce, Batali poaches a whole bird in water, reduces the flavor-infused cooking liquid until it's really rich, then combines it with wine, tomatoes and the shredded chicken.

TAGLIATELLE *with* CHICKEN RAGÙ

SERVES 8

One 4-pound chicken
16 cups water
4 tablespoons unsalted butter
½ cup extra-virgin olive oil
4 garlic cloves, thinly sliced
2 celery ribs, finely chopped
1 onion, finely chopped
2 cups dry white wine
One 28-ounce can whole
    tomatoes, crushed
1 tablespoon fresh thyme
    leaves
Kosher salt and freshly ground pepper
1½ pounds tagliatelle or
    fettuccine
Shredded Montasio or pecorino
    cheese, for serving

EDITOR'S NOTE

Montasio is a cow's-milk cheese from Italy's Friuli–Venezia Giulia region. Nutty and fruity-tasting, it becomes sharp and granular (like Parmesan) as it ages. Aged Montasio is wonderful for grating; buy it from a good cheese store or dibruno.com.

1 In a large pot, cover the chicken with the water. Bring to a simmer and cook over moderately low heat until the chicken is cooked through, about 1 hour. Remove the chicken from the broth and let stand until cool enough to handle. Discard the chicken skin and bones and finely shred the meat. Boil the broth over high heat until reduced to 1 cup, about 1 hour.

2 In a large saucepan, melt the butter in the olive oil. Add the garlic, celery and onion and cook over moderately high heat until the vegetables start to brown, about 10 minutes. Add the wine and bring to a boil. Add the tomatoes and their juices, the 1 cup of chicken broth, the shredded chicken and the thyme. Simmer over moderately low heat until the sauce thickens slightly, about 45 minutes. Season the ragù with salt and pepper.

3 In a large pot of boiling salted water, cook the tagliatelle until al dente. Drain well and return the pasta to the pot. Add the ragù and toss over low heat until the pasta is well coated, about 2 minutes. Transfer the pasta to warm bowls, top with the Montasio cheese and serve.

MAKE AHEAD The chicken ragù can be refrigerated for up to 3 days or frozen for up to 1 month.

Michelle Bernstein
adds chile peppers to
her chicken soup.

CUISINE À LATINA

by MICHELLE BERNSTEIN *and* ANDREW FRIEDMAN

iami chef Michelle Bernstein has an unusual background: She is of Jewish and Latin descent and has studied classical French cuisine. She has also traveled throughout Mexico, South America and the Caribbean. All those influences are clear in this, her first cookbook, an eclectic mix of Latin-American recipes often inspired by Jewish, Italian, French, Spanish and even Greek traditions. She's constantly rethinking classic recipes, and her twists are always smart and delicious, whether she's adding habanero, cilantro and chayote to dill-flecked chicken noodle soup or sautéing onions, peppers, chile and bacon for her riff on bouillabaisse.

Published by Houghton Mifflin Company, $30

Linguine with clam sauce is perfect in its simplicity, but the little additions here—the crunchy fennel, fresh basil and crème fraîche—make Bernstein's unique version absolutely worth trying.

LINGUINE *and* CLAMS, MY WAY

SERVES 4

- 1 cup dry white wine
- 1 cup Chicken Stock (recipe on p. 42) or low-sodium store-bought chicken broth
- 2 pounds littleneck, middleneck, or razor clams, scrubbed
- 1 tablespoon fennel seeds
- 8 ounces linguine
- 2 tablespoons olive oil
- 4 medium garlic cloves, minced
- 2 medium shallots, minced
- ½ medium fennel bulb, trimmed and minced
- ¼ cup crème fraîche
- 1 tablespoon unsalted butter
- 1 tablespoon minced fresh flat-leaf parsley
- 1 tablespoon minced fresh basil
- ½ teaspoon grated lemon zest

Kosher salt and freshly ground pepper

Crème fraîche and fennel bring an unexpected but very logical spin to the classic linguine and clams. The crème fraîche gives the sauce a creamy, tart quality, and the fennel fits right in, balancing the garlic.

For the clams, my favorite variety is razor clams, but they can be hard to find and have a short season. Littlenecks or other small clams are fine here.

Bring a large pot of salted water to a boil.

Meanwhile, bring the wine and stock to a simmer in a large heavy saucepan over medium-high heat. Add the clams and fennel seeds, cover, and steam just until the clams open, 4 to 5 minutes. As the clams open, use tongs or a slotted spoon to transfer them to a bowl. (Discard any that have not opened after 5 minutes.)

Raise the heat under the pan to high, bring the cooking liquid to a boil, and continue to boil until slightly thickened, about 5 minutes. Line a fine-mesh strainer with cheesecloth, set it over a bowl, and strain the cooking liquid through the cheesecloth.

Shuck the clams and set aside; discard the shells.

Add the linguine to the boiling water and cook until al dente.

Meanwhile, heat the oil in a large heavy skillet over medium heat. Add the garlic and shallots and cook, stirring occasionally, until softened but not browned, about 3 minutes. Add the strained clam broth and the minced fennel and cook for 4 minutes. Raise the heat to high and swirl in the crème fraîche, butter, parsley, basil, and lemon zest.

Drain the pasta and add it to the sauce. Add the clams and toss. Season to taste with salt and pepper and toss again to coat the pasta with the sauce.

Divide the pasta among four wide shallow bowls and serve.

This is not a classic grandmother-style chicken noodle soup, but it's still fantastic comfort food. The balanced heat from the little bit of minced habanero chile is warming, not jolting.

CHICKEN SOUP *with* DILL, CHAYOTE, CHILES *and* EGG NOODLES

SERVES 4 TO 6

- 1 chicken, about 4 pounds, patted dry, cut into 6 pieces (2 legs, 2 thighs, and 2 breasts), and skin removed
- 2 large Spanish onions, minced
- 1 celery stalk, finely diced
- 1 large carrot, finely diced
- 1 bay leaf
- About 4 quarts cold Chicken Stock (recipe follows), low-sodium store-bought chicken broth, or water
- 2 cups 1-inch chunks chayote (or substitute pumpkin, calabaza, or jicama)
- 2 cups diced (medium dice) peeled sweet potato (about 1 large potato)
- 2 medium ears corn, husked and cut into ¼-inch-thick rounds
- 1 cup fresh dill
- 1 teaspoon minced habanero or jalapeño chile
- 8 ounces egg noodles
- ¼ cup chopped fresh cilantro
- Kosher salt and freshly ground pepper
- 1 lime, quartered or cut into sixths (1 wedge per person)

EDITOR'S NOTE

The small quantity of chopped habanero in this soup provides a mild, fruity warmth. Habaneros are superspicy, however, so consider wearing rubber gloves while chopping them, and wash your board and knife well afterward.

This soup began with the chicken soup my mom made for me as a kid. She used Streit's matzo ball mix, both for the matzo balls and as a flavoring agent for the broth, and she floated egg noodles in the finished broth. By the time I was an adult, I had developed a real fondness for spicy foods, so I added chiles. I kept the egg noodles, but I also added chayote. Over time, I've incorporated other ingredients, such as cilantro and corn, while keeping some of my mom's signature touches, especially the dill. It's truly the history of my palate in a bowl.

I still crave my mother's chicken soup when I have a cold, but this one is all mine.

Put the chicken, onions, celery, carrot, and bay leaf in a large pot and add cold stock or water to cover by 1 inch. Bring to a boil, then lower the heat to a low simmer and simmer until the chicken is tender, about 1 hour.

Use tongs or a slotted spoon to transfer the chicken to a plate and set aside to cool. Add the chayote, sweet potato, corn, dill, and chile to the pot and simmer until the vegetables are cooked but still a little al dente, about 20 minutes.

Shred the cooled chicken meat and return it to the pot. Stir in the egg noodles and cilantro and cook for 8 to 10 minutes, or until the noodles are tender. Season with salt and pepper. Remove the bay leaf.

Ladle the soup into four to six bowls, making sure to get a good mix of vegetables in each bowl. Serve with the wedges of lime.

continued on p. 42

MAKES ABOUT 4 QUARTS

- 1 chicken, 3 to 4 pounds, cut into 10 pieces (2 wings, 2 legs, 2 thighs, and 2 breasts, split; you can ask your butcher to do this), skin removed
- 1 medium Spanish onion, coarsely chopped
- 2 medium carrots, peeled and coarsely chopped
- 2 garlic cloves, smashed with the side of a heavy knife
- 2 celery stalks, coarsely chopped
- 1 leek, trimmed, coarsely chopped, and well rinsed
- 2 bay leaves
- 3 sprigs fresh thyme
- 3 sprigs fresh flat-leaf parsley
- 1 teaspoon black peppercorns

About 6 quarts water

CHICKEN STOCK

Put all the ingredients except the water in a large heavy pot and add enough cold water to cover by 2 inches. Bring just barely to a boil over high heat, then reduce the heat and cook at a scant simmer for about 3½ hours, skimming any scum that rises to the surface.

Use tongs or a slotted spoon to remove and discard the chicken. Strain the stock through a fine-mesh strainer set over a bowl, pressing down on the solids to extract as much liquid as possible. Cool the stock quickly by setting the bowl in a larger bowl filled halfway with ice water and stirring it occasionally (do not cool it in the refrigerator). Once the stock is cool, skim off any fat on the surface. The stock can be refrigerated in an airtight container for up to 2 days or frozen for up to 2 months.

AUTHOR'S NOTE For a more strongly flavored stock, slowly reduce the strained stock by about one-quarter, simmering, never boiling it. Then cool as instructed and refrigerate or freeze.

This gingery caponata (an Italian relish traditionally made with eggplant) has a complex flavor but is ridiculously easy to prepare.

SALMON *with* GINGER CAPONATA

SERVES 4

- 2 tablespoons extra-virgin olive oil
- 1 medium shallot, minced
- 1 tablespoon minced peeled fresh ginger
- 2 tablespoons capers, rinsed and drained
- 2 tablespoons dried currants
- 1 tablespoon finely grated lemon zest
- 1 tablespoon minced fresh flat-leaf parsley
- 1 tablespoon minced fresh mint
- 1 tablespoon minced fresh cilantro
- ¼ cup pomegranate seeds (optional)
- 1 cup plain strained yogurt, preferably Greek-style

Kosher salt and freshly ground pepper
- 2 tablespoons canola oil
- 4 salmon fillets, 6 ounces each

EDITOR'S NOTE

Tart, juicy pomegranate seeds are delicious in this recipe. To extract the seeds without staining your hands with the red juice, halve the pomegranate, submerge it in a bowl of water and then pull out the seeds under the water.

This dish came about when I decided to make a version of caponata, the Italian eggplant relish. Don't ask me why, but I had the idea to base my version on ginger, tilting the recipe toward Asia instead of the Mediterranean. The peppery ginger goes well with the traditional caponata ingredients of currants and capers. The shallot adds an almost chutney-like intensity, and if you opt to use them, pomegranate seeds contribute a vibrant tang. It is delicious with seared sea scallops as well.

Heat a small heavy saucepan over medium-low heat. Add the olive oil, then the shallot and ginger, and cook, stirring, until softened but not browned, about 3 minutes. Add the capers, currants, and lemon zest and cook, stirring constantly, for 3 minutes.

Remove the pan from the heat and gently stir in the parsley, mint, cilantro, and pomegranate seeds, if using. Pour the caponata out onto a large plate, spread it out, and let it cool to room temperature. (The caponata can be refrigerated overnight in an airtight container; let come to room temperature before serving.)

Season the yogurt with salt and pepper; set aside.

Heat the canola oil in a large heavy skillet. Season the salmon with salt and pepper, add the fillets to the pan, and sauté for 3 to 4 minutes per side until medium-rare. Remove to a plate.

To serve, spoon some yogurt into the center of each of four dinner plates. Top with a piece of seared salmon and top each fillet with a spoonful of caponata.

Most cooks choose to grill or roast chicken rather than braise it. But braised chicken thighs like these are incredibly juicy and absorb all the flavors of the tomato sauce, spiked with spicy peperoncini.

BRAISED CHICKEN THIGHS
with "PIZZA SPICES"

SERVES 4

½	cup plus 3 tablespoons olive oil
8	chicken thighs
Kosher salt	
1	cup all-purpose flour
1	medium Spanish onion, diced
2	red bell peppers, cored, seeded, and diced
1	shallot, minced
½	cup dry white wine
1	cup tomato sauce
3	large garlic cloves, minced
2	tablespoons chopped fresh flat-leaf parsley
1½	teaspoons dried oregano
1½	teaspoons crushed red pepper flakes
4	jarred peperoncini, drained
Freshly ground pepper	

EDITOR'S NOTE

If Bernstein has any leftovers from this dish, she likes to turn them into a second meal. She shreds the chicken, adds it back to the sauce, then tosses it with pasta or gnocchi.

This recipe is a prime example of the charms of braising—chicken thighs slow-cooked in a tangy, well-seasoned tomato base that becomes the sauce. It's so efficient and easy, and it's also just plain delicious. If I had to choose one recipe in this book as my favorite, this would be it.

Preheat the oven to 350°F.

Line a large plate with paper towels. Heat ½ cup of the oil in a Dutch oven or very large skillet over medium-high heat. Season the chicken thighs with salt and dredge them in the flour, shaking off any excess. Working in batches if necessary, add the thighs to the pot, skin side down, and cook until golden on both sides, about 5 minutes per side. Drain the thighs on the paper-towel-lined plate.

Pour the fat out of the pot and carefully wipe it out with a paper towel. Add the remaining 3 tablespoons oil to the pot and heat over medium heat. Add the onion, bell peppers, and shallot and cook, stirring, until softened but not browned, 3 to 4 minutes. Add the wine, bring to a simmer, and cook until reduced by half, about 4 minutes. Add the tomato sauce and cook, stirring, for 3 to 4 minutes. Add the garlic, parsley, oregano, and pepper flakes and cook, stirring, for 5 minutes.

Return the chicken to the pot, skin side up, and spoon the sauce over it. Add the peperoncini and season with salt and pepper. Cover the pot, transfer it to the oven, and braise until the chicken is cooked through, 35 to 40 minutes.

To serve, put 2 thighs on each of four dinner plates and top with some sauce.

BEST OF THE BEST EXCLUSIVE

This chicken is ultracrispy, thanks to the mix of spices in the marinade. Instead of wiping the spices off before cooking, Bernstein leaves them on the skin to add more crunch.

SERIOUSLY AWESOME FRIED CHICKEN

SERVES 6

- 1 cup tarragon leaves, coarsely chopped
- 1 tablespoon fennel seeds
- 1 tablespoon mustard seeds
- 1 tablespoon celery seeds
- 1 tablespoon kosher salt
- 1 tablespoon black peppercorns, crushed
- 1 tablespoon finely grated lemon zest
- 6 chicken wings (about 1 pound)
- 4 whole chicken legs (about 2 pounds), split
- 1 quart buttermilk

About 2 pounds solid vegetable shortening, for frying

All-purpose flour, for dredging

Honey, for serving

1 In a large bowl, combine the tarragon, fennel seeds, mustard seeds, celery seeds, salt, peppercorns and lemon zest. Add the chicken and toss until well coated. Cover and refrigerate for 2 hours. Add the buttermilk and toss to coat. Cover and refrigerate overnight.

2 Preheat the oven to 200°F. In a large cast-iron skillet, heat 1 inch of vegetable shortening over moderately high heat until a deep-fry thermometer registers 325°F. Fill a large pie plate with flour. Remove the chicken from the buttermilk, letting the excess drip off (do not wipe off the spices), and dredge in the flour until well coated. Working in batches, fry the chicken over moderate heat, turning, until the crust is golden brown and the chicken is cooked through, about 15 minutes. Transfer the chicken to paper towels to drain. Keep the fried chicken warm in the oven while you fry the remaining chicken. Transfer to plates and serve with honey for drizzling.

FLAG-RAISING MIXED-BERRY
POTPIES, P. 48

BAKING FOR ALL OCCASIONS

by FLO BRAKER

f lo Braker describes herself as "part witch" when it comes to baking. The author of four baking books and a baking teacher for over 30 years, she characterizes her working style this way: "I'm a night owl and I like to bake late, late in the night . . . the grandkids are asleep, no phones ring, no interruptions . . . just me in the kitchen." Classic homespun American desserts are what she bakes, though she gives a modern twist to her recipes now and then—by glazing a coffee cake with butterscotch, for instance. Her detailed recipes are excellent for novice bakers who might be unsure of their skills: Braker's there every step of the way.

Published by Chronicle Books, $35

These little fruit pies stand out because of the filling, a generous amount of fresh fruit mixed with instant tapioca, spices and just enough heavy cream to give the tart berries a little richness.

FLAG-RAISING MIXED-BERRY POTPIES

SERVES 6

1 recipe Cream Cheese Pastry (recipe follows)

1 tablespoon finely minced crystallized ginger (optional)

FRUIT

6 cups (about 1¾ pounds/800 grams) mixed berries such as blueberries, blackberries, and red raspberries, picked over for stems

1 to 1¼ cups (7 ounces/200 grams to 8¾ ounces/250 grams) granulated sugar, depending on the sweetness of the berries

3 tablespoons cornstarch

4 teaspoons quick-cooking (instant) tapioca

1 teaspoon ground cinnamon

½ teaspoon nutmeg, preferably freshly grated

⅛ teaspoon salt

2 tablespoons heavy cream

2 tablespoons unsalted butter, cut into 6 slices

Granulated sugar for sprinkling

Make the pastry as directed, adding the crystallized ginger, if desired, when you scatter the cheese cubes over the mixture and then pulsing just until the ingredients come together in a ball.

Divide the dough in half, shape each half into a 5-inch disk about ¾ inch thick (12½ ounces/355 grams), wrap in plastic wrap, and refrigerate until firm, about 4 hours.

Before baking

Center a rack in the oven and preheat the oven to 375°F. Place six 1-cup ramekins or custard cups each about 4 inches in diameter on a large rimmed baking sheet.

To prepare the fruit

In a large bowl, gently toss together the berries, sugar, cornstarch, tapioca, cinnamon, nutmeg, and salt. Divide the fruit mixture evenly among the ramekins. Spoon 1 teaspoon of the cream over the fruit in each ramekin, and then top with a small pat of butter.

To top the potpies

On a lightly floured work surface, roll out 1 disk of the dough about 3/16 inch thick. Using a 4½-inch round cookie or biscuit cutter (or other template), cut out circles. (You need circles that are just a bit larger than the diameter of your ramekins, so adjust the size as needed if your ramekins are a different diameter.) Set a pastry circle on top of each fruit-filled ramekin and, using

MAKES 1 POUND, 9 OUNCES (710 GRAMS) DOUGH

- 2¼ cups (10¼ ounces/290 grams) all-purpose flour
- 2 tablespoons granulated sugar
- 1 teaspoon finely grated lemon zest
- ¼ teaspoon salt
- 8 ounces (2 sticks/225 grams) cold unsalted butter, cut into ¼-inch slices
- 6 ounces (170 grams) cold cream cheese, cut into small cubes

your fingertips, gently press the pastry down into the ramekin around the edges. (The pastry doesn't need to be sealed to the edges. As the potpies bake, the pastry will appear to "melt" and "hug" the fruit.) Roll out the second dough disk and cut out circles to cover the remaining ramekins.

With a pastry brush, apply a light coating of water to the pastry on each ramekin, and then sprinkle some sugar over the top. Using a small paring knife, make a couple of slits in the center of each pastry to allow steam to escape.

Bake the potpies until the pastry is golden and the fruit is bubbly, 30 to 35 minutes. Transfer to a wire rack to cool. Serve warm or at room temperature (the fruit filling will thicken as it cools).

CREAM CHEESE PASTRY

In a food processor, combine the flour, sugar, lemon zest, and salt and pulse 3 or 4 times to blend. Scatter the butter pieces over the flour mixture. Pulse until the mixture is the consistency of cornmeal. Scatter the cream cheese cubes over the mixture and pulse just until the ingredients come together in a ball.

On a clean work surface, divide the dough in half and shape each half into a 5-inch disk about ¾ inch thick (12½ ounces/355 grams), or divide as directed in individual recipes. Wrap each disk in plastic wrap and refrigerate until firm, about 4 hours, before using.

The dough can be refrigerated for up to 3 days. For longer storage, overwrap with aluminum foil, label with the contents and date, and freeze for up to 2 weeks. Thaw in the refrigerator for 4 hours or up to overnight and then use well chilled.

These sandwich cookies are phenomenal. The chocolate shortbread is crisp and buttery, while a bit of freshly grated lemon zest in the creamy filling keeps the sweetness of the white chocolate in check.

TRUFFLEWICHES

MAKES ABOUT 20 SANDWICH COOKIES

DARK CHOCOLATE SHORTBREAD

1¾ cups (8 ounces/225 grams) all-purpose flour
¾ cup (5¼ ounces/150 grams) granulated sugar
½ cup plus 1 tablespoon (2 ounces/ 55 grams) unsweetened Dutch-processed cocoa powder
⅛ teaspoon salt
7½ ounces (1½ sticks plus 3 tablespoons/215 grams) unsalted butter, softened
1 large egg
1 teaspoon pure vanilla extract

WHITE CHOCOLATE TRUFFLE FILLING

6 ounces (170 grams) white chocolate, finely chopped
¼ cup plus 2 tablespoons (3 fluid ounces/90 milliliters) heavy cream
1 teaspoon finely grated lemon zest

In the bowl of a stand mixer fitted with the paddle attachment, combine the flour, sugar, cocoa powder, and salt and beat on the lowest speed just to blend. Stop the mixer and place the butter on top of the flour mixture. Resume mixing on the lowest speed and mix just until the mixture starts to appear lumpy. You should see small clusters that are just beginning to show signs of coming together. Stop the mixer, add the egg and vanilla, and resume mixing on the lowest speed just until the mixture is thoroughly combined.

Divide the soft dough in half and shape each half into a disk. For easier handling, loosely wrap each disk in plastic wrap and freeze for 15 minutes or refrigerate for 30 minutes.

Place 1 dough portion between 2 sheets of waxed paper and roll out into a 10-inch circle about ¼ inch thick. Repeat with the remaining dough portion. Leaving the dough circles between the sheets of waxed paper, stack them on a baking sheet and refrigerate until firm, about 2 hours. Or, wrap plastic wrap around the dough circles and baking sheet and refrigerate for up to 3 days. For longer storage, overwrap with aluminum foil, label with the contents and date, and freeze for up to 1 month. To thaw, place the dough circles, still on the pan, in the refrigerator overnight.

Before baking

Center a rack in the oven and preheat the oven to 350°F. Line 2 large baking sheets with parchment paper.

Remove 1 dough package from the refrigerator. Peel off the top sheet of waxed paper, replace it loosely on top, and flip the entire package over. Discard the second sheet of waxed paper. Using a 1½-inch round fluted cutter, cut out circles of dough as closely together as possible. Arrange them on a prepared baking sheet ½ inch apart. Reserve the scraps, if desired.

Bake the cookies until their surface is dull and their tops are close to firm when touched gently, about 10 minutes. Be careful not to overbake. Transfer the baking sheet to a wire rack and let the cookies cool on the pan for 5 minutes. Using a metal spatula, transfer the cookies to the rack to cool completely. The cookies will firm up as they cool. Repeat with the remaining dough circle and baking sheet. Then, if desired, reroll the scraps between 2 sheets of waxed paper, chill, cut out additional cookies, and bake as directed.

To make the white chocolate truffle filling

Place the chocolate in a medium bowl. In a small, heavy saucepan, bring the cream with the lemon zest just to a boil over medium-low heat. Pour the hot cream over the chocolate and let stand for about 45 seconds. Whisk together until smooth and creamy. Cover with plastic wrap, pressing it directly onto the surface, and refrigerate just until the mixture is still creamy, yet firm enough to hold its shape, 35 to 45 minutes.

On a large tray or baking sheet, turn half of the cookies bottom side up. Using an ice cream scoop about 1⅛ inches in diameter (#100), scoop the truffle filling (about 1-inch balls) onto the cookies. Top with the remaining cookies, bottom side down. Press each sandwich cookie gently to secure the truffle between the 2 cookies, leaving a gap so the truffle is still round and visible. Refrigerate any leftover filling in a sturdy covered container for up to 1 week. To use as a filling or glaze, heat it over a bowl of hot water until it is the proper consistency.

TO STORE THE COOKIES Stack unfilled cookies in an airtight container and store at room temperature for up to 10 days. Arrange sandwiched cookies in a single layer in a covered foil-lined box and store at room temperature for up to 2 days.

This cake is an outrageous riff on crowd-pleasing cinnamon buns. Instead of individual buns, Braker makes one big cake wonderfully scented with sweet spices and glazed with gooey butterscotch.

BUTTERSCOTCH SPIRAL COFFEE CAKE

MAKES ONE 9-INCH ROUND CAKE, 14 TO 16 SERVINGS

DOUGH

- 2½ to 2¾ cups (11½ to 12¼ ounces/325 to 350 grams) all-purpose flour
- ¼ cup (1¾ ounces/50 grams) granulated sugar
- 2¼ teaspoons (1 envelope) instant yeast (see Editor's Note on p. 54)
- ½ teaspoon salt
- ½ teaspoon ground cardamom
- ⅛ teaspoon nutmeg, preferably freshly grated
- ⅛ teaspoon ground cinnamon
- ⅓ cup (2½ fluid ounces/75 milliliters) whole milk
- 2 ounces (½ stick/55 grams) unsalted butter
- ¼ cup (2 fluid ounces/60 milliliters) water
- 2 large eggs, at room temperature
- 1 teaspoon pure vanilla extract

BUTTERSCOTCH GLAZE

- ½ cup firmly packed (3½ ounces/100 grams) light brown sugar
- 2 ounces (½ stick/55 grams) unsalted butter
- 2 tablespoons dark corn syrup

CINNAMON-BUTTER FILLING

- ½ teaspoon ground cinnamon
- 2 tablespoons unsalted butter, melted

Imagine a cinnamon bun large enough to feed a crowd. Here's a giant one in coffee-cake form that's simple to make. The cinnamon-butter filling and butterscotch glaze pair beautifully, and an array of spices—cardamom, nutmeg, and cinnamon—gives the yeast dough an old-time flavor. Not one sweet tooth will be disappointed. You can also spread a thin layer of apple butter, homemade or store-bought, over the cinnamon butter and then bake as directed.

To make the dough

Stir together 2 cups (9 ounces/255 grams) of the flour, the sugar, yeast, salt, cardamom, nutmeg, and cinnamon in the bowl of a stand mixer; set aside. In a small, heavy saucepan, combine the milk and butter and heat over low heat just until the butter melts. Add the water and set aside until warm (120 to 130°F), about 1 minute.

Pour the milk mixture over the flour-yeast mixture and mix well with a rubber spatula until all of the dry ingredients are moistened. Attach the bowl to the mixer, and fit the mixer with the paddle attachment. With the mixer on low speed, add the eggs, one at a time, beating after each addition until incorporated. Add the vanilla in the final moments of mixing. Stop the mixer, add ½ cup (2¼ ounces/65 grams) more flour, and resume mixing on low speed until smooth, 30 to 45 seconds. Add 2 tablespoons additional flour and resume mixing on medium speed until the dough is smooth, still soft, and slightly sticky, about 45 seconds.

continued on p. 54

Sprinkle the work surface with 1 tablespoon of the flour, and center the dough on the flour. Knead the dough gently until it is smooth and no longer sticky, adding an additional 1 to 2 tablespoons flour only if necessary to prevent stickiness. Place the dough in a large bowl, cover the bowl securely with plastic wrap, and let the dough rise in a warm place (70°F) until doubled in bulk, 45 to 60 minutes. The dough is ready when a finger gently pressed into it leaves an indentation. Meanwhile, prepare the baking pan, the glaze, and the filling.

To make the butterscotch glaze

Lightly coat a 9 by 2-inch round cake pan with nonstick spray, or butter the pan. Combine the sugar, butter, and corn syrup in a small, heavy saucepan and set over low heat until the butter is completely melted. Pour the mixture into the prepared pan and tilt the pan to cover the bottom evenly; set aside. (The glaze might thicken slightly before it's time to place the dough in the pan, but it will liquefy again as the coffee cake bakes.)

To make the cinnamon-butter filling

In a small bowl or cup, stir the cinnamon into the butter; set aside.

Before baking

Center a rack in the oven and preheat the oven to 350°F.

To assemble the coffee cake

Gently deflate the dough. On a lightly floured work surface, roll out the dough into a 16 by 12-inch rectangle. Using a pastry brush, spread the butter-cinnamon mixture evenly over the dough. Cut the dough lengthwise into six 2-inch-wide strips. (A pizza cutter is helpful here.) Loosely (so the dough has some give as it expands in the oven) roll up 1 strip and place it, cut edge up, in the center of the prepared pan on top of the glaze.

One at a time, coil the remaining dough strips around the center strip, starting each strip at the end of the previous one, to make a single large spiral. As you roll the dough strips around the coffee cake, the butter-cinnamon side of the dough strips should be facing inside. (When you finish forming the spiral, there will be plenty of space left in the pan. The spaces around the dough will fill in as the dough bakes.) Loosely cover the pan with plastic wrap and let the cake rise in a warm place until it is almost doubled in size, about 30 minutes. The dough is ready when a finger gently pressed into it leaves an indentation.

Bake the coffee cake until the top is deep golden brown, about 35 minutes. Check after 20 minutes to make sure the cake is not browning too fast. If it is, cover the top loosely with aluminum foil the last 10 to 15 minutes of baking to prevent overbrowning. Transfer to a wire rack (if you have used foil, remove it) and let cool for 10 minutes.

Gently tilt the pan and tap the sides on a counter to release the cake sides, then invert a serving plate on top of the cake, and invert the pan and the plate. Leave the pan on the cake for 1 minute, so the glaze transfers to the cake, then gently lift off the pan. Using a rubber spatula, scrape out any butterscotch syrup remaining in the pan and spread it over the warm surface of the cake.

Serve the cake warm or at room temperature, cut into wedges gently with a serrated knife. This coffee cake is best eaten the day it is baked.

To prepare this moist, lemony coffee cake, Braker layers strips of dough in a loaf pan with citrus-scented butter. Once the cake is baked, it pulls apart easily, making this dessert incredibly fun to eat.

LEMON-SCENTED PULL-APART COFFEE CAKE

MAKES ONE 9 BY 5-INCH COFFEE CAKE, ABOUT 14 SERVINGS

SWEET YEAST DOUGH
About 2¾ cups (12¼ ounces/350 grams) all-purpose flour
¼ cup (1¾ ounces/50 grams) granulated sugar
2¼ teaspoons (1 envelope) instant yeast
½ teaspoon salt
⅓ cup (2½ fluid ounces/75 milliliters) whole milk
2 ounces (½ stick/55 grams) unsalted butter
¼ cup (2 fluid ounces/60 milliliters) water
1½ teaspoons pure vanilla extract
2 large eggs, at room temperature

LEMON PASTE FILLING
½ cup (3½ ounces/100 grams) granulated sugar
3 tablespoons finely grated lemon zest (3 lemons)
1 tablespoon finely grated orange zest
2 ounces (½ stick/55 grams) unsalted butter, melted

TANGY CREAM CHEESE ICING
3 ounces (85 grams) cream cheese, softened
⅓ cup (1¼ ounces/35 grams) powdered sugar
1 tablespoon whole milk
1 tablespoon fresh lemon juice

Lemon and cream cheese have long been classic companions in American baking, and this fun-to-assemble, sweet-tart filled coffee cake makes it easy to see why. Showcasing the lively flavors of fresh citrus, the sweet, buttery filling is made with fluffy, fragrant lemon and orange zest. The warm loaf is brushed with a zippy cream cheese icing, whose tangy flavor marries marvelously with the sunny taste of citrus. Enjoy a slice of this pull-apart coffee cake whenever you need an instant pick-me-up.

To make the sweet yeast dough

Stir together 2 cups (9 ounces/255 grams) of the flour, the sugar, the yeast, and the salt in the bowl of a stand mixer; set aside. In a small saucepan, heat the milk and butter over low heat just until the butter is melted. Remove from the heat, add the water, and set aside until warm (120 to 130°F), about 1 minute. Add the vanilla extract.

Pour the milk mixture over the flour-yeast mixture and, using a rubber spatula, mix until the dry ingredients are evenly moistened. Attach the bowl to the mixer, and fit the mixer with the paddle attachment. With the mixer on low speed, add the eggs, one at a time, mixing after each addition just until incorporated. Stop the mixer, add ½ cup (2¼ ounces/65 grams) of the remaining flour, and resume mixing on low speed until the dough is smooth, 30 to 45 seconds. Add 2 more tablespoons flour and mix on medium speed until the dough is smooth, soft, and slightly sticky, about 45 seconds.

Sprinkle a work surface with 1 tablespoon flour and center the dough on the flour. Knead gently until smooth and no longer sticky, about 1 minute, adding an additional 1 to 2 tablespoons flour only if necessary to lessen the stickiness. Place the dough in a large bowl, cover the bowl securely with plastic wrap, and let the dough rise in a warm place (about 70°F) until doubled in size, 45 to 60 minutes. Press the dough gently with a fingertip. If the indentation remains, the dough is ready for the next step. While the dough is rising, make the filling.

To make the lemon paste filling

In a small bowl, mix together the sugar and the lemon and orange zests. Set the sandy-wet mixture nearby (the sugar draws out moisture from the zests to create the consistency).

Before baking

Center a rack in the oven and preheat the oven to 350°F. Lightly butter a 9 by 5 by 3-inch loaf pan. Or, lightly coat the pan with nonstick spray.

To shape the coffee cake

Gently deflate the dough. On a lightly floured work surface, roll out the dough into a 20 by 12-inch rectangle. Using a pastry brush, spread the melted butter generously over the dough. Cut the dough crosswise into 5 strips, each about 12 by 4 inches. (A pizza cutter is helpful here.) Sprinkle 1½ tablespoons of the zest-sugar mixture over one of the buttered rectangles. Top with a second rectangle and sprinkle it with 1½ tablespoons of the zest-sugar mixture. Repeat with the remaining dough rectangles and zest-sugar mixture, ending with a stack of 5 rectangles. Work carefully when adding the crumbly zest filling, or it will fall off when you have to lift the stacked pastry later.

continued on p. 58

Slice the stack crosswise through the 5 layers to create 6 equal strips, each about 4 by 2 inches. Fit these layered strips into the prepared loaf pan, cut edges up and side by side. (While there is plenty of space on either side of the 6 strips widthwise in the pan, fitting the strips lengthwise is tight. But that's fine because the spaces between the dough and the sides of the pan fill in during baking.) Loosely cover the pan with plastic wrap and let the dough rise in a warm place (70°F) until puffy and almost doubled in size, 30 to 50 minutes. Press the dough gently with a fingertip. If the indentation remains, the dough is ready for baking.

Bake the coffee cake until the top is golden brown, 30 to 35 minutes. Transfer to a wire rack and let cool in the pan for 10 to 15 minutes.

While the coffee cake bakes, make the tangy cream cheese icing

In a medium bowl, using a rubber spatula, vigorously mix the cream cheese and sugar until smooth. Beat in the milk and lemon juice until the mixture is creamy and smooth.

To remove the coffee cake from the pan, tilt and rotate the pan while gently tapping it on a counter to release the cake sides. Invert a wire rack on top of the coffee cake, invert the cake onto the rack, and carefully lift off the pan. Invert another rack on top, invert the cake so it is right side up, and remove the original rack. Slip a sheet of waxed paper under the rack to catch any drips from the icing. Using a pastry brush, coat the top of the warm cake with the icing to glaze it. (Cover and refrigerate the leftover icing for another use. It will keep for up to 2 days.)

Serve the coffee cake warm or at room temperature. To serve, you can pull apart the layers, or you can cut the cake into 1-inch-thick slices on a slight diagonal with a long, serrated knife. If you decide to cut the cake, don't attempt to cut it until it is almost completely cool.

BEST OF THE BEST EXCLUSIVE

This is a stellar coconut cream pie in every way, from the mile-high whipped cream topping to the supercrunchy crust made with a combination of zwieback toasts and macadamia nuts.

DREAMY COCONUT CREAM PIE

MAKES ONE 10-INCH PIE

- 18 zwieback toasts (5¼ ounces), broken into pieces (see Editor's Note)
- ⅓ cup unsalted macadamia nuts, chopped
- ¾ cup sugar
- 1 stick (4 ounces) unsalted butter, melted, plus 2 tablespoons cold unsalted butter
- 2 cups sweetened coconut flakes
- 3 tablespoons water
- 1½ teaspoons unflavored gelatin
- 4 large egg yolks
- ⅓ cup plus 1 tablespoon cornstarch
- 2¼ cups whole milk
- ½ cup unsweetened coconut milk
- 1 tablespoon pure vanilla extract
- 1 cup heavy cream
- 2 teaspoons dark rum

EDITOR'S NOTE

Look for hard, crunchy zwieback toasts in the baby-products aisle of the supermarket, or use plain melba toasts plus an extra tablespoon of sugar.

1 Preheat the oven to 350°F. Lightly spray a 10-inch springform pan with nonstick spray. In a food processor, pulse the toasts and nuts with 2 tablespoons of the sugar until finely ground. Scrape into a bowl and mix in the melted butter until the crumbs are evenly moistened. Pat the crumbs over the bottom and 1 inch up the side of the pan. Bake for 10 minutes. Let cool. Spread the coconut flakes on a rimmed baking sheet and toast for about 10 minutes, stirring once, until golden. Let cool.

2 Pour the water into a bowl and sprinkle the gelatin over; let stand until the gelatin is softened, 5 minutes. Put the egg yolks in a bowl. In a saucepan, whisk ½ cup of the sugar with the cornstarch. Gradually whisk in the milk and coconut milk and cook over moderate heat, whisking, until smooth and thick, 6 minutes. Gradually pour the hot mixture into the yolks, whisking constantly. Scrape the filling back into the saucepan and bring just to a boil, whisking constantly. Remove from the heat. Add the cold butter, the gelatin, 2 teaspoons of the vanilla and ¾ cup of the toasted coconut; stir until the butter and gelatin are melted. Stir occasionally until cooled slightly, 15 minutes.

3 Sprinkle the crust with ½ cup of the coconut. Pour the custard into the crust and refrigerate until chilled, 2 hours.

4 In a bowl, using a handheld electric mixer, beat the cream with the remaining 2 tablespoons of sugar and 1 teaspoon of vanilla and the rum at medium-high speed until soft peaks form. Spread the whipped cream over the pie and refrigerate for 30 minutes. Sprinkle the remaining ¾ cup of coconut over the pie. Remove the side of the pan, cut the pie into wedges and serve.

ARLINE RYAN'S SWEDISH MEATBALLS
WITH SOUR CREAM SAUCE, P. 62

HEIRLOOM COOKING WITH THE BRASS SISTERS

by MARILYNN BRASS *and* SHEILA BRASS

marilynn and Sheila Brass's first cookbook, *Heirloom Baking,* was fantastic, and this follow-up is equally satisfying. This time, the sisters—self-described "roundish, bespectacled women who have a combined total of 114 years of home cooking experience"—explore the world of old-fashioned savory foods, gathering recipes for casseroles, dumplings and the like from vintage recipe boxes and handwritten cookbooks. This is a sweeping look back at nearly a century of North American cooking traditions, a fascinating collection of recipes (from crispy Norwegian potatoes to spicy Creole shrimp) that were brought by immigrants and that have evolved over the years.

Published by Black Dog & Leventhal, $29.95

Mild-flavored soda crackers (a New England classic akin to saltines) give these meatballs a pleasant saltiness and a slight toasty taste.

ARLINE RYAN'S SWEDISH MEATBALLS *with* SOUR CREAM SAUCE {1920s}

MAKES 40 MEATBALLS

- 1½ pounds ground veal
- ¾ pound ground pork
- 1 cup finely chopped onion
- ¾ cup light cream or half-and-half
- 2 tablespoons flour
- ¾ cup soda cracker crumbs
- ¾ teaspoon nutmeg
- ½ teaspoon salt
- ½ teaspoon coarsely ground black pepper

Pinch of summer savory (optional)

- 2 tablespoons butter, softened to room temperature
- 2 tablespoons vegetable oil
- ½ cup white wine
- 1 (14½-ounce) can low-sodium chicken stock
- 2 tablespoons flour
- 1 pint sour cream
- 2 tablespoons chopped fresh parsley, for garnish

This heirloom recipe was found handwritten on an index card from Indiana. These delicate meatballs in a sour cream sauce are a wonderful home plate served with wide noodles or rice to make the most of the gravy.

1 Place veal and pork in the bowl of a food processor fitted with the metal blade. Process until smooth. Add onion, cream or half-and-half, flour, cracker crumbs, nutmeg, salt, pepper, and summer savory. Pulse until texture is almost as smooth as a paste. Remove mixture from food processor and shape into balls, using about 2 tablespoons for each meatball.

2 Heat 1 tablespoon of the butter and 1 tablespoon of the oil in each of two large frying pans over medium heat. Add meatballs and cook, turning with tongs, until evenly browned, 5 to 7 minutes. Add ¼ cup white wine and ½ can of chicken stock to each pan and simmer 5 minutes.

3 Remove pans from heat. Remove meatballs to a platter and set aside. Consolidate all of the cooking juices in one pan. Whisk ¼ cup of the warm pan juices with the flour in a small bowl, return to pan, and whisk to blend. Set pan over low heat and bring to a bare simmer; do not allow sauce to boil. Whisk in sour cream a few tablespoons at a time. Return meatballs to pan and turn in sauce until completely heated through. Place on a serving dish and garnish with chopped fresh parsley.

Tips and Touches

Veal and pork should be ground twice if not using a food processor. Check sauce for lumps before adding sour cream and strain if necessary.

Chopped onion and sweet gherkins (mini pickles) add sweetness and crunch to this excellent, old-fashioned chicken liver paté.

NEW YORK PATÉ {1930s}

SERVES 8 TO 10

- 8 tablespoons butter, softened to room temperature, divided, plus more if needed
- 2 pounds chicken livers, rinsed and patted dry
- 1 cup finely chopped onion
- 1 cup finely chopped sweet gherkins
- 1 tablespoon prepared yellow mustard
- ¾ teaspoon salt
- ½ teaspoon coarsely ground black pepper

We found this living recipe for a sophisticated chicken liver paté on the personalized notepaper of Ione Ulrich Sutton, who was affiliated with the brokerage firm of Winslow, Cohu & Stetson, in New York. Further research told us that the personal papers of Ione, a career woman, writer, and active Republican, reside in the Eisenhower Library, in Abilene, Kansas.

1 Heat 2 tablespoons butter in a large frying pan over medium heat. Working in batches, add as many chicken livers as will comfortably fit in the pan and cook until well browned on one side, about 5 minutes. Turn with a spatula and cook until the second side is browned, another 5 minutes. Add more butter if needed. Remove pan from heat and mash livers with a fork in pan. Return pan to heat and continue cooking until livers are no longer pink, about 2 minutes more. Add chopped onion and cook an additional 2 minutes.

2 Place liver mixture in the bowl of a food processor fitted with the metal blade. Process until smooth. Add remaining 6 tablespoons butter, gherkins, mustard, salt, and pepper and pulse until blended. Line small molds or custard cups with plastic wrap with a 1-inch overhang, spoon paté into molds, and chill until firm. Unmold 15 minutes before serving by lifting plastic wrap and placing paté on plates.

HOW TO SELECT AND PREPARE CHICKEN LIVERS Buy chicken livers from a reputable butcher to insure freshness. Always choose livers that are free of green spots or discolorations. To clean, remove membranes and any fat adhering to livers and separate the lobes. Chicken livers should be rinsed and patted dry with paper towels before frying.

EDITOR'S NOTE
This paté is perfect for serving with cocktails. Set it out with rye bread, crackers or brioche toast and dishes of diced onion, chopped hard-cooked egg and capers.

Full-fat cottage cheese gives this soft, puffy bread a bit of richness, while onion flakes and dill seed contribute a wonderfully retro flavor.

AUNT RUTH'S DILLY CASSEROLE BREAD {1950s}

MAKES 1 ROUND LOAF

1 (¼-ounce) packet dry yeast
¼ cup water, warmed to 115°F
1 cup large curd cottage cheese, heated to lukewarm
2 tablespoons sugar
1 tablespoon onion flakes
1 tablespoon butter, softened to room temperature
2 teaspoons dill seed
½ teaspoon salt
¼ teaspoon baking soda
1 large egg
2 to 2½ cups flour
Softened butter, for brushing
Coarse sea salt, for sprinkling

This recipe came from our agent Karen Johnson's Aunt Ruth, a wonderful midwestern cook and baker. Ruth has been making her Dilly Casserole Bread for many years. This handwritten recipe was part of Karen's kitchen inheritance from her mother, Mary. Recently, at a flea market, Karen happily found a bowl to replace the one she broke that she had been using for baking her Dilly Bread.

1 Dissolve yeast in water and set aside in a warm place to proof for about 10 minutes. Mixture will bubble when yeast is proofed.

2 Mix cottage cheese, sugar, onion flakes, butter, dill seed, salt, baking soda, egg, and proofed yeast in the bowl of a standing mixer fitted with the paddle attachment. Add flour gradually, beating well after each addition, to make a stiff dough. Cover with a clean dish towel and allow to rise in a warm place until double in size, about 1 hour.

3 Punch down dough, and turn into well-buttered 8-inch round ovenproof casserole. Cover and let rise in a warm place for 1 hour.

4 Set the oven rack in the middle position. Preheat the oven to 350°F.

5 Bake 40 to 50 minutes, or until golden brown. Turn bread out of dish, brush top with soft butter, and sprinkle with salt. Cool bread on rack for at least 10 minutes before serving. Store leftover bread wrapped in wax paper at room temperature.

Tips and Touches

Use large curd creamed cottage cheese if you can find it because it has more moisture and gives the bread a richer flavor.

EDITOR'S NOTE

Ovens vary. When we made this bread, the top was fully browned before the loaf finished baking. If you find yourself in the same situation, tent the bread with foil until it's ready to come out of the oven.

Made with farina (a milled wheat cereal), these dumplings are the ultimate comfort food: They're light, fluffy and soothing. Serve them with honey for breakfast, or alongside a chicken or beef stew.

GRANDMA GAYDOS' GUM BOOTS {1920s to 1930s}
farina dumplings

MAKES 20 DUMPLINGS

- ⅓ cup butter, softened to room temperature
- 1 cup fine bread crumbs (see How to Make Fine Bread Crumbs)
- 1 pound farmer cheese or pot cheese (see Editor's Note)
- ½ cup dry farina (Cream of Wheat cereal)
- ¼ cup flour
- 1 egg, lightly beaten

Helen Gaydos, a young Slovakian girl who married a Greek Orthodox priest and raised five children during the Depression, fed her family these delicious hearty dumplings. Her children called them gum boots *because they couldn't pronounce the Slovakian name.*

1 Melt butter in a medium frying pan over low heat. Add bread crumbs and cook, stirring with wooden spoon, until bread crumbs absorb butter and turn light brown, about 5 minutes. Set aside on a platter in a warm place.

2 Bring a large pot of water to a boil. Mix cheese, farina, flour, and egg in a large bowl until dough forms. Roll golf ball–size pieces of dough between the palms of your hands to form dumplings. Drop dumplings into boiling water. Cover pot and cook 3 minutes. Remove cover and continue cooking until dumplings bob to top, 5 to 7 minutes total. Remove dumplings from pot with slotted spoon and transfer immediately to the platter with bread crumbs, rolling to coat. Serve immediately. Store leftover dumplings in a covered container in the refrigerator. Reheat gently in a frying pan with a little butter over low heat to warm through.

HOW TO MAKE FINE BREAD CRUMBS Set oven for 300°F. Place slices of dry white bread or brioche on jelly roll pans and set on middle and lower racks of oven. Bake 1 hour. Turn and bake until very dry, about 1 hour. Break into pieces and place in a food processor fitted with the metal blade. Pulse to form fine crumbs. Put through a strainer to remove hard pieces. Store crumbs in a plastic bag in the refrigerator or freezer. Dry bread crumbs can also be made using a grater or blender.

EDITOR'S NOTE
Pot cheese is made by pressing cottage cheese to remove some of its moisture. Pressed even further, the cottage cheese becomes farmer cheese, which has smaller curds and a denser texture.

BEST OF THE BEST EXCLUSIVE

These simple-seeming cookies get an extraordinarily deep chocolate flavor from the combination of cocoa powder and unsweetened chocolate. Cornmeal in the batter adds a satisfying crunchiness.

CRISPY DARK CHOCOLATE BUTTER COOKIES

MAKES 2½ DOZEN COOKIES

- 1 ounce unsweetened chocolate, finely chopped
- 1½ cups all-purpose flour
- ½ cup granulated sugar
- ½ cup confectioners' sugar
- ¼ cup cornmeal
- ¼ cup unsweetened cocoa powder
- ½ teaspoon salt
- ¼ teaspoon baking soda
- 2 sticks (½ pound) cold unsalted butter, cut into ½-inch dice
- 1 teaspoon pure vanilla extract

1 In a small glass bowl, microwave the chopped chocolate in 30-seconds intervals until melted, about 1 minute.

2 In a food processor, pulse the flour with both sugars and the cornmeal, cocoa powder, salt and baking soda. Add the butter and vanilla and pulse until the mixture resembles moist sand. Add the melted chocolate and pulse just until the dough comes together. Pat the dough into a disk, wrap in plastic and refrigerate until chilled, about 2 hours.

3 Preheat the oven to 325°F. Line 2 large rimmed baking sheets with parchment paper. Divide the dough in half and roll each half ¼ inch thick between 2 sheets of parchment paper. Using a 2½-inch round cookie cutter, stamp out cookies as close together as possible. Transfer the rounds to the prepared baking sheets 1 inch apart. Gather and reroll the scraps and stamp out more cookies.

4 Bake the cookies for about 18 minutes, rotating the pans from top to bottom and front to back halfway through baking, until the tops feel dry. Let the cookies cool completely on the baking sheets before serving.

MAKE AHEAD The cookies can be stored in an airtight container for up to 5 days.

MARINATED CHICKEN ALLA
GRIGLIA, P. 70

URBAN ITALIAN

by ANDREW CARMELLINI *and* GWEN HYMAN

Chef Andrew Carmellini began his career working under less than promising circumstances, in a red-sauce Italian joint in his hometown of Cleveland. But a trip to Italy in his late teens exposed him to the country's cuisine, and he proceeded to cook at some of the best—and worst—restaurants in both Italy and America (he shares the juicy details in his book). In 2000, he was named a FOOD & WINE Magazine Best New Chef for his work at New York's Café Boulud; he then went on to make elegant, earthy Italian food at A Voce. Between restaurant jobs, he wrote this book in his tiny Manhattan apartment kitchen, revealing a rare talent for coming up with approachable dishes based on classic Italian home recipes, with some brilliant chef ideas tossed in.

Published by Bloomsbury USA, $35

Because the marinade here is not wiped off the chicken before grilling or broiling, the herbs and garlic cook right into the crisp skin.

MARINATED CHICKEN *alla* GRIGLIA

SERVES 4

TIMING An overnight marinate, plus about ½ hour of cooking time

FOR THE MARINADE

- ¼ cup Roasted Garlic Puree (recipe follows)
- ½ cup rice vinegar or white wine vinegar
- ¼ cup extra-virgin olive oil
- ¼ cup grapeseed oil or corn oil
- 2 tablespoons dried oregano, preferably on the branch (Sicilian or Calabrian)
- 2 tablespoons chopped rosemary
- 1 lemon, thinly sliced
- 1 teaspoon red pepper flakes
- 2 tablespoons salt
- 1 teaspoon coarse-ground black pepper
- 1 tablespoon sugar

FOR THE CHICKEN

- 2 whole chickens, halved
- ½ teaspoon each of salt and coarse-ground black pepper

This is a simple marinated chicken—I used to make it all the time at home. Left overnight and grilled the next day, the chicken becomes tender, garlicky, and herbaceous, with a deep, tangy flavor.

1 Combine all the marinade ingredients in a bowl and mix well.

2 Place the chicken halves in a large container and pour the marinade over the top. Cover with plastic wrap and marinate in the fridge for at least 8 hours, or overnight.

3 Fire up the grill or preheat the broiler.

4 Remove the chickens from the marinade (but don't wipe the herbs off; they're delicious charred right on the skin). Season with more salt and pepper.

5 If you're using a grill: Place the chickens skin-side down and grill them on high. After 2 minutes, turn the halves 45°. After another 2 minutes, flip the halves over. After another 2 minutes, turn the halves 45° again. Turn the heat down to medium and cook the chicken until the juice runs clear when you stick a leg with a knife, about 20 minutes, depending on your grill.

Or

If you're using a broiler: Place the chickens on a roasting rack and broil them until the skins are crisp, about 5 minutes. Reduce the heat to 425°F and bake the chicken until the juice runs clear when you stick a leg with a knife, about 20 minutes.

6 Serve immediately, with the vegetables and accompaniments of your choice. Leftovers make great chicken salad.

ROASTED GARLIC PUREE

2 heads garlic
1 teaspoon extra-virgin
   olive oil
A pinch of kosher salt or
   sea salt
A pinch of coarse-ground
   black pepper
   (1 crack of the pepper mill)

1 Preheat the oven to 450°F.

2 Cut across the top of each head of garlic to expose some of the garlic flesh.

3 Place each garlic head cut-side up on a piece of tinfoil big enough to easily wrap it, about 3 inches by 3 inches. Sprinkle the garlic with the olive oil, salt, and pepper. Wrap the garlic up in the foil, making a Hershey's-Kiss shape.

4 Bake on a baking tray on the center rack in the oven until the cloves are soft and golden brown, about 1 hour. Cool the garlic in the fridge or freezer until it's cool to the touch. (The garlic can hold in the fridge for up to 3 days at this stage.)

5 Pick up each garlic head by the bottom and squeeze the meat into a fine sieve. With the back of a spoon, press the meat of the garlic through the sieve to get as much through as possible. Be sure to scoop the remnants from the underside of the sieve into the bowl. Discard the skins.

EDITOR'S NOTE
Carmellini's Roasted Garlic Puree is great in dressings or spread on grilled bread. To save time, you can also buy roasted garlic paste (it's sold in tubes, like premium tomato paste). The packaged version works just as well in marinades like this one.

by ANDREW CARMELLINI *and* GWEN HYMAN

Carmellini's Basic Tomato Sauce is key here; it's the most important recipe in his book, he says, because it's the base for so many of the dishes. The sauce cooks slowly, developing an intense tomato flavor.

RIGATONI PUGLIESE

SERVES 4 TO 6

TIMING About 30 minutes

FOR THE SAUCE
1 (15-ounce) can chickpeas
¼ cup plus 2 tablespoons
   extra-virgin olive oil
1 pound spicy Italian sausage
3 cups Basic Tomato Sauce
   (recipe follows)
½ teaspoon ground fennel seed

FOR THE BROCCOLI RABE
AND RIGATONI
1 bunch broccoli rabe, cleaned
   of outer leaves and bottom
   stems trimmed
1 pound rigatoni
2 tablespoons extra-virgin olive oil
1 clove garlic, sliced Goodfellas thin
¼ teaspoon red pepper flakes
Salt and pepper to taste

TO FINISH THE DISH
2 tablespoons butter
2 teaspoons extra-virgin olive oil
1 cup grated pecorino cheese

To prepare the sauce

1 Drain the chickpeas well, reserving the liquid. Blend half the chickpeas (about 1 cup) and all their liquid on high until the mixture forms a smooth paste, about 1 minute.

2 Heat the olive oil in a large saucepan over high heat. Squeeze the sausage out of the casing and add the meat to the pan. Brown it, stirring regularly and breaking the meat up into small pieces with a spoon or potato masher.

3 Add the tomato sauce and stir to combine.

4 Add the chickpea puree and the fennel seed and stir to combine. Cook over medium heat until the mixture forms a loose sauce and the flavors are combined, about 15 minutes.

To prepare the broccoli rabe and the rigatoni

1 Bring a large pot of salted water to a boil.

2 Blanch the broccoli rabe until the stems are just softened and the color has deepened, about 90 seconds. Remove with a slotted spoon or spider to a bowl of ice water to immediately stop the cooking process.

3 Return the water to a boil, add the rigatoni, and cook until it's al dente. Drain but do not rinse the pasta.

4 Warm the olive oil over medium-high heat in a medium sauté pan. Add the broccoli rabe, garlic, red pepper flakes, and the remaining half of the chickpeas. Season with salt and pepper and sauté until the greens are well coated, about 1 minute.

continued on p. 74

To finish the dish

1 Return the rigatoni to the pot. Add the sauce and cook on medium-high heat, mixing well, until the pasta is well coated, about 1 minute.

2 Remove the pot from the heat and stir in the butter, olive oil, and half the pecorino cheese. Transfer to a large serving dish and pour the broccoli rabe and chickpea mixture over the top. Top with the rest of the pecorino cheese and serve immediately.

BASIC TOMATO SAUCE

To peel the tomatoes

1 Bring a large pot of water to a boil. Wash and core the tomatoes, then cut an X in the bottom of each so the skins loosen as they cook.

2 Plunge the tomatoes into the boiling water for about 30 seconds. They're ready to come out when the skins start to shrink, split, and wrinkle; don't leave them in too long, or the tomatoes will start to cook. You'll probably have to do these in batches to avoid overcooking. Remove the tomatoes with a spider or strainer and immediately plunge them into a large bowl of ice water to stop the cooking process. Once the tomatoes have cooled down, pull the skins off with your fingers.

To prepare the sauce

1 Cut the tomatoes in half widthwise. Squeeze out the seeds and juice and discard. (This step is crucial. The key is to bring the sauce to the right consistency as quickly as possible, to preserve the fresh, bright tomato flavor. The more liquid there is, the longer you have to cook the sauce, and the less fresh and tomato-y it will taste.)

2 Roughly chop each tomato half into about 8 chunks—or if they're ripe enough, you can just pull the tomato halves apart into chunks with your fingers.

MAKES 4 CUPS

TIMING About 40 minutes if you're using canned tomatoes; 1 hour to 1½ hours if you're using fresh tomatoes

FOR THE BASE
12 beautifully ripe beefsteak tomatoes (about 5 pounds), washed, cored, and scored; or 10 cups (about 2½ 35-ounce cans) good-quality Italian canned tomatoes—I like San Marzano
1 heaping teaspoon sea salt or kosher salt

FOR THE FLAVORED OIL
1 head garlic
1¼ cups extra-virgin olive oil
1 packed cup basil leaves, washed, with stems on
1 teaspoon red pepper flakes

3 Place the chopped tomatoes in a large pot with a wide surface area. (If you're using the same pot you blanched the tomatoes in, be sure to cool it down—you want to start with a cold pot.) Top the tomatoes with the salt. The salt is absolutely integral to the recipe. It goes in at the beginning of the cooking process to help draw the moisture out of the tomatoes so it can evaporate. If you cut down the amount of salt, the sauce won't work.

4 Turn the heat to medium and let the tomatoes cook down at a lazy bubble, stirring occasionally to prevent sticking. This'll take 45 minutes to 1¼ hours, depending on season, ripeness, and the general quality of your tomatoes; 30 minutes for canned tomatoes. As the tomatoes cook, use a ladle to remove excess water. (The amount of excess could be anywhere from a cup to a quart, depending on how ripe the tomatoes are, but the sauce should be tomatoes and liquid, not tomatoes floating in liquid.) Smash the tomatoes with a wooden spoon as they cook so that the sauce gradually becomes smoother.

To prepare the flavored oil

1 Cut the top off the garlic head so that the skin stays on but the tops of the cloves are exposed. Combine the garlic, olive oil, basil leaves, and red pepper flakes in a small pot over medium heat and bring to a simmer. As soon as you hear the basil leaves "crack" (the sound is almost exactly like adding milk to Rice Krispies), take the mixture off the heat and reserve.

To finish the sauce

1 When the sauce is reduced by half to two-thirds and is thick but still bright red, strain the oil into the pot and stir to combine.

2 Cook the sauce for about 10 more minutes at a lazy bubble. Stir occasionally to keep it from sticking. When the oil and tomatoes have completely emulsified and the sauce looks "whole," turn off the heat and stir it up a bit in the pot with a masher or a hand blender set on low.

Carmellini flavors these juicy meatballs, intriguingly, with North African merguez sausage, which adds a complex spiciness.

LAMB MEATBALLS STUFFED *with* GOAT CHEESE

MAKES ABOUT 30 MEATBALLS; SERVES 6 FOR ANTIPASTI

TIMING About 1 hour, depending on whether you have Crumbs Yo! on hand. If you don't have any and don't have time to make them, you can leave them out: you'll just be missing a little crunch on the outside of the final product.

FOR THE MEATBALLS
- 3 tablespoons extra-virgin olive oil
- 1 small onion, chopped (about ½ cup)
- 1 clove garlic, finely chopped
- ½ teaspoon ground coriander seed
- 1 teaspoon ground fennel seed
- 1 tablespoon rosemary, finely chopped
- ¼ cup fresh goat cheese
- ½ pound merguez sausage, about 8 links (or 2 links hot Italian sausage, if you prefer), with casings cut away
- 1 pound ground lamb
- ½ cup dried bread crumbs
- 2 eggs
- ½ teaspoon salt

FOR THE SAUCE
- ¼ cup extra-virgin olive oil
- 1 medium onion, diced (about 1 cup)
- 1 (28-ounce) can Italian tomatoes (San Marzano, if possible) plus their juice
- ¼ teaspoon red pepper flakes
- ½ teaspoon salt
- ½ teaspoon sugar
- ½ teaspoon dried oregano, preferably on the branch

TO FINISH THE DISH
- ¼ cup Crumbs Yo! (recipe follows)
- ¼ cup grated pecorino cheese

This dish is kind of Middle East-meets-Little Italy: it's totally spaghetti-and-meatballs-style when it comes to the sauce, but then there's the lamb, not to mention the goat-cheese center, which oozes out of the meatballs—surprise!—when you cut into them. Serve these on their own as antipasti, or toss them with some penne or rigatoni as a main course, a great Sunday-night dish for family and friends.

To make the meatballs

1 Heat the olive oil in a sauté pan over medium heat. Add the onion and sweat for 3 minutes. Add the garlic and cook for 1 minute, stirring constantly.

2 Add the coriander, fennel, and rosemary. Cook together 1 minute, so that the aromas of the spices and herbs are released. Remove to a bowl and place in the fridge to cool (about 5 minutes), so that you're not combining hot onions with cold meat.

3 Meanwhile, roll the goat cheese between your palms to form ½-inch balls (the size of a pebble). Place them on a plate and reserve.

4 When the onion-herb mixture has cooled, combine it in a large bowl with the sausage, lamb, bread crumbs, eggs, and salt. Mix well with your hands.

5 Form the meatballs: for each meatball, scoop up about 2 tablespoons of lamb mixture and roll and press it into an oval, about the size of a distended Ping-Pong ball. Use your thumb

continued on p. 78

to create a goat-cheese-ball-sized dent in the middle, and drop a goat-cheese ball inside. Pinch the lamb mixture up around the goat cheese to close the hole, and roll the meatball between your hands till it's round and smooth. Repeat until you've used up all the goat cheese and the lamb mixture.

To make the sauce

1 Heat the olive oil in a large pot over medium-high heat. Add the onion and cook until it starts to soften, about 1 minute.

2 Crush the tomatoes in a bowl with the heel of your hand. Add them to the pot, then add the tomato juice, red pepper flakes, salt, sugar, and oregano. Mix to combine. Cook over medium-high heat for 10 minutes, until the flavors combine and the sauce is reduced.

3 Add the meatballs, being careful not to break them. Reduce the heat to low, so the sauce is at a very low simmer, and cover. It's very important that the liquid never come to a boil. You want as slow a simmer as possible, so the flavors really come together, the cheese melts, and the meat becomes rich and tender. Cook for 5 minutes, turn the meatballs with a spoon, and simmer another 5 minutes, until the meat is cooked and the sauce takes on the flavor of the meatballs. (Some goat cheese may find its way out during the cooking process—it depends on how tightly you've made your meatballs—but don't worry about this: the meatballs will still taste good.)

To finish the dish

Ladle the meatballs and sauce into 6 bowls. Sprinkle with the Crumbs Yo! and the grated cheese. Serve immediately.

CRUMBS YO!

MAKES 1 CUP

TIMING Superquick; no more than ½ hour if you're making homemade crumbs; about 6 minutes if you use panko crumbs

FOR THE BREAD CRUMBS

- 5 slices of 1- or 2-day-old bread

FOR THE CRUMBS YO!

- 2 tablespoons extra-virgin olive oil
- 1 cup bread crumbs (homemade or panko)
- ¼ teaspoon salt
- ¼ teaspoon pepper

OPTIONAL

You can use any one or any combination of these ingredients (or none at all) to flavor the Crumbs Yo! I'll leave it up to the inner chef in you.

- 1 tablespoon chopped fresh herbs (thyme or rosemary)
- Zest of 1 lemon or orange
- 1 teaspoon ground fennel seed or other spice
- ¼ cup bacon or pancetta (2 slices), diced
- A pinch of red pepper flakes
- A pinch of dried oregano

Toasted bread crumbs are one of my cooking secrets: I toss them in everything. They just make stuff taste better—they give everything a little bit of crunch, from salads to pastas (yes, that's right: pastas. This ain't yer Chef Boyardee supersoft pasta, kids). My crew and I named these bread crumbs Crumbs Yo! because we're always yelling to each other in the kitchen, "Pass me some crumbs, yo!"

This recipe is incredibly easy, but the simple move of toasting the bread crumbs in olive oil makes them taste exponentially better than just plain old ordinary bread crumbs. You can also flavor Crumbs Yo! with black pepper, herbs, grated citrus zest, grated cheese, bits of bacon or pancetta. I've given you the start-to-finish recipe here, but if you don't have day-old bread sitting around, panko bread crumbs will work just as well.

To make the bread crumbs

1 Preheat the oven to 300°F.

2 Cut the bread (including crusts) into 2-inch chunks and put the chunks on a baking tray. Bake for about 10 minutes, until the bread is thoroughly dried out.

3 Let the bread cool slightly—just enough to handle. Pulse the bread in a food processor until it is reduced to coarse crumbs.

To make the Crumbs Yo!

1 In a sauté pan, heat the olive oil over medium heat and toast the bread crumbs, salt, and pepper until golden brown, about 4 minutes. If you're flavoring your crumbs, toss your flavoring(s) of choice in the pan in the last minute of cooking.

2 Spread the Crumbs Yo! on a plate to cool. They'll keep for up to 2 days in the fridge, or for a long time in the freezer.

Delicious, easy-to-make spaghetti squash is a fantastic low-carb substitute for pasta. Here, Carmellini bakes the squash, then tosses it with butter flavored with sage, walnuts and Parmigiano-Reggiano.

SPAGHETTI SQUASH *with* SAGE *and* WALNUTS

SERVES 6 OR SO, DEPENDING ON THE SIZE OF YOUR SQUASH

TIMING Stupid-easy, yes—but I didn't say it was fast. Give yourself 2 hours, because every oven and every squash is different.

- 1 spaghetti squash (about 3 pounds; see Editor's Note on p. 82)
- ¾ teaspoon salt
- ½ teaspoon coarse-ground black pepper
- 5 tablespoons butter
- 15 fresh sage leaves
- ½ cup shelled walnuts, roughly chopped
- 1 tablespoon grated Parmigiano-Reggiano or pecorino cheese

Spaghetti squash is fun to eat: it's like kid food for grown-ups. The taste isn't kid stuff, though. This dish is aromatic and full of fall flavors, so it makes a great textural complement to meaty dishes. Plus it's stupid-easy to make.

1 Preheat the oven to 400°F.

2 Place the squash on a cutting board. Using a large, very sharp knife, cut the squash in half lengthwise. Scoop out the seeds with a spoon and discard them.

3 Place the squash halves on a roasting rack and season with ¼ teaspoon each of the salt and pepper. Place 1 tablespoon of butter and 2 sage leaves in the hollowed-out core of each half.

4 Bake the squash on a tray on the oven's middle rack until the flesh is just soft—about 1 hour (or longer—it all depends on your oven). Remove the squash and let it cool until you can work with the flesh comfortably, about 15 minutes.

5 Using a fork, scrape the meat of the squash away from the skin, so that you get fluffy spaghetti-like strands. Reserve these and discard the skins, unless you're saving them for the presentation (see p. 82). The squash will hold at this point up to a day ahead of time, in an airtight container in the fridge.

6 Heat the remaining 3 tablespoons of butter in a large saucepan over medium heat. When the butter has melted, add the walnuts. Toast the nuts and allow the butter to bubble, about 1 minute.

continued on p. 82

7 Add the remaining sage leaves. When the leaves release their aroma and begin to crackle in the pan (about 1 minute), add the squash and stir to coat it with the flavored butter. Cook for 2 minutes over medium heat until the squash is warm, stirring frequently so the flavors get inside the squash. Season with the rest of the salt and pepper.

8 Serve on a large plate or platter, topped with the cheese. Or if you're going for that fancy '70s-hostess-style thing, serve the squash inside its own skin.

BEST OF THE BEST EXCLUSIVE

Inspired by old-fashioned American crab boils, Carmellini cooks the crab for this luscious pasta with Old Bay (his father's favorite ingredient), a seasoning mix that includes bay leaves and celery salt.

SPAGHETTI *with* CRAB, SCALLIONS *and* MINT

SERVES 6

- 1 pound spaghetti
- 3 tablespoons extra-virgin olive oil
- 6 scallions, white and green parts thinly sliced separately
- 1 teaspoon Old Bay Seasoning
- 1 cup bottled clam broth
- ¼ cup fresh lemon juice
- 1 pound jumbo lump crabmeat, picked over
- 2 tablespoons unsalted butter

Kosher salt and freshly ground pepper

- ½ cup mint leaves, coarsely chopped

1 In a large pot of boiling salted water, cook the spaghetti until al dente. Drain well.

2 Meanwhile, in a large skillet, heat the olive oil. Add the scallion whites and cook over moderate heat until softened, about 2 minutes. Stir in the Old Bay. Add the clam broth, lemon juice, crabmeat and butter and cook, stirring constantly, until the butter is melted, about 1 minute.

3 Add the spaghetti and scallion greens to the skillet and toss over moderate heat until the sauce coats the spaghetti, about 2 minutes. Remove from the heat and add the mint. Season with salt and pepper. Transfer the spaghetti to shallow bowls and serve.

NOTE Carmellini likes to finish the dish with crisp bread crumbs. Use his recipe for Crumbs Yo! on p. 79.

Giada De Laurentiis making her savory corn muffins.

GIADA'S KITCHEN

by GIADA DE LAURENTIIS

television celebrity cook Giada De Laurentiis isn't afraid to combine cantaloupe, red onion and walnuts in a salad. That's one of the enticing recipes in this, her fourth book, which emphasizes the fresh, light side of traditional Italian cooking. "The recipes you'll find in this book represent a nice balance of exciting and healthy dishes," she writes. As always, De Laurentiis relies on supermarket ingredients, which makes her recipes super-accessible and clearly inspires her—whether she's inventing dishes for dinner parties (like Fresh Tomato and Goat Cheese Strata with Herb Oil) or meals for families with young children (Orecchiette with Mini Chicken Meatballs).

Published by Clarkson Potter, $32.50

This salmon recipe cleverly uses mint two ways: in both the lemon brodetto (broth) and the gorgeous green pea puree. The puree could stand on its own as a side dish; just double the recipe.

SALMON *in* LEMON BRODETTO *with* PEA PUREE

SERVES 4

LEMON BRODETTO
- 2 tablespoons olive oil
- 1 shallot, diced
- 2 lemons, one zested and both juiced
- 2 cups low-sodium chicken broth
- 1 tablespoon chopped fresh mint leaves

PEA PUREE
- 2 cups frozen peas, thawed (about 10 ounces)
- ¼ cup fresh mint leaves
- 1 garlic clove
- ½ teaspoon kosher salt
- ½ teaspoon freshly ground black pepper
- ½ cup extra-virgin olive oil
- ½ cup freshly grated Parmesan cheese

SALMON
- ¼ cup olive oil
- 4 (4- to 6-ounce) salmon fillets
- Kosher salt and freshly ground black pepper

EDITOR'S NOTE
Even if you're not a fan of fish skin, you may want to use skin-on salmon fillets here—the skin helps hold the fish together in the pan. Then peel off the skin before serving. We prefer wild salmon for its firm texture and clean flavor.

This dish is a perfect embodiment of the way I like to eat. The colors just say spring, it's light, and everything tastes really fresh and bright.

To make the lemon brodetto

Warm the olive oil in a medium saucepan over medium heat. Add the shallot and sauté until tender, about 7 minutes. Add the lemon zest and juice, and the broth. Bring to a simmer, cover, and keep warm over low heat.

To make the pea puree

Combine the peas, mint, garlic, salt, and pepper in a food processor and puree. With the machine running, add the extra-virgin olive oil in a steady drizzle. Transfer the pea puree to a small bowl and stir in the Parmesan. Set aside.

To make the salmon

Warm the olive oil in a large, heavy skillet over high heat. Season the salmon pieces with salt and pepper. Sear the salmon on one side until a golden crust forms, 4 to 5 minutes. Flip the fish and continue cooking until medium-rare, about 2 minutes more depending on the thickness of the fish.

To assemble the dish

Stir the tablespoon of chopped mint into the lemon brodetto and divide among 4 shallow bowls. Place a large spoonful of pea puree in the center of each bowl. Place a salmon piece atop each mound of pea puree and serve immediately.

Italian sausage adds lots of fast flavor to this speedy dish; its mild heat is especially good with the creamy ricotta and sweet peas.

TAGLIATELLE *with* SMASHED PEAS, SAUSAGE *and* RICOTTA CHEESE

SERVES 4 TO 6

- 1 pound fresh or dried tagliatelle (or other wide, long pasta)
- 2 tablespoons olive oil
- 2 garlic cloves, chopped
- 1 pound hot Italian sausage, casings removed
- 1 pound frozen peas, thawed
- 1 cup whole-milk ricotta cheese
- 1 bunch of fresh basil leaves, chopped (about ¾ cup)
- ¼ cup freshly grated Pecorino Romano cheese
- 1 teaspoon salt

EDITOR'S NOTE
This dish is great with supermarket ricotta, but fresh cow's- or sheep's-milk ricottas are even better because of their delicate milky flavor. Look for them at specialty food markets or cheese shops.

When you smash the peas, they release their starches into the sauce, making it thick and creamy. To make life a little easier, use a potato masher to smash the peas.

Bring a large pot of salted water to a boil over high heat. Add the pasta and cook until tender but still firm to the bite, stirring occasionally, 8 to 10 minutes if dry or according to package directions if fresh. Drain the pasta, reserving 1 cup of the pasta cooking water.

Meanwhile, heat the olive oil and garlic in a large, heavy skillet over medium-high heat until the garlic is fragrant. Add the sausage and cook, using a wooden spoon to break it up into bite-size bits. When the sausage has browned, about 5 minutes, push it over to one side of the pan. Add the peas to the pan and, using the back of the wooden spoon, smash the peas. Turn off the heat. Add the ricotta cheese to the pan and stir to combine, then add the cooked pasta and toss to coat. Add the pasta cooking water ¼ cup at a time, if needed, to make the pasta moist. Add the basil, pecorino, and salt. Toss gently to combine and serve immediately.

Every health-minded cook should be using more whole grains, so it's great to see De Laurentiis call for farro in place of the usual pasta.

FARRO *with* COARSE PESTO

SERVES 6 TO 8

- 8 cups low-sodium chicken broth
- 1 pound farro (about 2½ cups; see Editor's Note)
- 2 cups fresh flat-leaf parsley leaves
- ¼ cup fresh basil leaves
- 2 tablespoons fresh thyme leaves
- 2 garlic cloves
- ⅓ cup extra-virgin olive oil
- 1 tablespoon red wine vinegar
- ¾ teaspoon salt
- ½ teaspoon freshly ground black pepper
- Wedge of Pecorino Romano cheese, for garnish

EDITOR'S NOTE

Look for whole-grain farro at specialty food stores or order it from cybercucina.com. You can also substitute other large whole grains, such as wheat berries or barley; proceed as directed in the recipe, cooking until the grains are tender.

This is comfort food that's good for you. Farro is an ancient grain that was used to make cereals and pasta before wheat was widely available. It is somewhat similar to Israeli couscous in texture, but if you can't find it, any small pasta shape, such as orzo, makes a good substitute. Don't overwork the pesto; it should still have distinct pieces of the individual herbs, which keeps the flavors clearer and more distinct.

Bring the chicken broth to a boil in a large saucepan over high heat. Add the farro and stir to combine. Reduce the heat to low, cover the pan, and simmer the farro until tender, about 25 minutes. Drain the farro and set aside in a large bowl.

Meanwhile, in a food processor combine the parsley, basil, thyme, and garlic. Pulse until the herbs are coarsely chopped. Add the olive oil, vinegar, salt, and pepper. Pulse again until the herbs make a coarse mixture.

Toss the warm farro with the coarse pesto. Transfer to a serving bowl. Using a vegetable peeler, make about ½ cup of cheese shavings from the pecorino cheese wedge. Top the farro with the cheese shavings and serve.

GRILLED SALMON WITH OREGANO OIL, AVOCADO TZATZIKI SAUCE AND GRILLED LEMONS, P. 92

BOBBY FLAY'S GRILL IT!

by BOBBY FLAY *with* STEPHANIE BANYAS *and* SALLY JACKSON

this is the book to turn to when you know *what* you want but you don't know *how* you want it," writes celebrity chef Bobby Flay in this, his eighth book. Flay's approach is shopping-first: He urges readers to go to the farmers' market and buy whatever looks best, then refer to the book for ideas (it's organized by ingredient). So if you've come home with gorgeous corn, for instance, Flay has nine recipes for you to choose from, including an unconventional tabbouleh that includes balsamic vinegar and fresh basil. For anyone who seeks inspiration in ingredients—as so many of the world's most accomplished cooks do—this book is enormously helpful and encouraging.

Published by Clarkson Potter, $35

While this recipe may sound ambitious, it's really very doable: The most complicated component, the garlicky yogurt and avocado tzatziki sauce, comes together in seconds in a food processor.

GRILLED SALMON *with* OREGANO OIL, AVOCADO TZATZIKI SAUCE *and* GRILLED LEMONS

SERVES 4

- ¼ cup plus 2 tablespoons olive oil
- 2 tablespoons fresh oregano leaves

Kosher salt and freshly ground black pepper

- 4 (6-ounce) salmon fillets
- 2 lemons, halved

Avocado Tzatziki (recipe follows)

Salmon, not being native to the Mediterranean, is not typically used in Greek cuisine, but I like the flavor pairing here; the rich salmon stands up nicely to the pungent tzatziki.

1 Heat your grill to high.

2 Combine ¼ cup of the oil and the oregano in a blender and blend until smooth. Season with salt and pepper.

3 Brush the fillets on both sides with some of the oregano oil and season with salt and pepper. Grill the salmon for about 3 minutes per side, until slightly charred and cooked to medium, brushing with more of the oil every 30 seconds.

4 While the fish is grilling, brush the cut sides of the lemons with the remaining 2 tablespoons olive oil and grill, cut side down, until lightly golden brown, 2 minutes.

5 Serve the fillets with a dollop of Avocado Tzatziki and squeeze the juice from the grilled lemons on top.

AVOCADO TZATZIKI

MAKES 1 CUP

- 2 ripe Hass avocados, peeled, pitted and chopped
- 2 cloves garlic, chopped
- 1 serrano chile, chopped
- ¼ cup Greek yogurt

Grated zest and juice of 1 small lemon

- ½ English cucumber, finely diced
- ¼ cup chopped fresh flat-leaf parsley leaves

Kosher salt and freshly ground black pepper

Put the avocados, garlic, serrano, yogurt, lemon zest, and lemon juice in the bowl of a food processor and process until smooth. Transfer the mixture to a medium bowl, stir in the cucumber and parsley, and season with salt and pepper. Cover and refrigerate for at least 30 minutes and up to 2 hours before serving.

Cooks looking to get more whole grains into their diets should use more bulgur (wheat that's been steamed, dried and crushed). It adds delicious heft to this summery corn and tomato salad.

GRILLED CORN *and* TOMATO CRACKED WHEAT SALAD

SERVES 4

Kosher salt
1   cup bulgur wheat
4   ears Perfectly Grilled Corn (recipe follows)
3   tablespoons canola oil
Freshly ground black pepper
¼   cup finely chopped fresh flat-leaf parsley leaves
¼   cup finely chopped fresh chives
¼   cup finely chopped fresh basil leaves
2   ripe beefsteak or 4 plum tomatoes, halved, seeded, and finely diced
1   small red onion, finely diced
3   tablespoons balsamic vinegar
2   tablespoons fresh lemon juice
1   clove garlic, finely chopped
½   cup extra-virgin olive oil

You won't find corn, balsamic vinegar, and basil in the tabbouleh at Middle Eastern restaurants. The classic version is made with bulgur wheat combined with lots of mint and parsley, tomatoes, and lemon juice. But the bulgur wheat provides a blank canvas for any ingredient you want to use, and I love the combination of flavors in this great summer side dish.

1 Bring 3 cups of water to a boil in a medium saucepan. Add 1 tablespoon of salt and stir in the bulgur wheat. Cover the pot, turn off the heat, and let sit for 30 minutes or until the bulgur is tender. Drain well and press out any excess water. Place in a large bowl.

2 Heat your grill to high.

3 Remove the husks from the grilled corn and discard. Brush the ears of corn with the canola oil and season with salt and pepper. Grill the ears until the kernels are lightly golden brown on all sides, about 5 minutes.

4 Remove the kernels from the cobs and place the kernels in the bowl with the bulgur. Add the parsley, chives, basil, tomatoes, and onion and toss to combine.

5 Whisk together the vinegar, lemon juice, garlic, and extra-virgin olive oil in a small bowl and season with salt and pepper. Pour the mixture over the bulgur mixture and stir well to combine. Let sit at room temperature for at least 30 minutes before serving. The tabbouleh can be made 1 day in advance and stored, covered, in the refrigerator. Serve cold or at room temperature.

continued on p. 94

PERFECTLY GRILLED CORN

SERVES 4

8 ears corn
Kosher salt

Each year I wait for the end of summer so I can eat fresh Jersey corn on the cob until I burst. When I was growing up, my mom, like every mom at that time, would husk the corn and boil it in salted water. While I have fond memories of corn prepared that way, once I became a chef, I learned that grilling or roasting corn in its husks is a far superior way to prepare it. Boiling corn in water seems to leach out the flavor. It's also all too easy to overcook corn this way, giving the kernels a mushy consistency. Grilling it in the husks steams it and concentrates the natural sweet flavor while imparting the taste of the husk into the corn. Corn prepared this way is so good that all it needs is some butter and salt.

1 Heat your grill to medium.

2 Pull the outer husks down each ear to the stalk end. Strip away the silk from each ear of corn by hand. Fold the husks back into place and tie the ends together with kitchen string. Place the ears of corn in a large bowl of cold water with 1 tablespoon of salt for 10 minutes.

3 Remove the corn from the water and shake off the excess. Place the corn on the grill, close the cover, and grill for 15 to 20 minutes, turning every 5 minutes, or until the kernels are tender when pierced with a paring knife.

4 Remove the husks from the cobs before eating the corn.

To Remove Corn Kernels from the Cob

Stand the cob upright on its stalk end in a large bowl or pan. Hold the tip with your fingers and cut down the sides of the cob with a sharp paring knife, releasing the kernels without cutting into the cob. Run the dull edge of the knife down the naked cob to release any remaining corn and liquid.

After grilling the beef patties for this Spanish take on a bacon cheeseburger, Flay then grills the entire burger, pressing down with a spatula so the outside of the bun turns nice and crisp.

PRESSED BURGER *with* MANCHEGO, SERRANO HAM *and* PIQUILLO–SMOKED PAPRIKA AIOLI

SERVES 4

1½ pounds ground chuck,
    80 percent lean
3 tablespoons canola oil
Kosher salt and freshly ground
    black pepper
4 sesame seed hamburger buns
Piquillo–Smoked Paprika Aioli
    (recipe follows)
8 (¼-inch-thick) slices
    Manchego cheese
8 paper-thin slices Serrano ham

It's hard to take your time and be polite while eating this scrumptious burger. The rich, smoky, and spicy-sweet aioli is just the beginning. Layering that with nutty Manchego cheese and salty Serrano ham might be enough for a pretty good sandwich. But wrap that all around a juicy burger and press it into a crispy-on-the-outside, melted-on-the-inside, two-handed thing of wonder, and just try to hold yourself back.

1 Heat your grill to high.

2 Form the meat into 4 burgers, each 1 inch thick. Brush with 2 tablespoons of the oil and season liberally with salt and pepper on both sides. Place on the grill and grill until golden brown and slightly charred, 4 to 5 minutes. Turn the burgers over and continue cooking to medium-rare, about 3 minutes longer.

3 Place the bun bottoms on a flat surface and spread each one with a few tablespoons of the aioli. Top with a slice of cheese, then a slice of the ham, a burger, another slice of ham, and finally another slice of cheese.

continued on p. 98

EDITOR'S NOTE

Jarred piquillo peppers are roasted until they're sweet and silky. Buy them at specialty stores or from tienda.com. To turn them into tapas, stuff them with Spanish tuna or skewer them with olives, white anchovies and Manchego cheese.

MAKES ¾ CUP

- ½ cup mayonnaise
- 2 cloves garlic, chopped
- 2 piquillo peppers
- 2 teaspoons Spanish smoked paprika
- ½ teaspoon kosher salt

4 Brush the sesame seed side of the bun tops with the remaining oil and place the entire sandwich on the grill, oiled side down. Using a heavy-duty metal spatula, press down on the bottom of the buns and grill until the tops are lightly golden brown, 1 to 2 minutes. Turn the burgers over and press down on the top and continue grilling until the bottom is lightly golden brown and the cheese has melted, about 1 minute longer. Serve immediately.

PIQUILLO–SMOKED PAPRIKA AIOLI

Combine the mayonnaise, garlic, peppers, paprika, and salt in a food processor and process until smooth. Cover and refrigerate for at least 30 minutes or up to 1 day before serving.

BEST OF THE BEST EXCLUSIVE

Flay's fun version of steak sauce gets sweetness from honey and molasses and heat from horseradish and piquillo peppers.

BEEF SKEWERS *with* PIQUILLO STEAK SAUCE

SERVES 4

1½ cups packed flat-leaf
     parsley leaves
  6 garlic cloves
  ½ cup extra-virgin olive oil
  1 pound beef sirloin, cut
     into 1-inch cubes
  3 piquillo peppers, drained
  2 tablespoons sherry vinegar
1½ tablespoons Dijon mustard
  1 tablespoon prepared
     horseradish
  1 tablespoon honey
1½ teaspoons molasses
  1 teaspoon Worcestershire
     sauce
Kosher salt and freshly
     ground pepper
 12 scallions
  1 teaspoon canola oil

1 In a blender, puree the parsley with the garlic and olive oil. Transfer to a medium bowl and add the sirloin. Cover and refrigerate for at least 2 hours or up to 8 hours. Wipe out the blender.

2 In the blender, combine the piquillo peppers with the vinegar, mustard, horseradish, honey, molasses and Worcestershire sauce and puree until smooth. Season the steak sauce with salt and pepper.

3 Preheat a grill. Thread the sirloin onto pairs of skewers and season with salt and pepper.

4 Rub the scallions with the canola oil and season with salt and pepper. Grill the scallions over moderately high heat until lightly charred all over, about 2 minutes. Grill the skewers, turning once, until the sirloin is medium-rare, about 6 minutes. Transfer the skewers and scallions to plates and serve with the piquillo steak sauce.

MAKE AHEAD The steak sauce can be refrigerated for up to 1 week. Bring to room temperature before serving.

PONCHATOULA STRAWBERRY CUPCAKES, P. 102

SCREEN DOORS AND SWEET TEA

by MARTHA HALL FOOSE

martha Hall Foose was born and raised in the Mississippi Delta but only realized how special it was when she left: "When I went off to cooking school in France, I quickly found out that to some people, being from the Mississippi Delta was exotic—as different as my fellow students' provenances were to me." Foose returned home, opened two bakeries and became executive chef of the Viking Cooking School in Greenwood, Mississippi. Her book, a heartfelt tribute to real Southern cooking, is imbued with a sense of pride and full of stories about small-town citizens with big personalities. Best of all is the sheer originality of her recipes, like her pralines flavored with buttermilk and bacon.

Published by Clarkson Potter, $32.50

With strawberries in both the cake and frosting, these are heavenly when the fruit is in season. Plus, the icing is made with cream cheese, justifying the cupcakes' presence on the breakfast table.

PONCHATOULA STRAWBERRY CUPCAKES
really pink

MAKES 24 CUPCAKES

CUPCAKES

- 2½ cups cake flour
- 1 teaspoon baking soda
- ¼ teaspoon salt
- ⅓ cup buttermilk
- ¼ cup canola oil
- ½ teaspoon almond extract
- 1 teaspoon vanilla extract
- ½ cup (1 stick) unsalted butter
- 1½ cups granulated sugar
- 2 large eggs
- 1 cup mashed fresh or frozen strawberries
- 1 teaspoon grated orange zest

FROSTING

- ½ cup chopped fresh or frozen strawberries
- 2 tablespoons strawberry jam
- 1 teaspoon fresh lemon juice
- 1 (8-ounce) package cream cheese, softened
- 1½ cups (3 sticks) unsalted butter, softened
- 4 cups confectioners' sugar, sifted

The scent from a flat of Louisiana strawberries will fill a room. And I do think the small, deep red berries are profoundly the sweetest around. California ones seem too big and watery, and can be almost hollow when you bite into them. Florida's are pretty good and have a nice color, but can be a little insipid. They must keep the good ones for themselves.

These little cakes draped with pink, red-specked frosting are full of the springtime taste of ripe strawberries.

Make the cupcakes

Preheat the oven to 350°F. Spray a muffin tin with nonstick cooking spray or line with foil baking cups.

In a medium bowl, sift together the flour, baking soda, and salt. In another medium bowl, combine the buttermilk, oil, and almond and vanilla extracts; set aside.

In an electric mixer, beat the butter and granulated sugar until light and fluffy. Add the eggs one at a time, beating well after each addition. Gradually add the buttermilk mixture. Beat for 1 minute at medium speed.

Reduce the speed to low and add the flour mixture. Mix until just combined. Stir in the strawberries and orange zest. Spoon into the prepared muffin tins, filling them two-thirds full. Bake for 18 to 20 minutes, or until the cupcakes spring back when touched lightly in the center. Cool in the pans for 10 minutes, then unmold the cupcakes and cool on racks.

Make the frosting

In a small saucepan over medium heat, combine the strawberries, jam, and lemon juice. Cook and stir for 5 minutes, or until the jam is melted and the strawberries are soft. Press any big pieces with the back of the spoon to mash.

In an electric mixer fitted with the paddle attachment, mix the cream cheese and butter at medium speed until creamy. At low speed, slowly add the confectioners' sugar and mix until combined. Add the strawberries and mix at low speed until blended.

When the cupcakes are completely cool, spread with the frosting.

AUTHOR'S NOTES

Strawberries are an aggregate fruit, meaning the seeds are on the outside.

Like many other fruits, strawberries do not ripen any more once picked.

Wash strawberries right before you eat them. If damp when stored, they will mold and their skin will toughen.

If the strawberry jam mixture seems runny, cook for 5 more minutes.

Frosting beaten at too high a speed will be full of air bubbles and not have a smooth finish when spread.

These may be baked in paper, foil, or silicone liners, if desired.

Strawberry seedlings are planted in September in Louisiana for an early spring harvest. The 2005 Louisiana strawberry crop was almost decimated by flocks of cedar waxwings. In some areas the birds ate 50 percent of the crop, getting so fat some could not fly more than 50 feet.

Tangipahoa Parish in Louisiana is home to a wonderful Strawberry Festival each April.

A traditional New Orleans–style praline is made with sugar, butter and nuts. Foose's brilliant, sophisticated version adds bacon (a popular ingredient in desserts nowadays) and fresh orange zest.

BUTTERMILK BACON PRALINES
sweet, salty, ridiculous

MAKES 24 SMALL PRALINES

- 1 cup granulated sugar
- ½ cup packed light brown sugar
- ½ cup buttermilk
- 1 tablespoon light corn syrup
- ½ teaspoon baking soda
- ¼ teaspoon kosher salt
- 4 tablespoons (½ stick) unsalted butter
- ½ teaspoon vanilla extract
- 1 cup chopped pecans
- ½ teaspoon grated orange zest
- 4 slices bacon, cooked crisp and crumbled

These salty-sweet electuaries are brilliant paired with drinks before dinner. The outlandish combination of smoky bacon and pecans, scented with orange, in a brown sugar disk, is an amusing, tongue-teasing conversation starter—a true amuse-bouche.

In a heavy-bottomed, deep saucepan, combine the granulated and brown sugars, the buttermilk, corn syrup, baking soda, and salt. Cook slowly over medium heat for about 20 minutes, until the mixture reaches 235°F on a candy thermometer (see Author's Notes).

Remove from the heat and add the butter, vanilla, pecans, orange zest, and bacon. Being mindful of exposed skin as the mixture is very hot, beat like the dickens with a wooden spoon until smooth and creamy. Drop by teaspoonfuls onto a silicone mat or buttered parchment paper. Let stand for 30 minutes, or until cool and firm. Store in an airtight container.

AUTHOR'S NOTES

If you don't have a candy thermometer, drop a spoonful of the mixture into a cup of cool water. If the test drop can be formed into a pliable ball, then it is ready for the additional ingredients. If not, let the mixture cook a little longer and try again. Change water between tests for more accurate results.

Although I usually frown on the practice, cooking bacon in the microwave in this instance helps render it extra-crispy.

This fun, unusual cucumber salad—frozen just until it's refreshingly icy—would be great alongside barbecued ribs or chicken.

FROZEN CUCUMBER SALAD

tangy, chilling

SERVES 6

- 2 English cucumbers, skins scored, halved lengthwise, diced
- 1½ teaspoons fine sea salt
- 3 tablespoons sugar
- 1 cup sour cream
- 2 large egg whites, beaten to soft peaks
- ¼ cup champagne vinegar
- ¼ cup fresh lime juice
- 2 tablespoons chopped parsley
- 1 tablespoon snipped dill

Lime wedges, for garnish

Homegrown cucumbers, whether from your garden or someone else's, are one of the delights of summer. Cooling this salad way, way down by leaving it in the freezer for a few hours gives it a unique icy texture. Served in pitted avocado halves or hollowed-out cucumber boats, with a nice piece of cold poached salmon or gravlax, and with thin slices of buttered pumpernickel, this salad is quite good for a luncheon.

In a colander, combine the cucumbers and 1 teaspoon of the salt. Set in the sink to drain for 30 minutes, tossing occasionally. Rinse the cucumbers and set to drain on paper towels.

In a large resealable freezer bag, combine the remaining ½ teaspoon salt, the sugar, sour cream, beaten egg whites, vinegar, lime juice, 1 tablespoon water, the parsley, and dill. Add the prepared cucumber. Chill in the freezer for 1 hour.

Turn the salad into a large bowl and beat well. Return the mixture to the freezer bag and freeze for 2 hours, or until crystallized. Serve with lime wedges.

EDITOR'S NOTE

Softly whipped egg whites give this salad a light texture, even when it's frozen. To eliminate the (very small) risk of salmonella poisoning, seek out fresh pasteurized whites in the refrigerator section of a natural-food store or online at eggology.com.

AUTHOR'S NOTES

Long English cucumbers are rarely waxed and virtually seedless. I like to run a zester or channel knife down the sides of cucumbers to remove a little of the skin and create a corduroy look.

To make cucumber boats, slice the cucumbers lengthwise and hollow out the seedy core with a spoon.

BEST OF THE BEST EXCLUSIVE

This simple soup is lovely, but Foose improves it with a topping of lightly salted, softly whipped cream that's broiled until golden.

SWEET PEA SOUP *with* GOLDEN CREAM

SERVES 4 AS A FIRST COURSE

8 cups water
1 carrot, cut into ¼-inch dice
1 celery rib, cut into
 ¼-inch dice
½ small onion, cut into ¼-inch dice
1 teaspoon dry mustard
¼ teaspoon freshly ground
 white pepper
Two 9-ounce bags frozen baby peas
Kosher salt
¾ cup heavy cream

1 In a large saucepan, combine the water with the carrot, celery, onion, dry mustard and white pepper. Simmer over moderate heat for 45 minutes. Add the peas and simmer until thawed, about 2 minutes. Puree the soup in a blender until smooth.

2 Return the soup to the saucepan and simmer over moderate heat, stirring occasionally, until thickened, about 40 minutes. Season with salt.

3 Preheat the broiler. Ladle the soup into shallow ovenproof bowls and set the bowls on a rimmed baking sheet. In a medium bowl, whip the cream to soft peaks. Spoon the cream on top of the soup and season with salt. Broil the soup 3 inches from the heat for about 2 minutes, rotating, until the cream is melted and evenly golden. Serve.

MAKE AHEAD The soup can be refrigerated after Step 2 for up to 2 days. Reheat before broiling.

DUCK BREAST WITH PEARS, WALNUTS
AND BELGIAN ENDIVE, P. 110

MEDITERRANEAN FRESH

by JOYCE GOLDSTEIN

after writing 26 cookbooks and working as a chef for 28 years, Joyce Goldstein has established herself as a guru of Mediterranean cuisine. Her latest book zeroes in on salads of all kinds, with almost 150 recipes that go beyond leafy greens to include fruit, beans, grains, seafood, meat and more. There are wonderful recipes for classics like pasta salad with pesto and *salade niçoise,* as well as unusual dishes like cauliflower *zahlouk* (a chopped salad from Morocco) and Greek parsley salad with tahini. Almost every salad idea comes with at least one alternate dressing, making these recipes incredibly flexible.

Published by W. W. Norton & Company, $30

More cooks should try duck instead of the usual chicken. Goldstein scores the breasts so that the fat runs off and the skin becomes crisp, completely transforming all the other ingredients in this salad.

DUCK BREAST *with* PEARS, WALNUTS *and* BELGIAN ENDIVE

SERVES 4

VINAIGRETTE

- 2 tablespoons artisan-produced balsamic vinegar or condiment
- 2 tablespoons sherry vinegar
- ⅓ cup fresh orange juice
- 2 tablespoons freshly grated orange zest

Sea salt

- ⅓ cup toasted hazelnut oil
- ⅔ cup extra-virgin olive oil

DUCK

- 2 boneless Muscovy duck breast halves, about ½ to ¾ pound each, or 4 boneless Pekin duck breasts, 4 to 5 ounces each

Sea salt and freshly ground black pepper

Pinch of ground cinnamon or cloves (optional)

- 4 tablespoons walnuts or hazelnuts, toasted and coarsely chopped

2 or 3 heads Belgian endive, leaves separated and cut crosswise into 1-inch-wide pieces

- 1 head chicory, leaves separated
- 2 small Anjou or Comice pears, halved, cored, and sliced

Whenever I'm in Italy, instead of dining in restaurants all the time, I love to have a meal in a regional wine bar. It's a great way to sample local food products: specialty breads, salumi, cheeses, and oils, and of course the local wines from small producers. One of my favorite wine shops in Rome is the Enoteca Costantini, just off the Piazza Cavour. It has a small signature restaurant called Il Simposio, where I first tasted this dish. Sliced duck breast was dressed with orange balsamic vinaigrette and surrounded by slivers of pear and tiny leaves of wild arugula, a well-balanced contrast of bitter greens, rich duck, and sweet fruit. The duck was served warm. As wild arugula is not always easy to come by, I decided to make this at home with Belgian endive and chicory, but you can also use a mixture of bitter greens, even baby spinach.

At first the only duck breasts I could find at my market (without having to buy the whole duck) were giant Muscovy duck breasts, each big enough to feed two people. But the butcher at the meat counter directed me to the freezer case, where I found boneless Pekin duck breasts, each an ideal serving for one person. Both kinds of duck breast will work here. This dish requires last-minute attention, as it is best when the duck is served warm.

Make the Vinaigrette

Whisk all the ingredients together in a small bowl.

Make the Duck

Using a sharp knife, score the skin of the duck breasts in a crosshatch pattern, but do not cut into the meat. Rub the breasts with salt and pepper and a pinch of cinnamon, if you like. Let stand at room temperature for about 30 minutes.

Heat the oven to 350°F.

Place a large ovenproof sauté pan over medium heat. When it is hot, add the duck breasts, skin side down, and cook until the breasts render their fat, 8 to 10 minutes. Drain off the fat and slip the pan into the oven. Roast the duck for about 8 minutes for medium-rare. (If you like, you can finish the breasts on the stovetop, reducing the heat to low and sautéing, turning once, for 8 to 10 minutes.) Transfer the duck to a cutting board and let rest for 5 minutes. When the duck is cool enough to handle, cut it on the diagonal into ¼-inch-thick slices.

In a small bowl, macerate the nuts in 1 tablespoon dressing.

In a bowl, combine the Belgian endive and chicory. Sprinkle with salt to taste and toss with ¼ cup dressing. Arrange on 4 salad plates. Top with slices of duck and pear and drizzle with another ¼ cup of the the dressing (reserve the remaining dressing for another use). Sprinkle the nuts on top and serve.

Because chicken thighs can marinate longer than breasts without turning mealy, they can absorb more flavor. These come off the grill with the heady fragrance of garlic, red wine and paprika.

CHICKEN KEBABS *with* OREGANO GARLIC VINAIGRETTE MARINADE

SERVES 6

18 small boneless chicken thighs
1 large onion, cut in chunks (about 1½ cups)
2 cups Oregano Garlic Vinaigrette (recipe follows)
1 tablespoon sweet paprika or pimentón dulce
Sea salt and freshly ground black pepper

Although most recipes for chicken kebabs specify boneless, skinless, cubed chicken breasts, breasts are easily overcooked and can toughen on the grill. I prefer to use boned chicken thighs with the skin on. They remain moist and juicy throughout the broiling or grilling process, and the skin retains a wonderful flavor of the marinade. It is best to marinate the chicken for at least 6 hours and preferably overnight in the refrigerator. This recipe is an adaptation of jujeh kababe *and was given to me by an Iranian friend, but I have seen other versions of this dish in cookbooks from the Caucasus. Some use saffron instead of paprika; others use no herbs at all. If you like the smokiness of Spanish pimentón, by all means use it. Serve with rice pilaf or atop a rice salad.*

Place the chicken thighs in a nonreactive container.

Put the onion, dressing, and paprika in a blender or food processor. Puree until the ingredients are well mixed. Pour the marinade over the chicken and refrigerate overnight. Bring the chicken to room temperature before broiling or grilling.

Preheat the broiler or gas grill or make a charcoal fire. Soak the wooden skewers in water for 30 minutes.

Remove the chicken from the marinade and thread on skewers, 3 thighs per person. Sprinkle with salt and pepper to taste. Broil or grill for about 4 minutes on each side, or until the juices run clear and the chicken is cooked through. Serve immediately.

OREGANO GARLIC VINAIGRETTE

MAKES 1¾ CUPS

- 3 tablespoons dried oregano
- ½ cup red wine vinegar
- 2 to 3 cloves garlic, very finely minced
- Sea salt and freshly ground black pepper
- 1¼ cups mild and fruity olive oil

EDITOR'S NOTE

This flavorful vinaigrette is a great all-purpose marinade for grilling. Marinating time depends on the delicacy of the ingredients: Marinate lamb overnight, white-meat chicken for a few hours and shrimp for just 10 minutes.

Widely used in Greece, Italy, and Spain, this vinaigrette is delicious as a marinade for grilled vegetables, tossed in potato, rice, or bean salads, or spooned onto cherry tomatoes, regular tomatoes, mozzarella bocconcini, and cooked cauliflower and broccoli. It enhances salads where tuna, seafood, and hard-boiled eggs play a prominent role. It is also excellent as a marinade for lamb, chicken, and fish and may be drizzled on cooked chicken, fish, and lamb as a finishing sauce. In Sicily, it's known as salmoriglio or salmorigano sauce. And it's one of my favorite dressings.

Rub the oregano in your hands to warm it and release its oils. Toast it in a dry skillet over low heat for a minute or two.

Whisk all the ingredients together in a bowl. If you have time, warm the dressing over low heat for a few minutes to intensify the flavors.

Who knew that pita chips could be such a phenomenal salad ingredient? Here, triangles of toasted pita soak up the tangy dressing, making them a little tender and a little crispy.

FATTOUSH

SERVES 4 TO 6

 4 large or 8 small pita breads
1 to 1½ cups Basic Citrus Dressing
     (recipe follows)
 2 teaspoons ground sumac
     (optional)
Sea salt and freshly ground
     black pepper
2½ to 3 cups diced tomatoes,
     cut ½ inch thick
     (3 medium tomatoes)
 2 cups diced cucumbers, peeled
     and seeded if necessary,
     cut ½ inch thick
     (2 small cucumbers)
½ cup very finely diced red onion
 6 tablespoons finely chopped
     green onions (white and green
     parts)
 1 cup chopped fresh flat-leaf
     parsley
½ cup thinly slivered fresh mint
 2 cups chopped purslane
     (optional)
 4 cups loosely packed romaine
     strips, cut 1 inch wide

Fattoush was the most requested summer salad at my restaurant, Square One. Not just our customers but our staff too would start requesting it in late June. I'd say, "Please be patient. We have to wait until the tomatoes are perfect— ripe and perfumed."

Fattoush is a Lebanese variation of tabbouleh, the classic Middle Eastern wheat salad, but instead of using bulgur, it uses toasted pita bread. I love the textures in this salad and suggest that for the full crunch effect, you dress it just before serving, so the bread does not become soggy. Like tabbouleh, it typically takes a lemon and olive oil dressing, usually enhanced with tart sumac and lots of fresh mint and parsley. Adding the fleshy purslane and ground sumac is optional, as they are not readily found in many markets. They are, however, worth seeking out. Purslane is now considered a gourmet weed and is sold at many farmers' markets. Sumac is available at stores that specialize in Middle Eastern food or online from websites such as Penzeys.com and Vannsspices.com.

While the ingredients are not authentic, you can extend this salad by adding strips of cooked chicken or lamb, or even a few shrimp if you want to turn it into a full meal. Under the pan-Mediterranean umbrella, where ingredients from any region may be used, proprietary to the recipe or not, you'll find feta cheese added to fattoush—again, not authentic but tasty.

EDITOR'S NOTE
Sumac is a fruity, tart red berry that grows wild in the Middle East and Italy. It is ground into a deep red seasoning that Middle Eastern cooks use as a garnish to add a lemony flavor to dishes. A squeeze of lemon can be used in its place.

Heat the oven to 350°F. Place the pita breads on a baking sheet and bake until they are dry, about 15 minutes. Remove from the oven. When cool enough to handle, break the bread into large bite-sized pieces.

In a small bowl, whisk together the dressing and sumac, if using, and add salt and pepper to taste.

In a large salad bowl, combine the tomatoes, cucumber, red onion, green onion, parsley, and mint, then add the pita pieces, the purslane, if using, and the romaine, and toss with dressing. Serve immediately.

continued on p. 116

BASIC CITRUS DRESSING

MAKES ¾ CUP

½ cup mild and fruity extra-virgin
   olive oil
4 tablespoons fresh lemon juice
Sea salt and freshly ground
   black pepper

Citrus dressings are popular all over the Mediterranean but especially in the Middle East and North Africa. They are used to dress leafy and chopped salads, cooked vegetables such as beets, fennel, favas, and artichokes, and bean and grain salads. Citrus dressings are particularly good on fruit salads, salads with strong cheese components, and salads that are served with wine. They are ideal for seafood salads and raw fish dishes and may be spooned liberally over cooked fish and seafood as a finishing sauce. In Greece, the simple mixture of olive oil and lemon juice is called ladolemono.

Whisk all the ingredients together in a bowl.

Variation

For Garlic Citrus Dressing, add 2 teaspoons minced garlic.

BEST OF THE BEST EXCLUSIVE

This creamy risotto is a very satisfying one-dish meal. It's delicious with any kind of flaky white fish, such as branzino, trout or perch.

RISOTTO *with* SOLE

SERVES 6

1   stick (4 ounces) unsalted butter
1½ pounds sole fillets
Kosher salt and freshly
     ground pepper
2   cups bottled clam broth
1   onion, finely chopped
2   cups carnaroli rice
1   cup frozen baby peas, thawed
2   tablespoons snipped chives
2   tablespoons chopped
     flat-leaf parsley

1 In a large skillet, melt 4 tablespoons of the butter. Season the fillets with salt and pepper and cook over moderately high heat, turning once, until just white throughout, about 5 minutes. Transfer the fish to a plate and break it up into 1-inch chunks.

2 In a medium saucepan, mix the clam broth with 5 cups of water. Bring to a simmer and keep warm. In a large saucepan, melt 2 tablespoons of the butter. Add the onion and cook over moderate heat until tender, about 5 minutes. Add the rice and cook until well coated with butter, about 1 minute. Add 1 cup of the warm broth and cook over moderate heat, stirring constantly, until nearly absorbed. Continue adding the broth ½ cup at a time and stirring constantly until it is nearly absorbed between additions. The risotto is done when the rice is al dente and suspended in a thick, creamy sauce, about 20 minutes total. Season with salt and pepper.

3 Add the peas and the remaining 2 tablespoons of butter to the risotto and cook until the peas are warmed through and the butter is melted. Remove from the heat. Gently fold in the chives and parsley along with the fish and any accumulated fish juices. Ladle the risotto into shallow bowls and serve.

FENNEL AND PISTACHIO SALAD, P. 120

THE BOOK OF NEW ISRAELI FOOD

by JANNA GUR

even cooks who love Mediterranean food often know virtually nothing about the cuisine of Israel beyond hummus and falafel. Janna Gur, the editor of an Israeli food and wine magazine, seeks to remedy that by examining modern Israeli recipes in depth. They're a product, she explains, of both European and Arabic influences. "A society of immigrants from more than 70 countries, Israel is constantly changing, and so is its cuisine," she writes. Gur offers recipes for everything from Jerusalem bagels to lamb kebabs, as well as stories describing food traditions like the copious Israeli breakfast (a source of national pride). Gur's writing is enhanced by photographs of the markets, people and ingredients that represent the diversity of Israeli cooking today.

Published by Schocken Books, $35

Combining fennel and pistachios (a staple in Persian cooking) is a terrific idea for anyone in a salad rut. Chopped chile and lemon in the salad make the simple dressing taste more complex than it is.

FENNEL *and* PISTACHIO SALAD

SERVES 4 TO 6

3 to 4 small fennel bulbs
½ cup filleted lemon segments
   (see Editor's Note)
Coarse sea salt
¼ cup delicate olive oil
 1 hot green pepper, chopped finely
 2 tablespoons honey
½ cup pistachio nuts, roasted
   and crushed

1 Cut the fennel bulbs into thin longitudinal slices. Soak in ice water for about 30 minutes. Drain, mix the fennel slices with the lemon segments, sprinkle coarse sea salt on top and set aside to rest for 15 minutes.

2 Mix the fennel and lemon salad with the olive oil, hot pepper and honey. Sprinkle the roasted pistachio nuts on top and serve.

EDITOR'S NOTE

To fillet a lemon (a technique also known as supreming): Use a serrated knife to cut away all the skin and white pith from the fruit. Next, holding the skinned fruit over a bowl, slice between the segments to release them into the bowl.

Myriad recipes call for ricotta, Parmesan and feta, but few combine the three to such good effect. Incredibly easy to make, these pastries would be delicious either for breakfast or as a snack with wine.

CHEESE BOUREKAS

MAKES 20 LARGE BOUREKAS

THE CHEESE FILLING

500	grams (1 pound 2 ounces) *gvina levana* (fresh white cheese) or ricotta (5 percent fat)
250	grams (9 ounces) kashkaval or Parmesan cheese, grated
250	grams (9 ounces) brinza or feta cheese, crumbled
2	egg yolks
1	tablespoon cornstarch

Freshly ground black pepper

THE PASTRY

1½	kilograms (3 pounds 5 ounces) puff pastry dough
1	egg, beaten with 1 tablespoon water, for brushing

Sesame seeds for garnishing

EDITOR'S NOTE

Because they're made with purchased puff pastry, these flaky Balkan bourekas come together fast. For the best flavor, use all-butter puff pastry (look for it in the freezer section of specialty food stores). Thaw puff pastry in the refrigerator and roll it out while it's cool to keep it from sticking.

Crisp, golden pastry triangles filled with cheese—a Balkan classic.

1 Preheat the oven to 180°C (350°F).

2 Beat all the ingredients for the filling until smooth.

3 Roll the dough into a ½-centimeter (¼-inch) thick sheet. Cut into 12-centimeter (5-inch) squares. Put 1 tablespoon of the filling in the center of each square, fold diagonally to form a triangle and pinch the edges together. Arrange the bourekas with sufficient space between them on a tray lined with baking paper.

4 Brush the triangles with the beaten egg and sprinkle sesame seeds on top.

5 Bake for about 30 minutes, until the bourekas are golden and plump and smell delicious.

This dip comes together quickly—no food processor or blender necessary. Simply stir the roasted eggplant until it's creamy.

ROASTED EGGPLANT *with* TAHINI

½ cup raw tahini
3 to 4 tablespoons fresh lemon juice
2 cloves garlic, crushed
2 to 3 tablespoons chopped parsley
Salt and freshly ground black pepper
2 roasted eggplants
(see Flame-Roasting Eggplants)
Toasted sesame seeds or pine nuts

This classic combination always works. Use best-quality tahini.

Season the tahini with the lemon juice, crushed garlic, parsley and a pinch of salt and pepper. Stir the tahini into the flesh of the roasted eggplants. If the mixture is too thick, add water gradually and stir to desired texture. Sprinkle with toasted sesame seeds or pine nuts before serving.

Flame-Roasting Eggplants

Roasting eggplants on an open flame can be messy but is definitely worth the effort, as the smoky aroma adds immensely to the taste.

First line your stovetop with aluminum foil. Place a whole eggplant (or more than one if you are confident) on a rack over the open flame and roast, turning occasionally, until the skin is scorched and blackened and the flesh feels soft when pierced with a wooden skewer or a fork. The eggplant can also be broiled in the oven, or grilled on a charcoal barbecue. Cool slightly (to avoid burning your hands) and peel, carefully removing every last bit of scorched skin, or cut in half lengthwise and scoop out the flesh with a wooden spoon.

Ideally, roasted eggplant should be served shortly after roasting, and seasoned while still warm to ensure optimal absorption of every spicy nuance. But if you need to store it for later, drain the roasted flesh of excess liquid, cover with oil and refrigerate. Season before serving.

EDITOR'S NOTE
To serve this dish as part of a meze (appetizer) spread, set it out with olives, hummus, stuffed grape leaves and pickled turnips or other vegetables (available in Middle Eastern markets). Accompany with plenty of warm pita bread.

The oil in this recipe becomes more richly flavored as it's used first to fry the pine nuts, then the almonds, lamb and, finally, the rice.

MANSAF

SERVES 6 TO 8

1   cup olive oil
1   cup pine nuts
1   cup blanched almonds
6   lamb shanks, about 500 grams
    (1 pound) each
1   teaspoon ground cardamom
1   teaspoon Baharat Spice Mix
    (recipe follows)
1   teaspoon turmeric
1   teaspoon salt
½   teaspoon freshly ground
    black pepper
1   kilogram (2 pounds 4 ounces) rice

A traditional lamb casserole served at weddings as well as at the Eid El-Fitr feast. The dish is traditionally accompanied by warm yogurt.

1 Heat olive oil in a wide saucepan and fry the pine nuts until golden. Remove with a slotted spoon and drain on paper towel. Fry the almonds in the same oil and drain them too on paper towel.

2 Add the lamb shanks to the pan and seal on all sides, until the meat turns golden. Remove with a slotted spoon and save the oil.

3 Transfer the meat to a different pan and cover with water. Cook for 3 hours, until it is very tender and almost falls off the bone. Add all the seasonings toward the end of the cooking cycle. Strain and save the cooking liquid. Keep the meat warm.

4 Fry the rice in the saved oil for a few minutes. Add about 1½ liters (1½ quarts) of the cooking liquid, bring to a boil, lower the heat, cover and cook for 20 minutes.

5 To serve, spread the rice on a large tray or serving dish and arrange the meat on top. Sprinkle with the pine nuts and almonds and serve immediately.

BAHARAT SPICE MIX

1   tablespoon ground cardamom
1   tablespoon ground black pepper
½   tablespoon ground allspice
1   tablespoon ground cinnamon
1   tablespoon ground dry ginger
½   tablespoon ground nutmeg

It is best to use whole spices and roast and grind them prior to mixing, but quality ground spices can be used as well.

Mix all the ingredients and keep in an airtight jar.

Sesame in three forms—as thick tahini paste, toasty sesame oil and crunchy whole seeds—transforms this unusual cabbage slaw.

CABBAGE SLAW *with* ASIAN TAHINI DRESSING

SERVES 8

- 3 tablespoons tahini paste
- 2 tablespoons fresh lemon juice
- 2 tablespoons soy sauce
- 1½ tablespoons honey
- 2 teaspoons Asian sesame oil
- ½ head green cabbage, shredded (about 8 cups)
- 6 radishes, thinly sliced
- 5 medium button mushrooms, thinly sliced
- ⅔ cup mung bean sprouts
- ¼ cup toasted sesame seeds
- 2 scallions, white and green parts, thinly sliced

Kosher salt

In a small bowl, whisk the tahini with the lemon juice, soy sauce, honey and sesame oil. In a large bowl, combine the cabbage with the radishes, mushrooms, bean sprouts, sesame seeds and scallions. Add the tahini dressing and toss to coat. Season the slaw with salt and serve.

MAKE AHEAD The tahini dressing can be refrigerated for up to 5 days. The slaw can be refrigerated for up to 2 hours.

Typical curry ingredients, including tamarind pulp (on knife) and fresh curry leaves.

660 CURRIES

by RAGHAVAN IYER

What is curry, and why does anyone need 660 of them? Cookbook author and teacher Raghavan Iyer explains that curry is not only the powder in a bottle; he defines it broadly as "any dish that consists of meat, fish, poultry, legumes, vegetables, or fruits simmered in or covered with a sauce, gravy, or other liquid that is redolent of spices and/or herbs." From this starting point, Iyer provides hundreds of authentic yet accessible recipes from all over India. Most are one-dish dinners with aromatic, gorgeously spiced sauces (some hot, some not). These are the headily fragrant, deeply satisfying recipes that have made Indian cuisine so revered around the world, and any cook will be glad to have 660 to choose from.

Published by Workman, $22.95

This perfectly seasoned dal (a legume stew) comes together quickly. A generous amount of fresh ginger gives the lentils a nice warmth.

GINGERED RED LENTILS *with* GARLIC

MAKES 4 CUPS

- 1 cup skinned split brown lentils (salmon-colored in this form, masoor dal), picked over for stones
- 1 small red onion, coarsely chopped
- 4 large cloves garlic, coarsely chopped
- 4 lengthwise slices fresh ginger (each 2 inches long, 1 inch wide, and ⅛ inch thick), coarsely chopped
- 2 fresh green Thai, cayenne, or serrano chiles, stems removed
- 2 tablespoons ghee (see Editor's Note) or canola oil
- 1 teaspoon cumin seeds
- 2 dried red Thai or cayenne chiles, stems removed
- 1 medium-size tomato, cored and finely chopped
- 1 teaspoon coarse kosher or sea salt
- ¼ teaspoon ground turmeric
- ¼ cup finely chopped fresh cilantro leaves and tender stems

I love the gingery-garlic flavors in this dal—they provide depth to an otherwise ho-hum legume. For a more substantial and colorful presentation, spoon ¼ cup wilted greens (spinach, mustard, kale, or collard) over each serving of dal.

1 Place the lentils in a medium-size saucepan. Fill the pan halfway with water, and rinse the lentils by rubbing them between your fingertips. The water will become cloudy. Drain this water. Repeat three or four times, until the water remains relatively clear; drain. Now add 3 cups water and bring to a boil, uncovered, over medium heat. Skim off and discard any foam that forms on the surface. Reduce the heat to medium-low, cover the pan, and simmer, stirring occasionally, until the lentils are tender, 18 to 20 minutes.

2 While the lentils are cooking, combine the onion, garlic, ginger, and fresh chiles in a food processor. Mince the ingredients, using the pulsing action. (Letting the blades run constantly will yield a watery blend.)

3 Heat the ghee in a small skillet over medium-high heat. Add the cumin seeds and dried chiles, and cook until the chiles blacken and the seeds turn reddish brown, and smell nutty, 5 to 10 seconds. Immediately add the onion blend, reduce the heat to medium, and stir-fry until the mixture is light brown around the edges, 3 to 5 minutes.

EDITOR'S NOTE
Ghee is a form of clarified butter with a nutty flavor. It's great for frying because it doesn't burn easily. Buy it at Indian groceries or make your own: Melt unsalted butter in a heavy pan over low heat, skim the foam and cook until the solids fall to the bottom of the pan and turn golden. Strain, cool, cover and refrigerate.

4 Stir in the tomato, salt, and turmeric. Simmer, uncovered, stirring occasionally, until the tomato softens and the ghee starts to separate around the edges of the sauce, 3 to 6 minutes. Stir in the cilantro.

5 Stir the sauce into the cooked lentils. Ladle some of the lentil mixture into the skillet and stir it around to wash it out; add this to the lentils.

6 Cover the pan and simmer over medium heat, stirring occasionally, until the flavors mingle, about 5 minutes. Then serve.

Roasting dried chiles in a skillet before blending them with coconut milk gives this mildly tart Keralan curry a wonderfully deep flavor.

TART CHICKEN *with* ROASTED CHILES, TAMARIND *and* COCONUT MILK

SERVES 6

- 4 tablespoons canola oil
- 1 tablespoon yellow split peas (chana dal), picked over for stones
- 1 tablespoon coriander seeds
- 2 dried red Thai or cayenne chiles, stems removed
- 1 cup unsweetened coconut milk
- 2 teaspoons coarse kosher or sea salt
- 3 lengthwise slices fresh ginger (each 2½ inches long, 1 inch wide, and ⅛ inch thick)
- 4 large cloves garlic
- 1 chicken (3½ pounds), skin removed, cut into 8 pieces
- 1 medium-size red onion, cut in half lengthwise and thinly sliced
- 1 teaspoon tamarind paste or concentrate
- 12 to 15 medium-size to large fresh curry leaves (see Editor's Note)
- 2 tablespoons finely chopped fresh cilantro leaves and tender stems

The Moppalahs, inhabitants of the southwestern state of Kerala who follow the doctrines of the Islamic faith, consume chicken, mutton, fish, and other seafood as part of their special-occasion meals. This curry combines roasted and ground spices—a typically southern Indian technique—with coconut milk, the other Keralite staple, to provide the base for plump chicken. Serve it with aromatic basmati rice for a satisfying meal.

1 Heat 2 tablespoons of the oil in a large skillet over medium-high heat. Add the split peas, coriander seeds, and chiles, and roast the blend, stirring constantly, until the split peas and coriander are reddish brown and the chiles have blackened slightly, 1 to 2 minutes. Remove the pan from the heat, and use a slotted spoon to skim off the spice blend and transfer it to a blender jar. Set the pan aside.

2 Add ½ cup of the coconut milk to the blender jar, along with the salt, ginger, and garlic. Puree, scraping the inside of the jar as needed, to form a smooth, creamy yellow, red-speckled paste.

3 Transfer the nutty-smelling marinade to a medium-size bowl. Add the chicken pieces and thoroughly coat them with the marinade. Refrigerate, covered, for at least 30 minutes or as long as overnight, to allow the flavors to liven up the chicken.

4 Add the remaining 2 tablespoons oil to the skillet containing the residual spiced oil, and heat it over medium-high heat. Add the onion and stir-fry until its edges are light brown, 3 to 5 minutes. Add the chicken pieces in a single layer, saving the

EDITOR'S NOTE
Much as bay leaves are used in
Western cooking, aromatic curry
leaves are used in Indian kitchens to
flavor cooking oil, stews and sauces.
You can find fresh or frozen curry
leaves—both far superior to dried—
at Indian groceries. Tightly sealed
in a plastic bag, the leaves can be
frozen for up to 2 months.

residual marinade. Lower the heat to medium, and cook until the chicken is browned on the underside, 3 to 4 minutes. Turn the pieces over and brown on the other side, 3 to 4 minutes.

5 Pour the reserved marinade into the skillet and add the remaining ½ cup coconut milk and the tamarind paste. Stir, making sure the tamarind is thoroughly mixed in with the liquid. Lift the chicken pieces to ensure that the sauce runs underneath. Scrape the bottom to deglaze the pan, releasing all the cooked-on chicken bits, spices, and onion. Reduce the heat to medium-low, cover the skillet, and braise the chicken, basting it occasionally and turning the pieces every few minutes, until the meat in the thickest parts is no longer pink inside and the juices run clear, 15 to 20 minutes. Remove the chicken and arrange it on a serving platter.

6 Stir the curry leaves and cilantro into the sauce and raise the heat to medium. Simmer vigorously, uncovered, stirring occasionally, until the curry is gravy-thick, 5 to 8 minutes.

7 Pour the sauce over the chicken, and serve.

This adaptation of a classic Goan vindaloo is brilliant. Vinegar in the marinade tenderizes the meat and adds tang, while cayenne makes the dish superspicy (cut back on the cayenne for less heat).

TART-HOT BEEF *with* MALT VINEGAR *and* CAYENNE

SERVES 4

½ cup malt vinegar
2 teaspoons cayenne (ground red pepper)
½ teaspoon ground turmeric
1 pound boneless beef (chuck, or "stew meat"), cut into 1-inch cubes
2 tablespoons canola oil
4 ounces pearl onions, peeled and cut in half lengthwise
5 medium-size cloves garlic, finely chopped
6 dried red Thai or cayenne chiles, stems removed
1 teaspoon coriander seeds, ground
1 teaspoon cumin seeds, ground
1 teaspoon coarse kosher or sea salt
2 tablespoons finely chopped fresh cilantro leaves and tender stems for garnishing

Goan vindaloos rely on fermented palm vinegar or cashew vinegar to tone down (just a tad) the cayenne, found in two forms in this curry: whole and ground. In the absence of those two kinds of vinegar in this country, I am using sweet malt vinegar for an equally satisfying balance. I usually make sure there is a bowl of plain yogurt on the table for those who may not be bold enough to savor the heat of the vindaloo.

1 Combine the vinegar, cayenne, and turmeric in a medium-size stainless steel or glass bowl. Add the beef and toss to coat it with the mixture. Refrigerate, covered, for at least 1 hour or preferably overnight, to allow the acidic vinegar to tenderize the beef.

2 Heat the oil in a medium-size saucepan over medium-high heat. Add the onions, garlic, and chiles, and cook, stirring, until the onion halves are light honey-brown, about 5 minutes.

3 Add the beef and marinade. Cook, stirring occasionally, until the beef has absorbed the spiced vinegar and seared, and the oil is starting to separate from the meat, 12 to 15 minutes. Sprinkle in the coriander, cumin, and salt, and cook, stirring, for 1 to 2 minutes.

4 Pour in 1 cup water and bring to a boil. Reduce the heat to medium-low, cover the pan, and cook, stirring occasionally, until the meat is fork-tender and the sauce is reddish brown and thick, 40 to 45 minutes.

5 Remove the chiles if you like. Sprinkle with the cilantro, and serve.

These spinach and chickpea pancakes have the fluffy texture of omelets. They get their rich flavor from chickpea flour, which is available at natural-food stores and Indian groceries.

SPINACH *and* CHICKPEA FLOUR PANCAKES

SERVES 8

 1 cup chickpea flour
1½ teaspoons kosher salt
 ¼ teaspoon turmeric
 ¾ cup water
 1 cup packed baby spinach
   leaves, finely chopped
 1 tomato—halved, seeded
   and finely chopped
 ¼ cup finely chopped cilantro
 1 jalapeño, finely chopped
 3 tablespoons vegetable oil

1 In a medium bowl, whisk the chickpea flour with the salt and turmeric. Gradually whisk in the water until the batter is smooth. Stir in the spinach, tomato, cilantro and jalapeño.

2 In a large nonstick skillet, heat 1½ tablespoons of the vegetable oil until shimmering. For each pancake, ladle ¼ cup of the batter into the skillet and spread to a 4-inch round. Cook over moderate heat until light golden on both sides, about 6 minutes total. Transfer the pancakes to plates and cover with foil to keep warm. Repeat with the remaining oil and batter.

SERVE WITH Grilled lamb or chicken.

MAKE AHEAD The pancakes can be made up to 3 hours in advance. Reheat gently before serving.

COFFEE CARDAMOM CRÈME
CARAMEL, P. 136

OLIVES AND ORANGES

by SARA JENKINS *and* MINDY FOX

f or *Olives and Oranges,* her first book, Sara Jenkins taps into her childhood experiences living all over the Mediterranean (her father was a foreign correspondent) and her training as a chef. "The intent of this book," she writes, "is to show you how flavors work independently and together, so you can follow your own instincts and appetites, make the most out of the ingredients you have, cook without a recipe if you like, or change one to suit your needs." Jenkins makes classic Mediterranean recipes her own, then identifies them as quick- or slow-cooking dishes—a very practical approach. Her combinations are often ingenious, as in her spaghettini with ground lamb, yogurt and mint (a quintessential Turkish trio).

Published by Houghton Mifflin Company, $35

This clever variation on crème caramel is unbelievably creamy, and the balance of coffee and heady toasted cardamom is just right.

COFFEE CARDAMOM CRÈME CARAMEL

SERVES 6
SLOW-COOK RECIPE

CARAMEL
- ½ cup superfine sugar
- ¼ cup water

CUSTARD
- 1 heaping tablespoon green cardamom pods
- 1½ cups heavy cream
- ½ cup whole milk
- 3 tablespoons sugar
- 1 tablespoon instant coffee granules
- 1 large egg
- 3 large egg yolks
- Pinch of fine sea salt

SPECIAL EQUIPMENT
Six ½-cup ramekins

In Beirut, sweet dense coffee perfumed with cardamom is the beverage of choice for the men sitting around the coffeehouses playing backgammon and smoking their hookahs. Crème caramel, the French bistro staple, is perfectly suited to mixing with the flavors of the Old Colony.

Heat oven to 300°F. Set ramekins in a 9-by-13-inch baking dish.

For caramel

Heat sugar and water in a small saucepan over low heat, stirring until sugar dissolves, 2 to 3 minutes. Increase heat to medium-high and, without stirring, boil sugar mixture until it becomes a golden brown caramel, about 6 minutes, gently swirling once it starts to color. Remove from heat. Working quickly, distribute caramel evenly among ramekins, gently turning each ramekin to coat bottom.

For custard

Toast cardamom pods in a small skillet over medium-low heat until lightly golden and fragrant, about 5 minutes. Remove from heat and crack pods, using a mortar and pestle.

Combine cracked cardamom pods, cream, milk, and sugar in a medium saucepan and bring just to a boil. Remove from heat, add coffee, and whisk to dissolve coffee. Let steep, uncovered, for 10 minutes.

EDITOR'S NOTE
This caramel recipe calls for
superfine sugar, which dissolves
faster in water than granulated
white sugar. It's sold in boxes in
some supermarkets, but it can be
hard to find. Regular white sugar
will also work here; just stir until it
has dissolved thoroughly.

Strain cream mixture into a bowl and discard cardamom pods.

Lightly beat egg and egg yolks together in a medium bowl. Gradually add ¼ cup cream mixture to eggs and whisk to combine. Add remaining cream mixture and salt, whisking to combine.

Distribute custard evenly among ramekins. Add enough hot water to baking dish to come halfway up ramekins. Cover baking dish with foil and make a few slits in foil with the tip of a paring knife. Bake until custard is set, about 55 minutes.

Remove custards from water bath and let cool completely, then chill until very cold, at least 4 hours, or up to 2 days.

Serve from ramekins or unmold onto plates.

This side dish is great because it's so fast to prepare yet has enough bold flavor to accompany a plain piece of grilled fish or chicken.

GREEN BEANS *with* SHAVED ONION, FRIED ALMONDS *and* PARMIGIANO-REGGIANO

SERVES 4
QUICK-COOK RECIPE

- ¼ cup plus 2 tablespoons extra-virgin olive oil
- ½ cup whole raw almonds
- 1 teaspoon fleur de sel or other medium-coarse sea salt
- 1 pound green beans, trimmed
- 5 ounces Parmigiano-Reggiano cheese, any rind removed, cut into ⅓- to ½-inch irregular chunks
- 1 small red onion, thinly sliced or shaved on a mandoline or vegetable slicer
- ½ cup loosely packed fresh flat-leaf parsley leaves

Fresh-picked green beans are sublime and very different from not so fresh. In this dish, the onion is cooked just enough by the warmth of the beans to soften and sweeten its sharp piquancy. Even the cheese is transformed, as the warmth of the beans encourages it to give up its earthy tones to the dish. You can vary this dish in many ways. Try adding torn basil or other herb leaves, using scallions in place of the onion, or substituting Manchego cheese or Queso Iberico for the Parmesan.

Heat 2 tablespoons oil in a small skillet over medium heat. Add almonds and cook, shaking pan back and forth occasionally, until nuts are golden and start to pop, about 4 minutes. Remove from heat, sprinkle with ½ teaspoon salt, and stir. Remove nuts from oil with a slotted spoon and drain on paper towels, then coarsely chop.

Bring a large saucepan of well-salted water to a boil. Add beans and cook until crisp-tender, about 5 minutes. Drain, transfer to a large bowl, and immediately toss beans with remaining ¼ cup oil and ½ teaspoon salt.

Add cheese, onion, and parsley; toss well. Let sit for a few minutes, then toss with almonds and serve.

Flavor Tip

One of the simplest and best cooking techniques I learned in Italy is to toss vegetables just pulled from the oven or a pot of boiling water with a healthy pour of good extra-virgin olive oil. The heat of the vegetable brings out the perfume of the oil, allowing flavors to mingle in a way completely different from when a cold vegetable is dressed.

EDITOR'S NOTE
Seasoning the green beans with a squeeze of lemon immediately before serving them really enhances the flavor of the red onions, fried almonds and Parmesan cheese in this recipe.

Few pasta dishes call for yogurt, but it's fabulous in this luxurious spaghettini; whole-milk Greek yogurt would deliver even more tang.

SPAGHETTINI *with* GROUND LAMB, YOGURT *and* MINT

SERVES 4 TO 6
QUICK-COOK RECIPE

- 2 cups tangy plain whole-milk yogurt, such as Old Chatham sheep's-milk yogurt
- ½ teaspoon Aleppo pepper (see Editor's Note) or crushed dried red chile pepper
- 3 garlic cloves, minced
- 1 cup coarsely chopped mint leaves
- 2 tablespoons extra-virgin olive oil
- 1 medium onion, minced

Medium-coarse sea salt

- ¼ cup pine nuts
- 1 tablespoon unsalted butter
- 2 pounds ground lamb
- 1 pound spaghettini or other long pasta

Coarsely ground black pepper

EDITOR'S NOTE
Grown in Syria and Turkey, Aleppo pepper is a slightly sweet, mildly hot, oil-rich red chile with a complex, fruity flavor. It's usually sold coarsely ground in deep red, glossy flakes. Order Aleppo pepper from penzeys.com.

This may be the only pasta I make that is not Italian-inspired, but it's one that I really love. The flavor of cool, tangy yogurt with hot lamb, good as it is in a kebab-type sandwich, is just as terrific in this unusual recipe, which is originally from Turkey. Other long pastas also work well here, especially spaghetti, bucatini, and fresh tagliatelle.

Bring a large pot of salted water to a boil.

Stir together yogurt, Aleppo pepper, two-thirds of garlic, and half of mint in a medium bowl.

Heat oil in a large skillet over medium heat. Add onion, remaining garlic, and a pinch of salt and cook, stirring occasionally, until onion is becoming translucent, about 2 minutes. Add pine nuts and butter and cook until nuts begin to color, about 2 minutes more. Transfer mixture to bowl with yogurt.

Add one-third of lamb to skillet, increase heat to high, and cook until lamb starts to brown, about 5 minutes. Add remaining lamb in 2 batches, then cook, stirring occasionally, until well browned, crispy in spots, and cooked through, about 5 minutes more. The lamb should give off some liquid, but if not, add ¼ cup or so water, to give a little moisture, and stir to blend. Remove from heat.

Meanwhile, when lamb is close to done, cook pasta until al dente. Drain, transfer pasta to a large bowl, and immediately toss with half of lamb and half of yogurt mixture. Add remaining mint, lamb, and yogurt mixture and toss again. Season with salt to taste and abundant black pepper, and serve at once.

Unlike other greens, such as spinach and chard, escarole stays a little crunchy after it's been sautéed. It's quite good here with the chicken, smashed potatoes and (an unexpected addition) apples.

CHICKEN *with* ESCAROLE, APPLES *and* POTATOES

SERVES 4
QUICK-COOK RECIPE

- 12 ounces small new potatoes
- 4 (8-ounce) boneless chicken breasts with skin
- Fine sea salt and coarsely ground black pepper
- 3 tablespoons extra-virgin olive oil
- 5 tablespoons unsalted butter
- 2 semi-tart apples, such as Empire or Macoun, peeled, cored, and cut into eighths
- 1 garlic clove, smashed and peeled
- 1 pound escarole, leaves torn
- ½ cup dry white wine

Using one skillet to accomplish several steps, you build flavor in the pan as you cook. Use an interesting variety of fresh-dug potatoes from the farmers' market, if available. Fingerlings are one of my favorites; you can also try tiny purple potatoes or red-skinned ones.

Heat oven to 250°F.

Bring a large saucepan of salted water to a boil. Add potatoes and cook until tender, about 7 minutes. Drain and place on a plate in a single layer to cool.

When potatoes are just cool enough to handle, flatten each one slightly by gently pressing on it with the side of a chef's knife. Set aside.

Season chicken with salt and pepper. Heat oil in a large skillet over medium-high heat. Add chicken, skin side down, in batches if necessary, and cook until skin is golden, 5 to 7 minutes. Turn and cook until underside is lightly golden, about 3 minutes. Transfer to a baking pan, cover with foil, and place in oven.

Drain oil from skillet, return to medium-high heat, and add 2 tablespoons butter. Add only as many apples as will fit in a single layer and cook, turning apples as they brown, until golden on all sides, 3 to 4 minutes. Transfer to a plate. Repeat with any remaining apples.

continued on p. 142

Add 2 more tablespoons butter to skillet. Add only as many potatoes as will fit in a single layer, sprinkle with salt and pepper, and cook over medium-high heat, turning once, until potatoes are warmed through and golden, about 2 minutes per side. Transfer to a plate. Repeat with any remaining potatoes.

Add garlic and as much escarole as you can comfortably fit into skillet, increase heat to high, and cook, stirring, until escarole starts to wilt and you can add more, about 1 minute. Add remaining escarole and cook until just wilted, about 1 minute more. Add wine and cook until escarole is tender and wine is slightly reduced. Add apples and cook until warmed through, about 2 minutes. Remove from heat.

Remove chicken from oven and pour any juices from pan into skillet with escarole and apples. Stir to combine.

Divide potatoes among four plates, then add chicken and escarole mixture, leaving juices in skillet. Return skillet to high heat, bring juices to a boil, and boil for 1 minute. Whisk in remaining tablespoon butter. Season sauce with salt and pepper, pour over chicken, and serve.

Flavor Tip

Smashing boiled whole small potatoes, rather than cutting up large ones, and frying them in butter gives you lots of crispy brown edges and fluffy, tender centers.

BEST OF THE BEST EXCLUSIVE

These sweet, lemony brussels sprouts are minimalist—they're made with just five ingredients. Jenkins serves them at Porchetta, her new Manhattan sandwich spot focusing on slow-cooked pork.

ROASTED BRUSSELS SPROUTS *with* HONEY, LEMON *and* THYME DRESSING

SERVES 6

2½ pounds brussels sprouts, halved lengthwise
3 tablespoons extra-virgin olive oil
Kosher salt and freshly ground pepper
3 tablespoons honey
2 tablespoons fresh lemon juice
1 tablespoon thyme leaves

EDITOR'S NOTE
Choose brussels sprouts of uniform size so that they all cook in the same amount of time. Large brussels sprouts tend to have a cabbage-like flavor; small ones are milder and sweeter.

1 Preheat the oven to 400°F. In a large bowl, toss the brussels sprouts with 2 tablespoons of the olive oil and season generously with salt and pepper. Spread the brussels sprouts on a large rimmed baking sheet and roast for about 30 minutes, tossing halfway through, until browned and tender.

2 In a medium serving bowl, whisk the honey with the lemon juice, thyme and the remaining 1 tablespoon of olive oil. Add the brussels sprouts, toss to coat and serve.

MAKE AHEAD The brussels sprouts can be made up to 1 day in advance. Serve warm or at room temperature.

LEMON LEMON LOAF, P. 146

BAKED

by MATT LEWIS *and* RENATO POLIAFITO

When Matt Lewis and Renato Poliafito opened Brooklyn's Baked in 2005, they set out to prove that a bakery could be hip, cool and creative while also serving the old-fashioned cookies and cakes that everyone—hip or not—craves. In this, their first cookbook, the friends share their best recipes: chocolate chip cookies and brownies ("brownies are our thing," Lewis writes), their famous malt ball cake with milk chocolate frosting and their "signature creation," a tall chocolate cake layered with salted caramel, frosted with whipped caramel ganache and sprinkled with a pinch of sea salt. Recipes manage to be simultaneously nostalgic and modern: an unbeatable combination.

Published by Stewart, Tabori & Chang, $29.95

by MATT LEWIS *and* RENATO POLIAFITO

This superbly lemony cake—with three sources of lemon flavor—is beyond moist thanks to sour cream, butter and citrus syrup.

LEMON LEMON LOAF

MAKES TWO 9-BY-5-BY-3-INCH LOAVES

FOR THE LEMON CAKE
1½ cups cake flour
1½ cups all-purpose flour
2 teaspoons baking powder
¼ teaspoon baking soda
1 teaspoon salt
2¼ cups sugar
8 large eggs, at room temperature
¼ cup grated lemon zest
(from about 4 lemons;
see Authors' Note)
¼ cup fresh lemon juice
2 cups (4 sticks) unsalted butter,
melted and cooled
½ cup sour cream, at room
temperature
2 teaspoons pure vanilla extract

FOR THE LEMON SYRUP
⅓ cup fresh lemon juice
⅓ cup sugar

FOR THE LEMON GLAZE (OPTIONAL)
2 cups confectioners' sugar,
sifted, or more if needed
4 to 6 tablespoons fresh
lemon juice

Sometimes simplicity speaks volumes. Our lemon loaf recipe is very straightforward. We do not add poppy seeds, pecans, or any other extraneous ingredient. We really feel that the most important aspect of a lemon loaf is the zingy lemon flavor, and we accentuate it by using a combination of freshly squeezed lemon juice, freshly grated lemon zest, and a mildly sweet lemon syrup. The sour cream gives this loaf a subtle tang and a dense, moist crumb that cannot be achieved with yogurt. If you want to increase the lemony goodness of these cakes, add the simple glaze after the syrup has set and the cakes are cool. This loaf freezes extremely well, so you can double the recipe and make a few extra loaves.

Make the lemon cakes

Preheat the oven to 350°F. Spray the sides and bottom of two 9-by-5-by-3-inch loaf pans with nonstick cooking spray. Line the bottom with parchment paper and spray the paper.

Sift both flours, baking powder, baking soda, and salt together in a medium bowl.

Put the sugar, eggs, lemon zest, and lemon juice in a food processor and pulse until combined. With the motor running, drizzle the butter in through the feed tube. Add the sour cream and vanilla and pulse until combined. Transfer to a large bowl.

Sprinkle in the flour mixture, one-third at a time, folding gently after each addition until just combined. Do not overmix.

Divide the batter evenly between the prepared pans. Bake in the center of the oven for 20 minutes, rotate the pans, reduce the oven temperature to 325°F, and bake for another 30 to 35 minutes, or until a toothpick inserted in the center of the loaf comes out clean.

Let cool in the pans for 15 minutes.

Meanwhile, make the lemon syrup

In a small saucepan over medium heat, heat the lemon juice and sugar until the sugar is completely dissolved. Once dissolved, continue to cook for 3 more minutes. Remove from the heat and set aside.

Line a half sheet pan with parchment paper and invert the loaves onto the pan. Use a toothpick to poke holes in the tops and sides of the loaves.

Brush the tops and sides of the loaves with the lemon syrup. Let the syrup soak into the cake and brush again. Let the cakes cool completely, at least 30 minutes.

(The soaked but unglazed loaves will keep, wrapped in two layers of plastic wrap and frozen, for up to 6 weeks.)

If you like, make the lemon glaze

In a small bowl, whisk together the confectioners' sugar and 4 tablespoons of the lemon juice. The mixture should be thick but pourable. If the mixture is too stiff, add up to another 2 tablespoons lemon juice and whisk again, adding small amounts of lemon juice and/or confectioners' sugar until you get the right consistency. Pour the lemon glaze over the top of each loaf and let it drip down the sides. Let the lemon glaze harden, about 15 minutes, before serving.

The glazed loaves will keep for up to 3 days, wrapped tightly in plastic wrap, at room temperature.

AUTHORS' NOTE For zesting purposes, we always recommend using an organic fruit, free of chemicals or pesticides that might reside deep in the rind.

Salted desserts have become wildly popular, and the recipe for this one works better than any we've tried. The salted caramel used to layer the cake is so good you could even forgo the frosting.

SWEET *and* SALTY CAKE

MAKES ONE 8-INCH CAKE

FOR THE CLASSIC CHOCOLATE CAKE LAYERS

¾ cup dark unsweetened cocoa powder
1¼ cups hot water
⅔ cup sour cream
2⅔ cups all-purpose flour
2 teaspoons baking powder
1 teaspoon baking soda
½ teaspoon salt
¾ cup (1½ sticks) unsalted butter, softened
½ cup vegetable shortening
1½ cups granulated sugar
1 cup firmly packed dark brown sugar
3 large eggs, at room temperature
1 tablespoon pure vanilla extract

FOR THE SALTED CARAMEL

½ cup heavy cream
1 teaspoon fleur de sel (see Authors' Note on p. 151)
1 cup sugar
2 tablespoons light corn syrup
¼ cup sour cream

FOR THE WHIPPED CARAMEL GANACHE FROSTING

1 pound dark chocolate (60 to 70 percent cacao), chopped
1½ cups heavy cream
1 cup sugar
2 tablespoons light corn syrup
2 cups (4 sticks) unsalted butter, soft but cool, cut into ½-inch pieces

TO ASSEMBLE THE CAKE

2 teaspoons fleur de sel, plus more for garnish

This is our most loved cake and our most requested recipe. Is all this attention warranted? Absolutely. Our Sweet and Salty Cake is an indulgent but sophisticated adult sweet: The perfectly salted caramel contrasts beautifully with the rich chocolate layers, giving the cake balance and character.

Make the classic chocolate cake layers

Preheat the oven to 325°F. Butter three 8-inch round cake pans, line the bottoms with parchment paper, and butter the parchment. Dust with flour, and knock out the excess flour.

In a medium bowl, combine the cocoa powder, hot water, and sour cream and set aside to cool.

Sift the flour, baking powder, baking soda, and salt together into a medium bowl and set aside.

In the bowl of an electric mixer fitted with the paddle attachment, beat the butter and shortening on medium speed until ribbonlike, about 5 minutes. Add the sugars and beat until light and fluffy, about 5 minutes. Add the eggs, one at a time, beating well after each addition, then add the vanilla and beat until incorporated. Scrape down the bowl and mix again for 30 seconds.

Add the flour mixture, alternating with the cocoa mixture, in three additions, beginning and ending with the flour mixture.

Divide the batter among the prepared pans and smooth the tops. Bake for 35 to 40 minutes, rotating the pans halfway through the baking time, until a toothpick inserted in the

continued on p. 150

center of each cake comes out clean. Transfer the cakes to a wire rack and let cool for 20 minutes. Invert the cakes onto the rack, remove the pans, and let cool completely. Remove the parchment.

Make the salted caramel

In a small saucepan, combine the cream and fleur de sel. Bring to a simmer over very low heat until the salt is dissolved.

Meanwhile, keeping a close eye on the cream mixture so it doesn't burn, in a medium saucepan combine ¼ cup water, the sugar, and corn syrup, stirring them together carefully so you don't splash the sides of the pan. Cook over high heat until an instant-read thermometer reads 350°F, 6 to 8 minutes. Remove from the heat and let cool for 1 minute.

Add the cream mixture to the sugar mixture. Whisk in the sour cream. Let the caramel cool to room temperature, then transfer to an airtight container and refrigerate until you are ready to assemble the cake.

Make the whipped caramel ganache frosting

Put the chocolate in a large heatproof bowl and set aside.

In a small saucepan, bring the cream to a simmer over very low heat.

Meanwhile, keeping a close eye on the cream so it doesn't burn, in a medium saucepan combine ¼ cup water, the sugar, and corn syrup, stirring them together carefully so you don't splash the sides of the pan. Cook over high heat until an instant-read thermometer reads 350°F, 6 to 8 minutes. Remove from the heat and let the caramel cool for 1 minute.

Add the cream to the caramel and stir to combine. Stir slowly for 2 minutes, then pour the caramel over the chocolate. Let the caramel and chocolate sit for 1 minute, then, starting in the center of the bowl, and working your way out to the edges, slowly stir the chocolate and caramel mixture in a circle until the chocolate is completely melted. Let the mixture cool, then transfer it to the bowl of an electric mixer fitted with the paddle attachment. Mix on low speed until the bowl feels cool to the touch. Increase the speed to medium-high and gradually add the butter, beating until thoroughly incorporated. Scrape down the bowl and beat on high speed until the mixture is fluffy.

Assemble the cake

Place one cake layer on a serving platter. Spread ¼ cup of the caramel over the top. Let the caramel soak into the cake, then spread ¾ cup of the ganache frosting over the caramel. Sprinkle 1 teaspoon of the fleur de sel over the frosting, then top with the second cake layer. Spread with caramel frosting and sprinkle with 1 teaspoon of the fleur de sel. Then top with the third layer. Spread with caramel. Crumb coat the cake (see below) and put the cake in the refrigerator for 15 minutes to firm up the frosting. Frost the sides and top with the remaining frosting. Garnish with a sprinkle of fleur de sel.

This cake will keep beautifully in a cake saver at room temperature (cool and humidity free) for up to 3 days. If your room is not cool, place the cake in a cake saver and refrigerate for up to 3 days. Remove the cake from the refrigerator and let it sit at room temperature for at least 2 hours before serving.

AUTHORS' NOTE Fleur de sel, or sea salt, is readily available at grocery stores; however, there is a whole world of specialty salts now available online and at specialty food markets. Gray salt (*sel gris*), Hawaiian sea salt, Italian sea salt, and smoked sea salt will all work well in this recipe.

Crumb Coat

Essentially, a crumb coat is a very thin layer of frosting applied to the cake to keep the light crumbs suspended so they won't appear in the final layer of frosting. A crumb-coated cake should be refrigerated for at least 15 minutes prior to applying the next frosting layer.

Each component of these heavenly bars—the crust, the peanut butter layer and the chocolate icing—requires only a few ingredients. The result is much more than the sum of its parts.

PEANUT BUTTER CRISPY BARS

MAKES 9 BARS

FOR THE CRISPY CRUST
1¾ cups crisped rice cereal
¼ cup sugar
3 tablespoons light corn syrup
3 tablespoons unsalted
     butter, melted

FOR THE MILK CHOCOLATE
PEANUT BUTTER LAYER
5 ounces good-quality milk
     chocolate, coarsely chopped
1 cup creamy peanut butter

FOR THE CHOCOLATE ICING
3 ounces dark chocolate
     (60 to 72 percent cacao),
     coarsely chopped
½ teaspoon light corn syrup
4 tablespoons (½ stick)
     unsalted butter

This is, hands down, the most popular refrigerated bar we make at the bakery. Essentially, this is a very grown-up and very decadent Rice Krispies Treat. The "crispys" are candied, then layered with a generous amount of peanut butter milk chocolate and topped with a glossy dark chocolate icing. We adapted this recipe from the very talented chef and chocolatier Andrew Shotts, who makes the most amazing chocolate truffles for his company, Garrison Confections.

Make the crispy crust

Lightly spray a paper towel with nonstick cooking spray and use it to rub the bottom and sides of an 8-inch square baking pan.

Put the cereal in a large bowl and set aside.

Pour ¼ cup water into a small saucepan. Gently add the sugar and corn syrup (do not let any sugar or syrup get on the sides of the pan) and use a small wooden spoon to stir the mixture until just combined. Put a candy thermometer in the saucepan. Cook over medium-high heat and bring to a boil; cook until the mixture reaches the soft ball stage, 235°F.

Remove from the heat, stir in the butter, and pour the mixture over the cereal. Working quickly, stir until the cereal is thoroughly coated, then pour it into the prepared pan. Using your hands, press the mixture into the bottom of the pan (do not press up the sides). Let the crust cool to room temperature while you make the next layer.

continued on p. 154

EDITOR'S NOTE
To break up large blocks of baking chocolate, pastry chefs use a chocolate fork, a large, pronged tool available at cookware shops or from surlatable.com. To chop a block of chocolate with a knife, it helps to start at the corners.

Make the milk chocolate peanut butter layer

In a large nonreactive metal bowl, stir together the chocolate and the peanut butter.

Set the bowl over a saucepan of simmering water and cook, stirring with a rubber spatula, until the mixture is smooth. Remove the bowl from the pan and stir for about 30 seconds to cool slightly. Pour the mixture over the cooled crust. Put the pan in the refrigerator for 1 hour, or until the top layer hardens.

Make the chocolate icing

In a large nonreactive metal bowl, combine the chocolate, corn syrup, and butter.

Set the bowl over a saucepan of simmering water and cook, stirring with a rubber spatula, until the mixture is completely smooth. Remove the bowl from the pan and stir for 30 seconds to cool slightly. Pour the mixture over the chilled milk chocolate peanut butter layer and spread into an even layer. Put the pan in the refrigerator for 1 hour, or until the topping hardens.

Cut into 9 squares and serve. The bars can be stored in the refrigerator, covered tightly, for up to 4 days.

AUTHORS' NOTE This dessert is extremely rich and best served in small portions (hence the small pan); however, the recipe can be easily doubled or tripled for larger parties.

Pastry chefs have had fun reinventing the whoopie pie over the past few years, but this version—made with pumpkin and cream cheese instead of chocolate and marshmallow—is a true original.

PUMPKIN WHOOPIE PIES
with CREAM CHEESE FILLING

MAKES 12 WHOOPIE PIES

FOR THE PUMPKIN WHOOPIE COOKIES
- 3 cups all-purpose flour
- 1 teaspoon salt
- 1 teaspoon baking powder
- 1 teaspoon baking soda
- 2 tablespoons cinnamon
- 1 tablespoon ginger
- 1 tablespoon cloves
- 2 cups firmly packed dark brown sugar
- 1 cup vegetable oil
- 3 cups chilled pumpkin puree (see Authors' Note on p. 156)
- 2 large eggs
- 1 teaspoon pure vanilla extract

FOR THE CREAM CHEESE FILLING
- 3 cups confectioners' sugar
- ½ cup (1 stick) unsalted butter, softened
- 8 ounces cream cheese, softened
- 1 teaspoon pure vanilla extract

Try as we might, we were never huge fans of the traditional whoopie pie. We love the concept of two cakey chocolate cookies with a fair amount of cream sandwiched between them, but every execution we tried was always less than desirable. Maybe it was the cream filling with the shortening aftertaste. Maybe it was the too-wet cookie itself. After all, there is such a thing as being too moist. So we took some liberties with the whoopie pie and created our own version, which was named one of the top 100 tastes of 2007 by Time Out New York. *Our Pumpkin Whoopie Pie makes the perfect midnight snack, with its soft, cakelike cookie and chilled cream cheese filling. For bite-sized pies, use a melon baller to scoop the dough.*

Make the pumpkin whoopie cookies

Preheat the oven to 350°F. Line two baking sheets with parchment paper.

In a large bowl, whisk the flour, salt, baking powder, baking soda, cinnamon, ginger, and cloves together and set aside.

In a separate bowl, whisk the brown sugar and oil together until combined. Add the pumpkin puree and whisk to combine thoroughly. Add the eggs and vanilla and whisk until combined.

Sprinkle the flour mixture over the pumpkin mixture and whisk until completely combined.

Use a small ice cream scoop with a release mechanism to drop heaping tablespoons of the dough onto the prepared baking sheets, about 1 inch apart. Bake for 10 to 12 minutes, until the

continued on p. 156

cookies are just starting to crack on top and a toothpick inserted into the center of a cookie comes out clean. Remove from the oven and let the cookies cool completely on the pan while you make the filling.

Make the cream cheese filling

Sift the confectioners' sugar into a medium bowl and set aside.

In the bowl of an electric mixer fitted with the paddle attachment, beat the butter until it is completely smooth, with no visible lumps. Add the cream cheese and beat until combined.

Add the confectioners' sugar and vanilla and beat until smooth. Be careful not to overbeat the filling, or it will lose structure. (The filling can be made 1 day ahead. Cover the bowl tightly and put it in the refrigerator. Let the filling soften at room temperature before using.)

Assemble the whoopie pies

Turn half of the cooled cookies upside down (flat side facing up).

Use an ice cream scoop or a tablespoon to drop a large dollop of filling onto the flat side of the cookie. Place another cookie, flat side down, on top of the filling. Press down slightly so that the filling spreads to the edges of the cookie. Repeat until all the cookies are used. Put the whoopie pies in the refrigerator for about 30 minutes to firm up before serving.

The whoopie pies will keep for up to 3 days, on a parchment-lined baking sheet covered with plastic wrap, in the refrigerator.

AUTHORS' NOTE Make sure you chill the pumpkin puree thoroughly before making this recipe. The chilled puree will make your whoopies easier to scoop and give them a domed top.

More bakers are adding fresh herbs to desserts. Rosemary, used judiciously here, contributes a distinctive fragrance to these bars.

ROSEMARY-APRICOT SQUARES

MAKES 16 BARS

2¼   cups all-purpose flour
Salt
2½   teaspoons minced rosemary
1½   sticks (6 ounces) unsalted butter, at room temperature plus 3 tablespoons cold unsalted butter cut into cubes
½   cup confectioners' sugar
1   teaspoon pure vanilla extract
2   cups dried California apricots (8½ ounces)
1½   cups water
½   cup granulated sugar
3   tablespoons honey
2   tablespoons brandy
½   cup packed dark brown sugar
⅓   cup pecans, coarsely chopped

EDITOR'S NOTE
California and Turkish apricots are the types most commonly available. Turkish apricots are orange, plump and round, with a mild, sweet flavor; California apricots, sold halved, tend to have a deep vermilion color and an intense, sweet-tart flavor.

1 Preheat the oven to 350°F. Spray a 9-inch-square baking pan with nonstick cooking spray and line with parchment paper, allowing the parchment to hang over the edge.

2 In a small bowl, whisk 1¾ cups of the flour with ¼ teaspoon of salt and the rosemary. In a standing mixer fitted with the paddle, beat the 1½ sticks of butter with the confectioners' sugar and vanilla at medium speed until fluffy, about 2 minutes. At low speed, gradually beat in the flour mixture until just incorporated. Scrape the dough into the prepared pan; with lightly floured hands, press the dough evenly over the bottom. Refrigerate until chilled, about 30 minutes.

3 Bake the crust for 30 minutes, until light golden. Transfer to a rack and let cool, about 30 minutes.

4 Meanwhile, in a medium saucepan, combine the apricots, water, granulated sugar, honey, brandy and a pinch of salt. Bring to a simmer and cook over moderate heat until the apricots are very tender and the liquid has thickened, about 45 minutes. Scrape into a food processor and puree until smooth.

5 In a standing mixer fitted with the paddle, combine the remaining ½ cup of flour with the chilled butter and dark brown sugar, pecans and a pinch of salt. Beat at medium speed until the mixture resembles sand, about 1 minute.

6 Evenly spread the apricot mixture over the crust. Sprinkle the pecan topping over the filling; bake for 30 minutes, until browned on top. Transfer to a rack and let cool. Using the parchment overhang, transfer to a surface. Slice and serve.

INSALATA DI RISO, P. 160

BIG NIGHT IN

by DOMENICA MARCHETTI

With more people than ever cooking and entertaining at home, the timing is right for this book from Domenica Marchetti, a Virginia-based writer and cooking teacher who specializes in Italian recipes. Her goal here is to provide fantastic dishes for dinner parties, and she does so magnificently. "This is not everyday Italian food," she writes. "The recipes are creative and generous, and some are downright indulgent. Simply put, this is a book of great party food." Marchetti's right: *Big Night In* is a terrific compilation of festive dishes, from antipasti like a spinach and yogurt dip to dolci, including cheesecake sundaes with raspberries.

Published by Chronicle Books, $24.95

This fun, kitchen-sink-style salad of rice, tuna, eggs, pickled vegetables, peas, celery, olives, roasted peppers and capers is a great way to use pantry staples and refrigerator odds and ends.

INSALATA *di* RISO

SERVES 5 TO 6 AS A MAIN COURSE AND 10 TO 12 AS A SIDE DISH

1½   cups arborio, carnaroli, or other short-grain risotto rice
¼   cup extra-virgin olive oil
8   ounces best-quality canned or jarred tuna in olive oil, drained
3   hard-boiled eggs, quartered lengthwise or sliced crosswise
2   Rizzoli brand *alici in salsa piccante* or best-quality Italian anchovy fillets in olive oil, drained and chopped (see Editor's Note on p. 163)
1   cup diced jarred giardiniera (see Editor's Note on p. 166)
½   cup frozen peas, thawed
½   cup diced celery
½   cup pickled cocktail (pearl) onions, drained, and halved if they are any larger than a marble
⅓   cup diced jarred roasted red bell peppers or a combination of roasted red and yellow bell peppers if you can find them at your supermarket or gourmet food store
¼   cup green olives, such as Picholine
¼   cup purple olives, such as Gaeta or kalamata
2   tablespoons minced flat-leaf parsley
1   tablespoon capers, preferably in salt, rinsed, drained, and coarsely chopped
Juice of 1 large lemon
¼   cup mayonnaise (not mayonnaise-based salad dressing or sandwich spread)
Kosher or sea salt to taste
Freshly ground black pepper to taste

Of the many recipes in this book, this appetizing salad may be my favorite. It is based on a dish that my Zia Gilda, my mother's eldest sister, used to make every summer for my sister and me. I like to serve this as a refreshing alternative to potato salad at a backyard cookout, or as the main course at a casual summer luncheon.

Bring a large pot of salted water to a boil over medium-high heat. Pour in the rice. When the water returns to a boil, reduce the heat to medium-low, cover, and cook the rice at a gentle simmer for 20 minutes, or until it is al dente (tender but still a little firm and not at all mushy). Drain the rice in a colander in the sink and rinse it under cold water to stop the cooking process and to cool it. Drain thoroughly and transfer the rice to a large bowl. Toss the rice with the olive oil. Add the remaining ingredients except for the lemon juice, mayonnaise, and salt and pepper, and gently fold everything together. Stir in the lemon juice and mayonnaise and season to taste with salt and pepper. Spoon the rice salad into a decorative serving bowl, cover, and let it sit at room temperature for 30 to 60 minutes to allow the flavors to mingle. Just before serving, toss the salad again and bring it to the table with a large serving spoon to allow your guests to serve themselves.

DO AHEAD My sister and I agree that this salad is at its absolute best when made up to 1 hour in advance so that the rice has time to absorb the flavors but is still just the slightest bit warm. However, the ingredients may be chopped and prepared ahead of time and set aside or refrigerated until you are ready to use them. Bring them to room temperature before mixing them into the rice.

Classic spinach dip calls for any combination of cream cheese, sour cream and mayonnaise. This version, made with thick, tangy yogurt and a touch of cinnamon, is much healthier—and still delicious.

SPINACH *and* YOGURT DIP

MAKES ABOUT 1½ CUPS

- 3 tablespoons unsalted butter
- 1 garlic clove, minced
- ⅓ cup finely chopped yellow onion
- 1 (9-ounce) bag baby spinach leaves, cooked according to package instructions, squeezed to remove excess water, and chopped (about ⅔ cup)
- ¾ teaspoon kosher or sea salt
- 1 cup whole-milk Greek-style yogurt
- ¼ teaspoon ground cinnamon

Freshly ground pepper to taste

EDITOR'S NOTE
To make this streamlined spinach dip recipe even easier, replace the fresh baby spinach with frozen. Drain the thawed spinach well before chopping and measuring out the ⅔ cup needed.

Cinnamon adds a sweet, exotic note to this Middle Eastern–style dip, which I like to serve with both fresh pita bread and crispy pita chips, for a contrast in texture.

Melt the butter in a large skillet placed over medium heat. Add the garlic and onion and cook, stirring frequently, until the onion is soft and translucent, about 7 minutes. Remove the pan from the heat and stir in the spinach and salt. Mix well to combine. Set the mixture aside to cool.

In a medium bowl, combine the yogurt, cinnamon, and a generous grinding of pepper. Fold in the cooled spinach mixture and mix until thoroughly combined. Let the dip sit for 30 minutes to allow the flavors to mingle. Refrigerate until thoroughly chilled.

DO AHEAD This dip can be made up to 2 days in advance and refrigerated in a tightly lidded container. Transfer the dip to a decorative bowl before serving.

The lemon-anchovy butter here gives the steaks fabulous flavor. Freeze any extra and use it on all sorts of grilled foods—it would be tasty with chicken, fish, vegetables or even bread.

GRILLED CAESAR FLANK STEAKS
with LEMON-ANCHOVY BUTTER

SERVES 12

FOR THE STEAKS
- 4 cloves garlic, pressed
- ¾ cup soy sauce
- ½ cup red wine vinegar
- ¼ cup freshly squeezed lemon juice
- 3 tablespoons Worcestershire sauce
- 3 tablespoons smooth Dijon mustard
- Freshly ground black pepper to taste
- ¾ cup extra-virgin olive oil
- 3 flank steaks (about 4 pounds total)

FOR THE LEMON-ANCHOVY BUTTER
- 4 tablespoons unsalted butter, softened to room temperature
- 4 anchovy fillets, preferably Rizzoli brand *alici in salsa piccante,* mashed with a fork (see Editor's Note)
- 1 small clove garlic, minced
- 1 teaspoon lemon zest
- Freshly ground black pepper

TO SERVE
- Whole leaves of red leaf or red romaine lettuce

All the bright, assertive flavors that make up a great Caesar salad come together in this delicious entrée: fresh lemon, Worcestershire sauce, garlic, and anchovies. It has the added appeal of being quick and easy to make; the little prep work involved is done a day in advance. Marinating the flank steak overnight not only gives you a jump start, it enhances the meat's flavor and tenderizes it.

To marinate the steaks

In a medium bowl, whisk together the garlic, soy sauce, vinegar, lemon juice, Worcestershire sauce, mustard, and black pepper. Slowly whisk in the olive oil. Place two of the flank steaks in a gallon-size zipper-lock freezer storage bag and the third in another gallon-size freezer bag. Hold the bags upright and divide the marinade between them, adding a little more to the bag that contains two steaks. Carefully seal the bags shut, pressing out as much air as you can without letting any of the marinade escape. Flatten the bags out and place them on a small rimmed baking sheet or in a baking dish (in case of leakage) and refrigerate overnight.

To make the lemon-anchovy butter

In a small bowl, combine the softened butter, anchovies, garlic, lemon zest, and black pepper to taste. Spoon the butter onto a sheet of waxed paper and roll the paper around the butter, forming the butter into a 2-inch-thick cylinder as you roll. Tightly twist the ends of the paper shut. Place the cylinder

EDITOR'S NOTE
Marchetti favors tins of rolled anchovies in spiced oil, but you can use any good-quality anchovies packed in olive oil here. To keep oil-packed anchovies from getting too fishy-tasting in your fridge, top off the container with olive oil so they're always completely submerged.

of butter in the refrigerator to harden overnight. (I usually set the cylinder in a concave dish that is meant to hold a corn cob; this allows the butter to keep its cylinder shape as it hardens.)

To grill the steaks

Remove the steaks from the refrigerator up to 1 hour before you plan to grill them. Remove the lemon-anchovy butter from the refrigerator 15 to 20 minutes before you plan to serve the steaks.

Prepare a charcoal grill (see Author's Note) or preheat a gas grill to medium-high and lightly oil the grate. Set the steaks on the grill over direct heat and grill them for 5 to 8 minutes per side, or until an instant-read thermometer registers 120°F for rare and 130°F for medium-rare. Remove the steaks to a carving board and loosely tent them with foil. Let them sit for about 10 minutes before slicing.

To serve, cut the steaks across the grain into ½-inch-thick slices, or thinner if you like. Arrange the slices on a large serving platter lined with the lettuce leaves. Cut the cylinder of lemon-anchovy butter into thin disks and place the disks here and there over the slices of steak (you may not use all the butter; return the unused portion to the refrigerator for another use, or freeze it).

AUTHOR'S NOTE I like to use natural hardwood lump charcoal rather than pressed carbon charcoal briquettes as the hardwood imparts an alluring smokiness to the meat. For some reason I am also (oddly) drawn to the delicate glass tinkling sound of the wood as it burns.

DO AHEAD Both the flank steak and the lemon-anchovy butter should be made a day in advance but may be made up to 2 days in advance.

These are the best stuffed peppers you'll ever taste. The mix of bread crumbs, pickled vegetables and cheeses in the filling is divine; baking the peppers in tangy tomato sauce makes them soft and delectable.

THREE-CHEESE-STUFFED RED *and* YELLOW PEPPERS

**SERVES 4 AS A MAIN COURSE
AND 8 AS A SIDE DISH**

- ¼ cup plus 4 tablespoons extra-virgin olive oil
- 4 cups lightly packed fresh bread crumbs (see Author's Note on p. 166)
- 3 tablespoons minced flat-leaf parsley
- 2 cloves garlic, minced
- ½ cup finely chopped mixed giardiniera (see Editor's Note on p. 166)
- 2 tablespoons capers, preferably in salt, rinsed, drained, and coarsely chopped
- ½ cup freshly grated Parmigiano-Reggiano
- ½ cup freshly grated Pecorino Romano
- ½ cup freshly shredded Asiago
- 1 teaspoon kosher or sea salt, or to taste
- Freshly ground black pepper
- Pinch of ground cayenne pepper (optional)
- 2 large red bell peppers
- 2 large yellow bell peppers
- 1 (14.5-ounce) can stewed tomatoes, crushed with a potato masher or coarsely chopped

I know a lot of people who have never tasted a good stuffed pepper. They are usually made with unripe green peppers, filled with bland, pasty stuffing or gristly sausage, and doused with a heavy-duty sauce. These peppers are a revelation in comparison: sweet red and yellow peppers take the place of green, and the savory cheese-and-bread stuffing is at once substantial and light. Serve them as the entrée at a casual luncheon or supper party.

Heat the oven to 375°F.

Heat ¼ cup of the olive oil in a large skillet or sauté pan placed over medium heat. Add the bread crumbs, parsley, and minced garlic and sauté, stirring frequently, for 8 minutes, or until the bread crumbs are pale golden and starting to crisp. Transfer the bread crumbs to a large bowl. Add the giardiniera, capers, cheeses, salt, pepper, and cayenne, if using. Mix everything together with a large wooden spoon or silicone spatula. Set the stuffing aside while you prepare the peppers.

Cut the peppers in half lengthwise, cutting right through the stems so that each pepper half has a decorative stem end. With a paring knife, remove the seeds and the white pithy ribs. Spoon the filling into the hollowed-out pepper halves. Fill them generously but don't overstuff them. Reserve any leftover stuffing for sprinkling over the peppers before baking.

Coat the bottom of a baking dish that is just large enough to hold the peppers snugly with 2 tablespoons of olive oil. Pour about three-quarters of the tomatoes into the dish and spread them out with a spatula. Arrange the peppers on top of the

continued on p. 166

EDITOR'S NOTE
Giardiniera, Italian-style pickled vegetables, usually contains cauliflower, carrots, red peppers and pearl onions in vinegar. It's sold in jars in Italian specialty stores and some supermarkets. The drained vegetables make a nice addition to an antipasto platter along with olives, cheeses and cured meats.

tomatoes. Spoon the remaining tomatoes over the tops of the peppers. Sprinkle with any remaining bread crumbs, and drizzle the remaining 2 tablespoons of olive oil over the peppers.

Bake the peppers for about 1 hour or slightly longer, until the tops are nicely browned and the peppers themselves are just tender. Turn off the oven and let the peppers sit inside for another 15 minutes to 30 minutes, until they are completely tender. Serve immediately.

AUTHOR'S NOTE To make fresh bread crumbs, cut away the crusts from a large chunk of ciabatta or other rustic Italian bread (about one-third of a 1-pound loaf). Tear the chunk into large pieces, place in a food processor, and pulse until coarse crumbs form. You should have about 2 cups' worth.

DO AHEAD The stuffing may be made several hours or up to a day in advance and stored in a tightly lidded container in the refrigerator. Bring it to room temperature before stuffing the peppers. The peppers may be cleaned and sliced in half several hours in advance, and stored in a zipper-lock plastic bag in the refrigerator. The stuffed peppers may be baked several hours in advance and served at room temperature or reheated in a low (300°F) oven just until warmed through.

BEST OF THE BEST EXCLUSIVE

Marchetti tosses supersweet roasted tomatoes with pasta and creamy robiola cheese. However, it's the fennel seed on the tomatoes that gives this rich dish its distinctive flavor.

PAPPARDELLE *with* SLOW-ROASTED TOMATOES *and* ROBIOLA CHEESE

SERVES 6

2½ pounds plum tomatoes, halved
½ cup extra-virgin olive oil
3 large garlic cloves, thinly sliced
1 tablespoon fennel seeds
Kosher salt and freshly ground pepper
1 pound pappardelle
One 9-ounce square aged robiola cheese, cut into 1-inch dice

1 Preheat the oven to 275°F. Arrange the tomato halves cut side up on a rimmed baking sheet and drizzle with the olive oil. Scatter the garlic slices and fennel seeds over the tomatoes and season generously with salt and pepper. Bake the tomatoes for about 3 hours, until they begin to brown and wrinkle. When the tomatoes are cool enough to handle, chop coarsely and transfer to a large bowl along with any accumulated juices.

2 In a large pot of boiling salted water, cook the pasta until al dente; drain, reserving ½ cup of the pasta cooking water. Add the pasta and the reserved cooking water to the tomatoes and toss to coat. Add the robiola and toss until the cheese is slightly melted and coats the pasta. Season with salt and pepper and serve at once.

MAKE AHEAD The roasted tomatoes can be refrigerated for up to 2 days. Rewarm gently before tossing with the pasta.

POTATO, ONION AND GRUYÈRE
GALETTE, P. 170

THE ART AND SOUL OF BAKING

by SUR LA TABLE *with* CINDY MUSHET

f irst and foremost, this huge baking book is "a tool for learning." That description comes from author Cindy Mushet, a veteran pastry chef and a baking instructor at Sur La Table, the Seattle-based cookware store. In this book, Mushet provides incredibly detailed tips, techniques and tidbits of knowledge that demystify baking, leaving virtually no question unanswered. But despite Mushet's precision, her overall attitude is appealingly low-key: "Hey," she writes, "it's food, not world peace." With over 275 recipes—savory (onion tarts) and sweet (fruit bars)—*The Art and Soul of Baking* has much to offer both novice and experienced cooks.

Published by Andrews McMeel, $40

Anybody interested in saving time should make free-form tarts like this sensational rustic galette instead of tarts that require a mold.

POTATO, ONION *and* GRUYÈRE GALETTE

**MAKES 1 (10-INCH) GALETTE,
SERVING 8 TO 10**

  1 recipe Flaky Pie or Tart Dough
     (recipe follows), prepared through
     Step 4
1½ tablespoons olive oil, plus
     1 tablespoon for drizzling
  1 large onion (12 ounces), thinly sliced
½ teaspoon finely chopped fresh
     thyme or rosemary
¼ teaspoon plus 1 pinch kosher salt
Black pepper
  4 ounces Gruyère cheese,
     coarsely grated
  1 pound red potatoes, washed
     (left unpeeled) and cut into
     ¼-inch-thick slices
  1 egg, lightly beaten
Crème fraîche, for serving (optional)
Golden caviar, for serving (optional)

EQUIPMENT
Baking sheet
Parchment paper or
    a silicone mat
Rolling pin
Medium sauté pan
Large bowl
Pastry brush
Paring knife
Metal spatula
Cooling rack
Cake lifter or 2 metal spatulas
    or tart pan bottom
Chef's knife

Here is a savory version of the free-form fruit tart known in France as a galette. Onions, sautéed until soft and sweet, are combined with sliced potatoes and grated Gruyère, an aged, wonderfully nutty cheese from Switzerland, for a comforting, all-season tart that is as welcome at the brunch table as it is at dinner.

1 Preheat the oven to 400°F and position an oven rack in the lower third. Line the baking sheet with parchment paper or a silicone mat. Following the general instructions in Steps 5 through 7 on page 173, roll the dough into a 13-inch round and transfer it to the baking sheet. Chill for 1 hour.

2 Heat the 1½ tablespoons olive oil in the medium sauté pan over medium-high heat. Add the onion and cook, stirring occasionally, until soft and lightly colored, 8 to 10 minutes. Stir in the thyme, ¼ teaspoon salt, and 5 grinds of pepper and blend well. Transfer to a plate and set aside to cool.

3 Combine the cooled onion mixture, cheese, and potatoes in the large bowl. Mound the filling in the center of the chilled tart shell, leaving a 1½-inch border at the edge. Fold that border up around the filling, pleating it to make a pretty, circular enclosure and leaving the center open. Drizzle the filling with the remaining 1 tablespoon olive oil and sprinkle lightly with salt and 3 grinds of pepper. Lightly brush the pleated dough with the beaten egg to give it shine and help it brown in the oven.

EDITOR'S NOTE

Chilling the filled galette before baking ensures that the crust won't "weep" butter as it bakes and instead emerges from the oven nice and flaky. Cover and refrigerate the galette for at least 30 minutes or up to a day before baking.

4 Bake the galette for 45 to 50 minutes, until the pastry is golden brown and the potatoes are soft when tested with a paring knife or skewer. Use the metal spatula to lift the edge of the galette slightly and check underneath. The bottom crust should be a beautiful brown color. Transfer to a rack to cool for 5 to 10 minutes.

5 Transfer the galette to a serving plate with the cake lifter, 2 spatulas, or a tart pan bottom supporting the bottom as you move it. Slice with a chef's knife and serve warm. If you like, serve with dollops of crème fraîche and spoonfuls of caviar.

STORING Store uncovered at room temperature for up to 6 hours. Or cover with plastic wrap and refrigerate for up to 2 days. Reheat in a 400°F oven for 10 to 15 minutes before serving.

GETTING AHEAD The dough can be rolled out up to 2 days ahead, covered with plastic wrap, and refrigerated.

continued on p. 172

FLAKY PIE OR TART DOUGH

MAKES 1 (9- OR 10-INCH) PIE SHELL

1 stick (4 ounces) cold
  unsalted butter, cut into
  ½-inch pieces
3 to 4 tablespoons cold water
1¼ cups (6¼ ounces) unbleached
  all-purpose flour
1½ teaspoons sugar
  (omit for a savory crust)
¼ teaspoon saltt

EQUIPMENT
Small measuring cup
Food processor fitted with
  a metal blade
Large bowl
Rolling pin
Pastry brush
9- or 10-inch pie or tart pan
Kitchen scissors

Many bakers are so intimidated by the idea of making flaky pie crust that they either settle for the prepared dough from the grocery store or don't make pie at all. But, like all baking, pie crust is quite straightforward once you know how the ingredients work together. If you're new to pie dough, take a deep breath and follow the steps below for a beautifully crisp, golden brown, flaky pie crust. This recipe doesn't call for shortening, as the flavor, aroma, and color of an all-butter crust can't be beat. The drawback to butter is that it can soften quickly at room temperature, which is why it's best to use the food processor to ensure great results every time. Weigh your dry ingredients if you can, but if you don't have a scale, you can measure by the dip-and-sweep method.

1 Place the butter pieces in a bowl or on a plate and freeze for at least 20 minutes. Refrigerate the water in a small measuring cup until needed.

2 Mix the dough: Place the flour, sugar, and salt in the bowl of the food processor. Process for 10 seconds to blend the ingredients. Add the frozen butter pieces and pulse 6 to 10 times (in 1-second bursts), until the butter and flour mixture looks like crushed crackers and peas.

3 Immediately transfer the butter-flour mixture to the large bowl. Sprinkle a tablespoon of the cold water over the mixture and "fluff" it in, then add another, and another, until 3 tablespoons have been added. Continue to fluff and stir 10 or 12 times. It will not be a cohesive dough at this point but a bowl of shaggy crumbs and clumps of dough. Before bringing the dough together, you need to test it for the correct moisture content. Take a handful of the mixture and squeeze firmly. Open your hand. If the clump falls apart and looks dry, remove any large, moist clumps from the bowl, then add more water, one teaspoon at a time, sprinkling it over the top of the mixture

EDITOR'S NOTE
If you don't have a kitchen scale, Mushet says to measure flour in a measuring cup using the "dip and sweep" method: Stir the flour up a bit before dipping the cup in, then level the top by sweeping across it with a butter knife or offset spatula.

and immediately stirring or mixing it in. Test again before adding any more water. Repeat, if needed. The dough is done when it holds together (even if a few small pieces fall off). If the butter feels soft and squishy, refrigerate before continuing. If the butter is still cold and firm, continue to the next step. (Note: Adding the liquid may also be done on low speed in a stand mixer fitted with the paddle attachment—add three-fourths of the liquid, test for moistness, then add the remaining liquid if needed.)

4 Knead and chill the dough: Turn the dough onto a work surface and knead gently 3 to 6 times. If it won't come together and looks very dry, return it to the bowl and add another teaspoon or two of water (one at a time), mixing in as above, and try again. Flatten the dough into a 6- or 7-inch disk, wrap in plastic or parchment paper, and refrigerate for 30 minutes. This allows time for the dough to hydrate fully and for the butter to firm up again.

5 Roll the dough: If the dough has been refrigerated for more than 30 minutes, it may be very firm and hard and will crack if you try to roll it. Let it sit on the counter for 10 to 15 minutes until it is malleable but still cold. Dust your work surface generously with flour and set the disk on the flour. Dust the top with flour. Roll, turning the dough, until you've got a 14- to 15-inch circle about ⅛ inch thick. If at any point the dough becomes warm and sticky, gently fold it into quarters, unfold it onto a baking sheet, and refrigerate for 15 minutes, or until the butter is firm again.

6 If a crack or hole forms while rolling, brush any flour away and patch the area.

7 Transfer the dough: Fold the dough circle into quarters, brushing off any excess flour as you fold. Put the point of the folded dough in the center of the pie pan, tart pan, or baking

continued on p. 174

sheet and unfold the dough, lifting it slightly as necessary to ease it into the crevices of the pan. Do not stretch or pull the dough, which can cause thin spots, holes, and/or shrinkage during baking.

8 Trim the dough: Use a pair of kitchen scissors to trim the dough so it overhangs the edge of the pan by 1 inch. Fold the overhanging dough under itself around the pan edge, then crimp or form a decorative border. Chill for 30 minutes before baking.

STORING The dough can be wrapped in plastic and refrigerated for up to 2 days, or double-wrapped in plastic, slipped into a freezer bag, and frozen for up to 1 month.

What the Pros Know

When doubling or tripling a batch of pie dough, whether for a double-crusted pie or simply to have some extra dough in the freezer for another day, it can be difficult to fit all the ingredients into your food processor (unless you have a large model). No problem. Take a tip from pastry chefs who have to make 20 times the recipe—use your stand mixer for the whole process. Simply chop the butter and freeze it for a couple of hours, then cut it into the dry ingredients, using the low speed and paddle attachment. Add the cold water just as the butter pieces reach the "peas and crushed crackers" stage, and continue to mix on low until the dough holds together in large, shaggy clumps. Once you've finished the dough, divide it into equal pieces, wrap in plastic, and refrigerate for 30 minutes. Roll each piece into a ⅛-inch-thick round and layer between sheets of parchment paper on a baking sheet. Wrap the entire sheet in plastic, then refrigerate or freeze until needed.

Any baked good with an ingredient list this short is worth trying. These happen to be the ultimate crumble bars, with great fruit flavor and an incredible crust that includes butter, brown sugar and oats.

RASPBERRY-CHERRY CRUMBLE BARS

MAKES 36 (3 BY 1-INCH) BARS

- 1¾ cups (8¾ ounces) unbleached all-purpose flour
- 1¾ cups (6 ounces) old-fashioned or quick oats (not instant)
- 1 cup (8 ounces) firmly packed light brown sugar
- ¼ teaspoon salt
- 2 sticks (8 ounces) cold unsalted butter, cut into ½-inch pieces
- 1 (16-ounce) jar good-quality seedless raspberry jam
- 1 cup (5½ ounces) dried sour cherries
- Confectioners' sugar, for dusting

EQUIPMENT
9 by 13-inch baking pan
Stand mixer fitted with a paddle attachment or a food processor fitted with a metal blade
Silicone or rubber spatula
Cooling rack
Medium bowl
Thin knife or flexible spatula
Fine-mesh strainer

These homey, irresistible bars can be put together in no time, will feed a crowd, and are loved by everyone. The brown sugar–oatmeal crust provides just the right sweetness and crunch against the soft, tart, lightly chewy filling in the center, which is simply a mixture of raspberry jam and dried sour cherries. Pack them in lunches, bring them to bake sales, or serve them warm with ice cream—this is a good recipe to have in your repertoire. Use old-fashioned oats when you want a hearty crunch, or quick oats for a more tender bite, but don't use instant oats or you'll have mush.

1 Preheat the oven to 350°F and position an oven rack in the center. Line the baking pan with foil across the bottom and up the two long sides, then lightly coat with melted butter, oil, or high-heat canola-oil spray.

2 Mix the crumble dough: Place the flour, oats, brown sugar, and salt in the bowl of the stand mixer and beat on low speed until evenly mixed (or place in the food processor and process for 5 seconds). Add the cold butter and mix on low speed until the mixture looks like wet sand and starts to form clumps, 5 to 6 minutes (or process for 45 to 60 seconds, pausing to scrape down once with the spatula).

3 Bake the bottom crust: Divide the dough in half. Pat one half into an even layer in the prepared pan. Set the other half aside. Bake for 20 to 25 minutes, until golden and crisp. Transfer to a rack and cool for 20 minutes. Leave the oven on.

continued on p. 176

4 Make the filling: Empty the jar of jam into the medium bowl and stir well to break up any lumps. Add the cherries and stir until well mixed and all the cherries are coated with jam. Spread evenly over the cooled crust, all the way to the edges. Sprinkle the remaining dough evenly over the filling.

5 Bake for 35 to 40 minutes, until the topping is golden brown and the filling is bubbling. Transfer to a rack and cool completely, 1½ to 2 hours.

6 Unmold the cookies: To serve, run a thin knife or spatula around the edges of the pan to loosen any dough or filling. Lift the cookies out using the foil as handles and place on a cutting surface. Cut into 3 by 1-inch bars. Just before serving, use the fine-mesh strainer to lightly dust confectioners' sugar over the cookies.

STORING Keep the bars in an airtight container between layers of parchment or waxed paper for up to 4 days at room temperature. Dust with confectioners' sugar just before serving.

GETTING AHEAD The bottom crust can be baked and the bars assembled (but not baked) and frozen in the pan for up to 6 weeks. Wrap tightly with two layers of plastic reaching all the way around the pan. To bake, do not defrost; simply unwrap the pan and bake for a few extra minutes.

What the Pros Know

These bar cookies are a template for your creativity in the kitchen. While this recipe is sure to please, you can use the dough as a starting point, then change the filling flavors to suit your tastes and the occasion. Use only jam in the center, and leave out the dried fruit, filling it with your favorite preserve. Or try a layer of quince paste, fig spread, or poppy seed filling instead. Change the jam and fruit pairing to other tasty combinations such as apricot jam and snipped dried mango; orange marmalade with dried, sweet-tart cranberries; or cherry jam with snipped apricots.

Too many muffins are like sugar bombs, but these light, moist, savory ones are more like a cheesy herbed bread. Studded with pieces of red pepper, they make a pretty addition to a bread basket.

FETA, ROASTED PEPPER *and* BASIL MUFFINS

MAKES 12 MUFFINS

- 2 cups (10 ounces) unbleached all-purpose flour
- 2 teaspoons baking powder
- ½ teaspoon baking soda
- ½ teaspoon salt
- ¾ cup (3 ounces) crumbled feta cheese
- ½ cup (4 ounces) jarred roasted red bell pepper, patted dry and chopped into ¼-inch dice
- 3 tablespoons finely chopped fresh basil
- 1 cup (8 ounces) buttermilk
- ¼ cup (2 ounces) olive oil
- 1 large egg

EQUIPMENT

Standard 12-cup muffin tin
Whisk
Large bowl
Medium bowl
2-cup liquid measuring cup
Silicone or rubber spatula
Large ice cream scoop
    or 2 soup spoons
Cooling rack
Thin knife or spatula

Who says muffins have to be sweet? These are a great savory accompaniment to eggs or bacon on the breakfast table, and just as good alongside soup, salad, or roasted chicken. Do not substitute dried basil, because it just doesn't have the punch of flavor these muffins require. If fresh basil is unavailable, substitute a tablespoon of fresh thyme or a teaspoon of dried thyme instead.

1 Preheat the oven to 375°F and position an oven rack in the center. Lightly coat the muffin tin with melted butter, oil, or high-heat canola-oil spray. Whisk the flour, baking powder, baking soda, and salt in the large mixing bowl. Set aside. In the medium bowl, stir together the feta cheese, roasted bell pepper, and chopped basil. Set aside.

2 Pour the buttermilk into the measuring cup. Add the olive oil and the egg and whisk together until well blended. Make a well in the center of the dry ingredients. Pour the buttermilk mixture into the well and stir gently with a spatula. Mix only until there are no more streaks of flour or pools of liquid and the batter looks fairly smooth. A few small lumps scattered throughout are fine—they will disappear during baking. Gently fold in the feta cheese mixture until evenly distributed in the batter.

3 Use the large ice cream scoop or 2 soup spoons to divide the batter evenly among the prepared muffin cups. Bake for 18 to 20 minutes, until the tops feel firm and a skewer inserted into the centers comes out clean. Transfer the muffin tin to a rack and let cool for 5 minutes. Gently run a thin knife or

continued on p. 179

spatula around each muffin to free it from the pan, lift out the muffins, and transfer them to a rack to finish cooling (careful, these are tender while hot). Serve warm.

STORING When completely cool, the muffins can be stored at room temperature, wrapped in plastic or sealed in a resealable plastic bag, for 2 days. Reheat, wrapped in foil, in a 325°F oven for 8 to 10 minutes, until warmed through.

The muffins can also be frozen for up to 1 month, wrapped tightly in plastic wrap and then sealed in a resealable plastic freezer bag. Thaw, still wrapped, for 30 minutes before reheating.

What the Pros Know

To use parchment in the muffin pan instead of the traditional pleated paper muffin liners, cut twelve 5 by 5-inch squares of parchment. Fit one into each muffin cup in the pan, pleating the sides slightly where they overlap so they lie flat against the pan walls. The parchment will extend above the top of the muffin cup. Put a spoonful of muffin batter into each liner to anchor it in the pan. Adjust each paper as necessary so they are centered and even. Finish filling with the muffin batter. Bake as directed.

Part banana bread, part marble cake, this is a new classic. To make it extra-decadent, smear slices with a little store-bought dulce de leche.

CHOCOLATE-BANANA MARBLE BREAD

MAKES 1 LOAF

- 2 large or 3 medium very ripe bananas, at room temperature
- ¼ cup (2 ounces) buttermilk, at room temperature
- 2 teaspoons pure vanilla extract
- 2 cups (7 ounces) sifted cake flour
- 1 teaspoon baking soda
- ¾ teaspoon baking powder
- ¼ cup (1 ounce) unsifted unsweetened Dutch-process cocoa powder
- 3 tablespoons (1½ ounces) boiling water, plus more if needed
- 1½ sticks (6 ounces) unsalted butter, softened (65° to 68°F)
- 1 cup (7 ounces) sugar
- 2 large eggs at room temperature, lightly beaten

EQUIPMENT
9 by 5-inch loaf pan
Parchment paper
Food processor fitted with a
    metal blade (optional)
2 medium bowls
Whisk
Fine-mesh strainer
Small bowl
Stand mixer fitted with a paddle
    attachment
Silicone or rubber spatula
Cooling rack

Here's a banana bread that's soft, tender, and bursting with bananas, yet not overly sweet as so many versions are. The key is an intensely bitter cocoa-powder paste added to half of the batter, resulting in a deep, rich chocolate flavor that pairs perfectly with the sweetness of the bananas. The two batters are marbled together, producing a beautiful pattern and adding a sophisticated note to this all-American favorite. Because of the moisture that the bananas add, the loaf keeps well for at least 4 to 5 days at room temperature, and it freezes so well that you can put a couple of them away for unexpected visitors. Be sure the bananas are ripe and soft, with plenty of black spots speckling their skins, or you won't have the burst of banana flavor you want. Whirl them in the food processor for an ultra-smooth puree, or mash thoroughly with a fork if you prefer.

1 Preheat the oven to 350°F and position an oven rack in the center. Lightly coat the loaf pan with melted butter or high-heat canola-oil spray and line it with a piece of parchment paper that extends 1 inch beyond the long edge of both sides of the pan. Peel the bananas and place them in the bowl of the food processor. Process to a smooth puree. (Alternatively, mash them in a bowl using a fork.) Measure out 1 cup of the puree and transfer it to a medium bowl, discarding the rest of the puree or saving it for another use. Add the buttermilk and vanilla and whisk just until blended. Set aside.

2 Use a fine-mesh strainer to sift the cake flour, baking soda, and baking powder together into a medium bowl. Whisk to blend well. Set aside. Place the cocoa powder in the small bowl. Pour

continued on p. 182

the boiling water over the cocoa and stir until it forms a smooth paste—it should run thickly off the spoon. If it is too thick, add another tablespoon of boiling water and stir again. Set aside.

3 Place the butter and sugar in the bowl of the stand mixer. Beat on medium-high speed until the butter is very light, almost white in color, 4 to 5 minutes. Scrape down the bowl with a spatula. Turn the mixer to medium speed and add the eggs, 1 tablespoon at a time, completely blending in each addition before adding the next. About halfway through the eggs, turn off the mixer and scrape down the bowl with the spatula, then continue adding the rest of the eggs. Scrape down the bowl again.

4 With the mixer running on the lowest speed, add one-third of the flour mixture. Just as it is barely blended and you can still see a few patches of flour, add half the banana mixture. Repeat with the remaining flour and banana mixtures, ending with the flour. Scrape down the bowl and finish blending the batter by hand.

5 Transfer half of the batter to the second medium bowl. Add the cocoa paste and, using the rubber spatula, gently but thoroughly blend it into the batter.

6 Drop alternating spoonfuls of dark and light batters into the prepared pan, then marbleize by using a spoon to gently turn the batter over in 3 places down the length of the pan.

7 Bake the banana bread for 55 to 65 minutes, until firm to the touch and a toothpick inserted into the center of the loaf comes out clean. Transfer to a rack to cool completely. When cool, remove from the pan, peel off the parchment paper, and cut slices by sawing gently with a serrated knife.

STORING Chocolate-Banana Marble Bread can be made 4 or 5 days ahead and kept at room temperature, wrapped in plastic wrap. It freezes beautifully for up to 8 weeks when double-wrapped in plastic and placed inside a resealable plastic freezer bag. Defrost, still wrapped in plastic to avoid condensation on the loaf, for 2 hours before serving.

BEST OF THE BEST EXCLUSIVE

Some brownies are dense and fudgy, others—like these—are more fluffy and cakelike. Mushet sprinkles store-bought toffee bits on top, which melt in the oven to form a deliciously crisp, caramelly crust.

TRIPLE CHOCOLATE–TOFFEE BROWNIES

MAKES 24 BROWNIES

- 6 ounces semisweet chocolate, chopped
- 3 ounces unsweetened chocolate, chopped
- 1 cup all-purpose flour
- 1 teaspoon baking powder
- ½ teaspoon salt
- 1 stick (4 ounces) unsalted butter, at room temperature
- 1½ cups sugar
- 4 large eggs, at room temperature
- ½ cup whole milk, at room temperature
- 2 teaspoons pure vanilla extract
- 1 cup toffee bits
- ⅓ cup mini chocolate chips

EDITOR'S NOTE

Toffee bits are available in the baking aisle of most supermarkets, but you can also crush up a toffee bar for this recipe (even a chocolate-covered one will work well here). Pulse it in a food processor until the pieces are about the size of chocolate chips, or put the bar in a heavy bag and crush it with a mallet or rolling pin.

1 Preheat the oven to 350°F. Spray a 9-by-13-inch baking pan with nonstick cooking spray and line with parchment paper, allowing the parchment to hang over the edges.

2 In a medium glass bowl, microwave the semisweet and unsweetened chocolates at high power in 30-second intervals until melted, about 2 minutes. In a small bowl, whisk the flour with the baking powder and salt.

3 In a standing mixer fitted with the paddle, beat the butter with the sugar at medium-high speed until pale yellow, about 3 minutes. Add the eggs one at a time, beating well between additions. Scrape down the side of the bowl. Add the melted chocolate and beat until incorporated. Beat in the milk and vanilla at low speed. Beat in the flour mixture, then beat in ⅔ cup of the toffee bits and the mini chocolate chips until evenly distributed.

4 Scrape the batter into the prepared pan and smooth the surface. Sprinkle with the remaining ⅓ cup of toffee bits. Bake the brownies for about 35 minutes, until a toothpick inserted in the center comes out with a few moist crumbs.

5 Set the brownies on a rack to cool completely, about 2 hours. Refrigerate for 30 minutes before cutting. Use the parchment overhang to lift the brownie out of the baking pan; cut into squares and serve.

MAKE AHEAD The brownies can be stored in an airtight container at room temperature for up to 3 days.

BEEF, MUSHROOM AND GLASS
NOODLE SALAD, P. 186

SECRETS OF THE RED LANTERN

by PAULINE NGUYEN *with recipes by* LUKE NGUYEN *and* MARK JENSEN

Pauline Nguyen's family expresses emotions through food. "A dish of bitter melon soup is a dish of reconciliation," she writes. "When we quarrel, we cannot speak the words 'I am sorry'— we give this bittersweet soup instead." At Red Lantern, the stellar Vietnamese restaurant in Sydney that she runs with her partner, chef Mark Jensen, and her brother Luke, the cooking also expresses emotion: a refugee's feelings of love and longing. *Secrets of the Red Lantern* shares her family's complex history and the classic dishes that sustained them, translated here into unintimidating recipes that make sense in Western kitchens. As Nguyen writes, "Vietnamese food is easy—there is no mystery to it. It is simple to prepare; and the cooking methods are straightforward."

Published by Andrews McMeel, $40

This refreshing noodle salad includes juicy, exceptionally tender pieces of grilled sirloin, which makes it a great main-course dish.

BEEF, MUSHROOM *and* GLASS NOODLE SALAD

SERVES 4 AS PART OF A SHARED FEAST

- 1 (½-pound) sirloin steak
- 3½ ounces bean thread noodles
- ¼ cup dried mushroom strips, such as wood ear mushrooms or Chinese black fungus
- 1 small handful mint leaves
- 1 small handful basil leaves
- 1 small handful cilantro leaves
- 1 small handful Vietnamese mint
- 2 Kaffir lime leaves, finely sliced
- 2 long red chiles, julienned
- 1 red onion, sliced
- 1 small cucumber, halved lengthwise and sliced into 1/16-inch-wide pieces
- 1 teaspoon Roasted Rice Powder (recipe follows)
- 1 tablespoon chopped Roasted Peanuts (recipe follows)
- 1 tablespoon Fried Shallots (recipe follows)

BEEF MARINADE

- 1 clove garlic, crushed
- 1 tablespoon soy sauce
- 1 tablespoon Asian fish sauce
- 2 teaspoons sugar
- 1 teaspoon sesame oil

SALAD DRESSING

- ⅓ cup grated palm sugar
- ¼ cup lime juice
- 2 tablespoons Asian fish sauce
- 2 tablespoons soy sauce
- 1 clove garlic
- 1 tablespoon chile oil
- 1 tablespoon sliced lemongrass, white part only
- 1 small handful cilantro leaves
- 2 tablespoons olive oil

To marinate the beef, mix all the marinade ingredients together in a bowl, add the sirloin steak, and coat well. Refrigerate for 2 hours.

Soak the bean thread noodles and mushrooms separately in hot water for 20 minutes, strain, and dry with a paper towel. Cut the bean thread noodles into 1½-inch lengths and set aside. Put all of the salad dressing ingredients in a food processor and blend to combine.

Cook the sirloin to your liking on a grill pan or in a skillet. Allow to rest for 5 minutes, then finely cut the sirloin across the grain into ¼-inch slices. Combine the beef with the rest of the salad ingredients, except the peanuts and shallots, in a large bowl. Add the dressing, then toss well to combine. Turn out the salad onto a serving platter and garnish with the Roasted Peanuts and Fried Shallots.

ROASTED RICE POWDER

1 cup jasmine rice

In a dry wok, stir-fry the rice over medium heat until it is toasted a soft brown color. Allow to cool, then place in a mortar and pound to a fine powder.

This powder will keep indefinitely in an airtight container.

ROASTED PEANUTS

1²⁄₃ cups raw shelled peanuts

In a dry wok, stir-fry the peanuts over medium heat until the peanuts are cooked to a soft brown color. Crush the peanuts in a mortar until coarsely ground.

The roasted nuts will keep in an airtight container for up to 2 weeks.

FRIED SHALLOTS

½ pound shallots
4 cups vegetable oil

Finely slice the shallots and wash under cold water. Dry the shallots with a cloth, then set them aside on some paper towel until they are completely dry.

Put the oil in a wok and heat to 350°F, or until a cube of bread dropped in the oil browns in 15 seconds. Fry the shallots in small batches until they turn golden brown, then remove with a slotted spoon to a paper towel.

The fried shallots are best eaten freshly fried, but will keep for up to 2 days in an airtight container.

These incredibly fragrant, succulent drumsticks require some time in the kitchen, but the ingredients aren't hard to find: Coconut juice (also known as coconut water) is available at many supermarkets.

SOY CHICKEN DRUMSTICKS

SERVES 4 AS A MAIN, OR 6 AS PART OF A SHARED FEAST

- 4½ pounds chicken drumsticks
- 3 tablespoons Asian fish sauce
- 3 tablespoons soy sauce
- ½ cup Shaoxing (Chinese cooking wine)
- 1 cup coconut juice
- 1 tablespoon sesame oil
- ½ cup soft brown sugar
- 1 tablespoon cracked black pepper
- 1 onion, diced
- 8 cloves garlic, chopped
- 1 tablespoon finely sliced ginger
- 1 cup oil, for frying the drumsticks, plus 2 tablespoons extra
- 2 cups Chicken Stock (recipe on p. 191)
- 2 scallions, sliced
- 1 handful cilantro leaves

Clean the drumsticks of excess fat, wash, and pat dry with a paper towel, and put in a large bowl with the fish sauce, soy sauce, Shaoxing, coconut juice, sesame oil, brown sugar, black pepper, 1 tablespoon of the diced onion, 1 tablespoon of the chopped garlic, and the ginger. Mix to combine the ingredients well and marinate for 4 hours in the refrigerator.

Remove the drumsticks from the marinade and pat dry with a paper towel, reserving the marinade for later use. Add the oil to a wok or large saucepan over high heat and fry the chicken in small batches until golden brown. Remove and set aside.

Once all the chicken is cooked, discard the oil and clean the wok. Pour the extra oil into the wok and fry the remaining onion and garlic until golden. Return all of the chicken to the wok along with the reserved marinade and Chicken Stock. Cover with a lid and simmer for 15 minutes.

Remove the lid and increase the heat slightly. Reduce the sauce by half, turning the drumsticks regularly as the sauce reduces, about 30 minutes.

Once cooked, the chicken should fall off the bone. Transfer the chicken to a serving platter and boil the sauce for an additional 5 minutes before pouring it over. Garnish with the sliced scallions and cilantro. Serve with jasmine rice, sticky rice, or a fresh baguette.

Fish sauce, lemongrass and chile give these mussels an unusual sweet-salty-spicy taste. The recipe is very simple: Just combine all the ingredients in a wok, cover and let them steam.

MUSSELS *with* LEMONGRASS, CHILE *and* GARLIC

SERVES 2

- 1 pound black mussels
- 1 cup Chicken Stock (recipe follows)
- 2 tablespoons oil
- 2 lemongrass stems, white part only, finely sliced
- ½ onion, chopped
- 2 cloves garlic, chopped
- 1 bird's-eye chile, sliced
- 1 tablespoon oyster sauce
- 1 tablespoon Asian fish sauce
- 1 teaspoon potato starch
- 2 teaspoons sugar
- ½ teaspoon salt
- ½ teaspoon black pepper
- 1 handful cilantro leaves
- ½ lemon

Scrub and debeard the mussels, then set aside. In a wok over high heat, place the Chicken Stock and mussels, cover with a lid, and cook for 5 minutes, or until the mussels open. (Discard any that do not open.) Strain the mussels, reserving the cooking liquid for later use.

Put the wok back over medium heat, add the oil, and gently fry the lemongrass, onion, garlic, and chile. Once golden, add the mussels and increase the heat. Toss with the oyster sauce and fish sauce, then add ½ cup of the reserved cooking liquid. Mix the potato starch with 1 tablespoon water and toss it with the mussels to thicken the sauce. Season the mussels with the sugar, salt, and pepper, turn out onto a serving platter, garnish with the cilantro, and squeeze the lemon over them.

CHICKEN STOCK

MAKES 5 QUARTS

- 6 cloves garlic
- 8 scallions, white part only
- 1 whole chicken (about 3½ pounds)
- 1½-inch piece of ginger, sliced

Crush the garlic and scallions into a paste in a mortar. Wash the chicken thoroughly under cold running water, making sure to remove all traces of blood, guts, and fat from the cavity. Place the chicken in a large saucepan with 6 quarts of water and bring to a boil. Decrease the heat of the stock to a slow simmer and skim the surface. Continue to skim for 10 minutes, until you have removed most of the fat, then add the ginger, garlic, and scallions. Cook for a further 2 hours, then strain and allow the stock to cool. Refrigerate for up to 3 days or freeze until needed.

This quintessential Vietnamese dish offers the perfect balance of sweet and salty. Superquick and supremely easy to make, it would be a great option for a dinner party.

SHRIMP SAUTÉED *with* TOMATO, FISH SAUCE *and* BLACK PEPPER

SERVES 4

- 2 tablespoons vegetable oil
- 1 tablespoon ground garlic
- 2 bird's-eye chiles, chopped
- 1 teaspoon tomato paste
- 12 jumbo shrimp, peeled, deveined, with tails intact
- 3 tablespoons sugar
- 1 teaspoon cracked black pepper
- ¼ cup Asian fish sauce
- ¾ cup Fish Stock (recipe follows) or water
- ½ very ripe tomato, diced
- 1 scallion, finely sliced
- 1 small handful cilantro leaves

Luke Nguyen: Mom used to cook this dish at Pho Cay Du. I remember getting excited every time a customer ordered it— it was the most expensive dish on the menu. Mom would send me across to the fresh fish markets to look for the biggest and freshest jumbo shrimp or scampi that I could find.

I always thought to myself, why don't they just keep a few in the fridge in case we get an order? Sometimes the customer was left waiting for over 20 minutes while I scoured the streets. As I learned later on, the customer never minded waiting as the shrimp were so fresh and the flavors so good. The aroma of the sautéed shrimp with the tomato has been implanted in my memory. Every time we cook this dish at Red Lantern, I think of the times at Pho Cay Du.

Place the oil, garlic, and chiles in a wok over medium heat and stir until fragrant but not colored. Add the tomato paste, shrimp, and sugar. Toss to combine, then add the pepper, fish sauce, Fish Stock or water, and diced tomato.

Increase the heat, bring to a simmer, and cook for 3 minutes, or until the shrimp are cooked through. Transfer the shrimp to a serving platter, then reduce the sauce slightly and pour over the shrimp. Garnish with the scallion and cilantro.

continued on p. 194

FISH STOCK

MAKES 4 QUARTS

4½ pounds white fish bones
      (such as snapper or cod)
  1 large leek
1½-inch piece of ginger, sliced
  4 cloves garlic
  2 Kaffir lime leaves
  1 bunch cilantro, stems
      and roots only

Place the fish bones in a large saucepan with 4 quarts of water and bring to a boil. Skim off any impurities, then add the remaining ingredients. Return to a boil, then decrease the heat and simmer for 30 minutes. Strain through a fine sieve and allow to cool. Store in the refrigerator for up to 3 days, or freeze until needed.

EDITOR'S NOTE

Ask your fishmonger for bones for the stock, or look for frozen fish stock. Extra fish stock can be kept in the freezer and used for paellas, fish soups and stews, seafood sauces or shellfish risottos.

BEST OF THE BEST EXCLUSIVE

These sweet, peppery ribs—marinated, roasted, then simmered in coconut water—are from Luke Nguyen's forthcoming cookbook.

VIETNAMESE BRAISED PORK SPARERIBS

SERVES 4

¼ cup Asian fish sauce
¼ cup sugar
2 shallots, minced
2 teaspoons salt
2 teaspoons oyster sauce
¼ cup minced garlic
One 2½-pound rack of spareribs, halved crosswise and cut into individual ribs (see Note)
2 cups coconut water
2 medium onions, cut into ½-inch wedges
2 teaspoons black peppercorns, crushed
1 tablespoon Sriracha or other Asian chile sauce
Cilantro leaves, for garnish

1 In a large bowl, whisk the fish sauce with the sugar, shallots, salt, oyster sauce and 2 tablespoons of the garlic until the sugar is dissolved. Add the ribs, toss to coat and let stand for 30 minutes.

2 Preheat the oven to 450°F. Line a large rimmed baking sheet with foil. Using a slotted spoon, transfer the ribs to the baking sheet and roast for about 30 minutes, until browned.

3 In a large saucepan, bring the coconut water to a simmer. Add the ribs and onions and simmer over moderately high heat until the coconut water is reduced by half, about 10 minutes. Using a slotted spoon, transfer the ribs to a serving bowl.

4 Add the crushed black pepper, chile sauce and the remaining 2 tablespoons of garlic to the coconut water and simmer over moderately low heat for 5 minutes. Pour the sauce over the ribs, garnish with cilantro leaves and serve.

SERVE WITH Steamed jasmine rice.

NOTE Have your butcher cut the spareribs for you.

MAKE AHEAD The braised ribs can be refrigerated for up to 2 days. Reheat before serving.

Clockwise from top: honey, white sugar, confectioners' sugar, turbinado sugar, palm sugar, muscovado sugar, maple syrup, organic raw cane sugar and (in the center) molasses.

SWEET!

by MANI NIALL

a re treacle and agave syrup the sweeteners of the future? If veteran California baker Mani Niall has his way, we'll all be using a repertoire that goes way beyond white sugar. "When I bake, I choose the right sweetener for the job, and it may or may not be granulated sugar," he writes. "If I want a moist, chewy texture, I might add molasses or maple syrup. For a deeper, richer flavor, I may experiment with a brown sugar." While Niall doesn't demonize white sugar, he emphasizes minimally processed varieties, which are richer in minerals and less likely to cause blood-sugar spikes. Because *Sweet!* shows how to improve familiar recipes simply by varying the sweetener, it's terrific for anyone interested in good food, whether health-minded or not.

Published by Da Capo Press, $18.95

Granulated white sugar is the perfect neutral sweetener for these buttery cookies delightfully scented with ground cardamom.

CINNAMON-CARDAMOM SNICKERDOODLES

MAKES ABOUT 3 DOZEN COOKIES

2⅔ cups unbleached all-purpose flour, preferably organic
2 teaspoons cream of tartar
1 teaspoon baking soda
½ teaspoon fine sea salt
16 tablespoons (2 sticks) unsalted butter, at room temperature
1½ cups granulated sugar
2 large eggs, at room temperature
1½ teaspoons vanilla extract

SPICED SUGAR

2 teaspoons ground cardamom seeds, from about 20 pods (see Author's Note)
½ cup granulated sugar
2 teaspoons ground cinnamon

Snickerdoodles are an American cookie stalwart—they have been around for much longer than their chocolate chip cousins. They are always rolled in cinnamon sugar before baking to give them a crackled, crunchy glaze, but I like to literally spice things up with ground cardamom. The resulting aroma and flavor are incredible. The best snickerdoodles are crisp around the edges with a chewy center that may look a bit sunken.

Position oven racks in the center and top third of the oven and preheat to 375°F. Line two baking sheets with parchment paper or silicone baking mats.

Sift together the flour, cream of tartar, baking soda, and salt. (This is important, to completely combine the cream of tartar and baking soda, and to break up any clumps of the latter.) Beat the butter and sugar in a medium-size bowl with an electric mixer at high speed until the mixture is light in color and texture, about 3 minutes. One at a time, beat in the eggs, then the vanilla. Reduce the speed to low. In four equal additions, add the flour mixture, beating the dough until it is smooth after each addition.

To make the spiced sugar, combine the ground cardamom, sugar, and cinnamon in a small bowl.

Using a level tablespoon of dough for each cookie, roll the dough into walnut-size balls. A few at a time, toss the balls in the spiced sugar to coat, and place about 2 inches apart on the cookie sheets. Sprinkle the top of each cookie with about ⅛ teaspoon of the spiced sugar.

EDITOR'S NOTE
Cream of tartar, an acidic white powder that's a by-product of winemaking, can be combined with baking soda to make baking powder; this classic New England recipe likely predates store-bought baking powder. The ratio of cream of tartar to baking soda helps create a crackled top in these snickerdoodles.

Bake until the edges of the cookies are crisp and lightly browned, but the centers are still a bit soft, switching the positions of the sheets from top to bottom and front to back halfway through baking, about 10 minutes. Cool on the sheets for a few minutes, then carefully transfer to a wire cake rack to cool completely. (The cookies can be stored in an airtight container at room temperature for up to 5 days.)

AUTHOR'S NOTE Cardamom seeds lose their flavor soon after grinding, so it is always best to grind your own, even if you find ground cardamom at a spice shop. Break open the green cardamom pods and grind the seeds in an electric spice grinder, mini food processor, or a mortar and pestle. Use immediately.

This light, crisp pumpkin seed brittle sweetened with white sugar and corn syrup gets its exotic flavor from Spanish smoked paprika.

SMOKY PUMPKIN SEED BRITTLE

MAKES ABOUT 1½ POUNDS BRITTLE

Vegetable oil, for the baking sheet
1½ cups granulated sugar
¾ cup light corn syrup
2 cups (8 ounces) raw green pumpkin seeds (*pepitas*)
1½ teaspoons smoked paprika (*pimentón de La Vera*) or chile powder
2 teaspoons kosher salt
1 tablespoon butter
1½ teaspoons baking soda, sifted

I find the combination of sweet and spicy tantalizing, and this riff on peanut brittle tells the story in broad, flavorful strokes. The brittle gets its light texture from the chemical reaction between the alkaline baking soda and the acidic syrup—be sure to use a tall saucepan to allow room for the syrup to foam when the baking soda is added. Pimentón de La Vera, made from oak-smoked peppers, provides the underlying smoky note. Look for it labeled simply "smoked paprika" in the spice section of your supermarket, at specialty food stores, or online.

Lightly yet thoroughly brush a baking sheet and a metal spatula with the vegetable oil.

Stir together the sugar, 1 cup of water, and corn syrup in a tall, heavy-bottomed medium-size saucepan. Bring to a boil over low heat, stirring to help dissolve the sugar. Stop stirring, cover, and cook for 3 minutes. Uncover and attach a candy thermometer and boil until the thermometer reads 260°F.

Meanwhile, toss together the pumpkin seeds, smoked paprika, and salt in a small bowl. When the syrup reaches 260°F, add to the saucepan, along with the butter. Cook, stirring almost constantly, until the syrup reaches 295°F.

Remove from the heat and carefully stir in the baking soda, which will make the syrup foam and sputter. Immediately pour the mixture onto the baking sheet, using your other hand to spread it as thinly as possible with the metal spatula as you pour. Cool for 5 minutes, then run the spatula under the candy to prevent sticking. Cool completely. Crack into bite-size pieces. (The brittle can be stored in an airtight container at room temperature for up to 1 week.)

Made with turbinado sugar as well as whole wheat flour and wheat germ, these cookies are at once wholesome and decadent.

WHOLE WHEAT GINGER COOKIES

MAKES ABOUT 3½ DOZEN COOKIES

- 1 cup unbleached all-purpose flour, preferably organic
- 1 cup whole wheat flour
- 1⅔ cups dark, grainy sugar, such as turbinado, demerara, or raw sugar
- 3 tablespoons wheat germ or rolled quinoa
- 1 teaspoon baking powder
- ½ teaspoon freshly grated nutmeg
- ¼ teaspoon fine sea salt
- 8 tablespoons (1 stick) unsalted butter, cut into ½-inch pieces, chilled
- ½ cup sliced crystallized ginger
- ½ cup heavy cream, as needed

When I was a private chef in England, these crisp little cookies were my employer's kid's favorites. But when I made them in the United States, I discovered that British wholemeal (whole wheat) flour is both lighter and grainier than ours. I adjusted by using a combination of whole wheat and unbleached flours, and by adding wheat germ. Those alterations give these cookies a hearty whole-grain flavor, accented by equally robust dark sugar. The dough is best made in a food processor, which blends the ingredients and cuts the ginger into very fine pieces at the same time. Be sure to allow time for the dough to chill.

Combine the all-purpose and whole wheat flours, ⅔ cup of the sugar, and the wheat germ, baking powder, nutmeg, and salt in a food processor fitted with the metal chopping blade. Pulse a couple of times to combine. With the machine running, add a few butter pieces at a time through the feed tube, and process until the mixture looks sandy. Add all of the ginger at once. Gradually add the cream, and process, adding more cream if needed, until the mixture comes together into a stiff dough. (To make the dough by hand, finely chop the ginger. Combine the flours, ⅔ cup of the sugar, and the wheat germ, baking powder, nutmeg, and salt in a medium-size bowl. Add the butter. Using a pastry blender, cut the butter into the dry ingredients until the mixture looks sandy. Add the ginger. Gradually stir in enough of the cream to make a stiff dough. You may have to work in the last of the cream with your hands. Transfer to a very lightly floured work surface and knead briefly.)

EDITOR'S NOTE
While white flour keeps well in the pantry, whole grains don't because they contain more of the nutritious oils naturally present in the kernel. Store whole-grain flours and wheat germ in the freezer and use within a few months to ensure freshness.

Divide the dough in half. Place each half on a piece of plastic wrap, form into a 9-inch-long log about 1½ inches in diameter, and wrap in the plastic. Refrigerate until chilled and firm, at least 2 hours and up to 2 days.

Position racks in the center and upper third of the oven and preheat to 350°F. Line two baking sheets with parchment paper or silicone baking mats.

Place the remaining sugar in a small bowl. Slice the dough into ⅓-inch-thick disks. Roll the edges of each in the sugar, pressing in the sugar to help it adhere, and place 1 inch apart on the baking sheets. Bake, switching the position of the racks from top to bottom and front to back halfway through baking, until the cookies are dark golden brown, about 14 minutes. Cool on the sheets for a few minutes, then transfer to wire cake racks and cool completely. (The cookies can be stored in an airtight container at room temperature for up to 1 week.)

Mexican agave syrup (made from the agave plant, which also produces mezcal and tequila) gives this juicy, spicy chicken a delicate sweetness. Ground ancho chiles make it nice and smoky.

CHILE-RUBBED AGAVE CHICKEN

SERVES 4

- 3 tablespoons pure ground ancho chile
- 2 teaspoons ground cumin
- 1 teaspoon garlic powder
- ⅛ teaspoon cayenne
- 1 teaspoon fine sea salt
- 4 chicken breast halves, with skin and bone (about 10 ounces each)
- 1½ tablespoons canola oil
- ½ cup chicken stock, preferably homemade, or use low-sodium broth
- 3 tablespoons agave syrup (see Note on p. 205)

Lime wedges, for garnish

At opposite ends of the taste spectrum, hot and sweet can harmonize together very nicely. In this case, ancho chile already has a sweet note of its own that is accented by the agave syrup. This simple chicken dish will bring lots of bold flavor to the table, especially when served with a side dish of roasted sweet potatoes.

Mix together the ground chile, cumin, garlic powder, cayenne, and salt. Using a small paring knife, working with one breast at a time, cut the meat away from the bones in one piece, keeping the skin attached. Place a boned breast between two pieces of plastic wrap, and pound gently with a flat meat pounder until the breast is about ¾ inch thick. Rub the chile mixture all over the breasts.

Heat the oil in a large skillet over medium heat until the oil is hot but not smoking. Place the chicken in the skillet, skin side down. Cook until the underside is well browned, about 4 minutes. Turn and cook until the other side is browned, about 3 minutes longer. Add the stock and agave syrup, being careful that the liquid doesn't boil over. Lower the heat to medium-low and cover. Cook until the chicken feels firm when pressed in the center, about 3 minutes longer.

Transfer the chicken to dinner plates and pour the juices on top. Serve immediately with the lime wedges.

BEST OF THE BEST EXCLUSIVE

Most frozen desserts require an ice cream maker. Granitas like the refreshingly tart one here, however, are the ultimate low-tech recipe: Aside from a freezer, all you need is a pan and a fork.

CITRUS *and* AGAVE GRANITA

SERVES 4

- 1 cup fresh orange juice
- ¼ cup plus 2 tablespoons fresh lemon juice
- ¼ cup plus 2 tablespoons fresh lime juice
- ½ cup agave syrup (see Note)

In a large bowl, whisk the orange, lemon and lime juices with the agave syrup until well blended. Pour into an 8-inch round or square cake pan and freeze for 30 minutes. Using a fork, stir the granita; continue stirring every 30 minutes until frozen and fluffy, about 3 hours. Fluff the granita with a fork, scoop into bowls and serve immediately.

NOTE Agave syrup is available at natural-food stores and online from wholesomesweeteners.com.

MAKE AHEAD The granita can be frozen for up to 1 week. Scrape with a fork before serving.

PROVENÇAL TOMATO CASSEROLE, P. 208

THE BEST CASSEROLE COOKBOOK EVER

by BEATRICE OJAKANGAS

there is a casserole for everyone in this massive tribute to America's homiest dish. The introduction states boldly that "the casserole is back." This makes sense, because a casserole is one of the most practical dishes a cook can make: It's affordable, can be prepared in advance, is good for a crowd and usually leaves only one pot to wash. Beatrice Ojakangas, a prolific cookbook author and food consultant, also loves how easy it is to make casseroles with all kinds of ingredients, a blend of inspiration and what's on hand. In this book, that translates into over 500 dishes, arranged in basic chapters like appetizers, breakfast and brunch and poultry and also in categories such as casseroles for crowds, casseroles for two and casseroles for kids.

Published by Chronicle Books, $24.95

This appealing casserole makes great use of tomatoes. It's particularly gorgeous with different-colored heirloom varieties.

PROVENÇAL TOMATO CASSEROLE

SERVES 6

6 medium tomatoes
1½ cups fresh bread crumbs (see Author's Note)
¼ cup minced green onions (white and green parts)
¼ cup minced fresh basil, or 2 tablespoons dried
2 tablespoons minced fresh parsley
2 teaspoons minced garlic
1 teaspoon chopped fresh thyme, or ½ teaspoon dried
1 teaspoon coarse kosher salt
2 tablespoons balsamic vinegar
½ cup shredded Gruyère cheese
2 to 3 tablespoons olive oil

EDITOR'S NOTE
To vary this recipe, try it with Fontina or fresh goat cheese in place of the Gruyère, or mix in a teaspoon or two of other chopped fresh herbs like rosemary or tarragon.

This casserole is best in summer, when the tomatoes ripen on the vine. But the herbs and the drizzle of balsamic vinegar perk up winter tomatoes, too, and we enjoy the casserole then, as well. If you like, assemble it ahead of time, and bake it at the last minute.

1 Preheat the oven to 400°F. Coat a shallow 3-quart casserole with cooking spray.

2 Cut the tomatoes into 4 slices each and overlap the slices in the casserole to cover the bottom of the dish.

3 In a small bowl, mix the bread crumbs, green onions, basil, parsley, garlic, thyme, and salt and sprinkle the mixture evenly over the tomatoes. Drizzle with the balsamic vinegar and sprinkle with the cheese. Drizzle with olive oil. (At this point the casserole can be covered and held at room temperature for up to 2 hours, or refrigerated overnight. If chilled, add 10 minutes to the baking time.)

4 Bake for 15 to 20 minutes, until the crumbs are crisp. Serve warm.

AUTHOR'S NOTE To make fresh bread crumbs, tear 1 or 2 slices of fresh bread into pieces and put in the food processor with the steel blade in place. Process with on/off pulses until the bread is broken down into crumbs.

Unlike many cheese-based dips, this one is spicy, thanks to the combination of two kinds of chiles: poblano and jalapeño.

JALAPEÑO CHILE *con* QUESO

SERVES 10

 2   tablespoons butter
 2   green onions, minced
     (white and green parts)
 1   poblano pepper, seeded
     and diced
 1   teaspoon ground cumin
 1   large tomato, diced
 1   can (4 ounces) diced
     green chiles
 1   jalapeño pepper, seeded
     and diced (optional)
 1   package (8 ounces) cream
     cheese, cubed
 ½   cup heavy cream or sour cream
 1   cup shredded Monterey
     Jack cheese
Chopped fresh cilantro for
     garnish
Tortilla chips or raw vegetables
     for serving

Jalapeño pepper can make this version of chile con queso spicy hot. Remember, though, when handling hot peppers, to wear rubber gloves and keep your hands away from your face, especially your eyes!

1 Preheat the oven to 350°F.

2 Melt the butter in a small skillet and add the green onions and poblano pepper. Sauté for about 5 minutes, until tender.

3 In a 1-quart casserole, combine the green onion mixture, cumin, tomato, diced chiles, jalapeño pepper (if using), cream cheese, and heavy or sour cream. (At this point the casserole can be covered and refrigerated for up to 1 day. Add 5 minutes to the baking time.)

4 Bake, uncovered, for 30 minutes, or until bubbly. Sprinkle with the Monterey Jack cheese and cilantro. Serve hot with tortilla chips or raw vegetables for dipping.

With its creamy Alfredo sauce, frozen peas and crunchy bread crumb topping, this retro noodle casserole is the epitome of comfort food. For an extra zap of flavor, serve it with a tangy hot sauce.

PASTA *and* CHICKEN ALFREDO

SERVES 6

- 3 tablespoons butter, melted, plus extra for the dish
- 1 recipe Quick Alfredo Sauce (recipe follows), or 2 jars (10 ounces each) prepared sauce
- 8 ounces farfalle, fettuccine, or your favorite pasta
- 2 cups diced cooked chicken or turkey, or 1 can (13 ounces) chicken or turkey breast, drained
- 1 bunch green onions, thinly sliced (white and green parts)
- 2 cups frozen peas, thawed
- 1 teaspoon poultry seasoning (see Editor's Note)
- ½ cup seasoned fine dry bread crumbs
- ½ cup grated Parmesan cheese

Fettuccine Alfredo is a classic pasta dish. I've converted it into a casserole and included chicken or turkey meat; it's a great way to use leftovers. I often make this on Friday after Thanksgiving with almost any kind of pasta I happen to have on hand. Alfredo sauce is made with butter, Parmesan, and cream. Quick Alfredo Sauce deviates from that recipe but produces a creamy sauce that is easily made and better than the bottled variety you can buy.

1 Preheat the oven to 400°F. Butter a deep 3-quart casserole. Prepare the Alfredo sauce and have it ready.

2 Cook the pasta in a large pot of boiling water for 12 minutes, or until just tender but still firm to bite. Drain and transfer to a large bowl. Mix in the Alfredo sauce, chicken, green onions, peas, and poultry seasoning.

3 In a small bowl, mix the bread crumbs, Parmesan, and 3 tablespoons melted butter.

4 Transfer the pasta mixture to the baking dish. Sprinkle with the crumb mixture. (At this point the casserole can be covered and refrigerated overnight. Add about 10 extra minutes to the oven time.) Bake, uncovered, until the pasta is hot and the topping is golden brown, about 25 minutes.

QUICK ALFREDO SAUCE

MAKES ABOUT 2¾ CUPS

1 package (8 ounces)
   cream cheese
1 cup milk
4 tablespoons butter
1 cup grated Parmesan
   cheese

Alfredo sauce is credited to Chef Alfredo di Lello, who combined it with cooked fettuccine in the early 1900s. Since then, we've found many ways to use this sauce and even make changes in its preparation. In this simple-to-make version, cream cheese replaces the cream in the original sauce.

1 Combine all of the ingredients in a medium saucepan and place over low heat.

2 Heat until the ingredients are melted and well combined, stirring frequently, approximately 15 minutes. Use in a casserole or simply pour over the pasta of your choice. Use the sauce hot, or cover and refrigerate until ready to use.

EDITOR'S NOTE
If you don't have prepared poultry seasoning (a blend that varies from brand to brand), substitute ¼ teaspoon each of dried, crumbled rosemary, thyme and sage and a pinch of black pepper here.

The reason people make streusel is to celebrate whatever fruit is in season. This recipe, with its supersimple butter–and–brown sugar topping and warmly spiced apples, is a perfect example.

CRISP APPLE STREUSEL

SERVES 8

FOR THE STREUSEL TOPPING
- ⅓ cup butter, plus extra for the dish
- ⅔ cup all-purpose flour
- ⅓ cup packed light or dark brown sugar

FOR THE FRUIT FILLING
- 8 cups sliced apples (about 3 pounds)
- ¾ cup granulated sugar
- 2 tablespoons all-purpose flour
- 1 teaspoon ground cinnamon
- ½ teaspoon ground nutmeg

Whipped cream for serving

EDITOR'S NOTE

A mix of apples like Fuji and McIntosh would be delicious here, but our year-round favorite is the Granny Smith. It retains its shape when baked and gives dishes just the right sweet-tart flavor.

The German word streusel *means "to sprinkle" or "strew." Here, the streusel forms a crunchy topping for baked apples. This popular dessert is also known as "apple crisp."*

1 Preheat the oven to 350°F. Butter a shallow 1½-quart casserole.

2 To make the topping: In a large bowl, mix the flour and brown sugar. With a pastry blender, cut the ⅓ cup butter into the flour until the mixture resembles coarse crumbs. Set aside.

3 To make the fruit filling: Put the sliced apples in a large bowl and toss with the granulated sugar, flour, cinnamon, and nutmeg. Spread in an even layer in the buttered casserole.

4 Sprinkle the topping over the apples, patting it down evenly. Bake, uncovered, for 45 minutes to 1 hour, or until the apples are tender and juices bubble around the edge and the topping is browned. Serve warm or at room temperature with whipped cream.

BEST OF THE BEST EXCLUSIVE

The dough for this hearty bread is mixed with nutty grains of cooked wild rice, which add an appealing chewiness. A great all-purpose bread, it can be spread with jam or a ripe, creamy cheese.

WILD RICE, CRANBERRY *and* PECAN BREAD

MAKES TWO 9-INCH LOAVES

- 1 **cup wild rice**
- 1½ **cups pecans**
- 2 **cups warm water**
- One ¾-**ounce package active dry yeast (2½ teaspoons)**
- ¼ **cup honey**
- 1 **cup whole wheat flour**
- 2 **teaspoons salt**
- 4 **cups bread flour**
- 1 **cup dried cranberries**

1 In a large pot, cover the wild rice with water and bring to a boil. Cook over moderate heat until tender, 45 minutes. Drain.

2 Preheat the oven to 350°F. Spread the pecans on a rimmed baking sheet and toast for about 8 minutes, until fragrant. Let cool, then coarsely chop.

3 In the bowl of a standing mixer fitted with the paddle, mix the warm water with the yeast and honey until the honey is dissolved. Let stand for 5 minutes, until bubbly. In a small bowl, mix the whole wheat flour with the salt; add to the mixer and beat until a smooth dough forms. Mix in 2 cups of the bread flour until smooth. Add the wild rice, pecans and cranberries and mix until incorporated. Switch to the dough hook. Add the remaining 2 cups of bread flour and mix at medium speed until a soft, springy dough forms, about 10 minutes. Cover with plastic wrap and let stand in a warm place until doubled in volume, about 1 hour.

4 Turn the dough out onto a lightly oiled surface and divide it in half. Form each half into a round loaf. Place each loaf on a lightly oiled baking sheet. Cover and let stand until doubled in volume, about 45 minutes.

5 Preheat the oven to 375°F. Bake the bread for about 35 minutes, until a wooden skewer inserted in the center of each loaf comes out clean. Let the loaves stand until cooled slightly, about 30 minutes. Serve warm or at room temperature.

MAKE AHEAD The bread can be stored in an airtight container for up to 5 days or frozen for up to 1 month. Toast to serve.

Joël Robuchon cooking at his flagship Vegas restaurant, Joël Robuchon at The Mansion.

THE COMPLETE ROBUCHON

by JOËL ROBUCHON

despite his 25 Michelin stars, legendary chef Joël Robuchon can write great recipes for home cooks, and he proves this in his gigantic compendium of classic French dishes. With over 800 recipes, *The Complete Robuchon* includes every single French recipe anyone could ever want, from hollandaise sauce and rouille to grilled veal kidneys and roast duck. There are no human-interest stories here, no insights into the chef's home life. Save for Robuchon's impassioned plea to eat seasonally, this book has the impersonal tone of a reference work. But the recipes are remarkably spot-on; Robuchon is a stickler for precision and perfection, and the same dedication that earned him all those Michelin stars makes him a terrific cookbook author.

Published by Alfred A. Knopf, $35

Don't be fooled by this recipe's name: This is a rich baked custard with zucchini in it. Sautéing the zucchini with cumin and nutmeg before adding it to the eggs gives the dish a wonderful complexity.

ZUCCHINI GRATIN *with* FRESH CHEESE

SERVES 4

PREPARATION AND COOKING 45 minutes

Butter
2 tablespoons olive oil
1 pound (500 grams) small zucchini, washed and sliced into rounds ⅛ inch (3 millimeters) thick
Salt
Pepper
Powdered cumin
Grated nutmeg
½ pound (200 grams) fresh sheep's- or goat's-milk cheese or *fromage blanc*
2 tablespoons crème fraîche or heavy cream
5 eggs
1 tablespoon small sage leaves sliced into thin strips

1 Remove the butter from the refrigerator. Preheat the oven to 300°F/150°C and place a rack in the lower third.

2 Line a dish with several layers of paper towels. Heat the olive oil in a skillet over medium-high heat. One minute later, when the oil is quite hot, sauté the zucchini slices, still over rather high heat. Season with salt, pepper, a pinch of cumin, and a pinch of nutmeg. Flip and stir with a wooden spoon for about 4 minutes of total cooking. Lift out with a slotted spoon and lay the zucchini slices on the paper towel–lined dish.

3 In a bowl, whisk together the cheese and crème fraîche. Whisk in the eggs one by one and then the sage. Add a pinch of salt and a pinch of pepper.

4 Pour 1 quart (1 liter) water into a deep baking sheet or dish large enough to hold the gratin dish. Place it on the oven rack. Put the zucchini slices in the bowl of cheese, eggs, and cream and stir with a wooden spoon.

5 Brush the gratin dish with the softened butter. Pour the zucchini-cheese mixture into the dish evenly. Place the gratin dish in the pan of water and cook for 30 minutes. Serve hot.

Do home cooks usually peel asparagus? Maybe not, but this step makes the spears exceptionally tender. The "shower" of herbs here, particularly the chervil, really brings out the flavor of the asparagus.

GREEN ASPARAGUS TIPS *with* MIXED HERBS

SERVES 2 AS A SIDE DISH

PREPARATION 10 minutes

COOKING 6 minutes

- ½ pound (250 grams) green asparagus tips
- 2½ tablespoons plus 1 teaspoon olive oil
- ½ cup (10 centiliters) chicken broth (homemade or made with a bouillon cube)

Lemon juice

- 1 tablespoon minced chervil
- 1 tablespoon minced chives
- 1 tablespoon minced flat-leaf parsley

Salt

Pepper

This makes a fine side dish for scrambled eggs, omelettes, duck breast, and rib steak (côte de boeuf)*, among other foods.*

1 Peel and carefully wash the asparagus tips. Warm 2½ tablespoons oil in a pot over low heat. When it is hot, add the asparagus and stir well to coat with oil. Add the chicken broth, cover, and cook for 3 minutes over low heat.

2 Check to see whether the stock has evaporated. If it has, add a little water. Cover and cook 3 minutes more.

3 Turn off the heat. Sprinkle with a few drops of lemon juice and shower with the herbs. Taste for salt and pepper. Remove to a plate, drizzle with 1 teaspoon olive oil, and serve.

EDITOR'S NOTE

The tips of the asparagus, meaning the bud and about 2 inches of the stalk, are the most flavorful and delicate part. But don't waste the rest of the stalks; peeled, they're great in stir-fries, soups or risottos.

Searing beef, then cooking it in the oven in a salt crust, creates the most tender, juicy, well-seasoned meat imaginable. The crust locks in moisture and insulates the roast from the oven's extreme heat.

ROAST BEEF *in an* HERBED SALT CRUST

SERVES 6 TO 8

PREPARATION 15 minutes
(The salt crust must be prepared at least 2 hours in advance or the night before if possible.)

COOKING rare, 30 minutes
(count on 12 minutes per pound);
medium-rare, 35 to 40 minutes
(count on 15 to 16 minutes per pound)

RESTING 20 minutes

  1   pound (500 grams) coarse salt
  3   tablespoons plus 1 teaspoon
       thyme leaves
  1   tablespoon rosemary leaves
  2   large eggs, separated
3½ cups (400 grams) flour,
       plus a little more for working
       with the dough
  1   whole fillet of beef, 2½ pounds
       (1.2 kilograms)
  1   tablespoon olive oil
  1   tablespoon butter
Pepper

Fillet is a particularly delicate piece of beef and as such must be served rare; it certainly should not be cooked past medium-rare. More than that and the meat toughens. In this recipe the meat is seared at a very high temperature and then roasted at a lower temperature so that it absorbs the aroma of the herbs and stays tender.

1 Put the coarse salt in the bowl of a food processor (fitted with a dough blade if possible). Add 3 tablespoons thyme leaves and the rosemary and pulse to mix. With the machine running, add 2 egg whites and ⅔ cup (15 centiliters) water. Add the flour bit by bit until it is combined. Dump the dough out onto a lightly floured work surface and knead for 2 or 3 minutes, until it is homogeneous. The dough should be firm, not soft and sticky, or the beef will steam instead of roasting. If necessary, add a little more flour to make it less sticky. Put the dough in a lightly oiled bowl, cover it with plastic wrap, and leave it to rest, refrigerated, for at least 2 hours or up to 24. This resting time will make the dough less sticky and easier to work with.

2 Thirty minutes before you plan to begin cooking, remove the beef from the refrigerator. Remove a rack from the oven. If it isn't clean, rinse it under hot running water and wipe it clean with paper towels. Place it over a large plate or platter.

3 Preheat the oven to 370°F/190°C. Prepare a sheet pan or roasting dish large enough to hold the beef and line it with parchment paper.

4 Pat the meat dry with paper towels. Do not salt it; this will draw out its juices, and it will not brown properly.

5 Heat the oil in a pot large enough to hold the meat over medium heat. Add the butter. A minute later, when the butter begins to foam, lay the meat in the pot and sear for 2 minutes. The heat should be quite high. Give the meat a quarter turn, being careful not to pierce it, and sear 2 minutes more. Repeat twice so that all 4 sides are evenly browned. Remove the seared roast to the oven rack over the plate, still careful not to puncture it.

6 Lightly flour a rolling pin and a work surface. Remove the dough from the refrigerator and roll it out into a 10-by-12-inch (26-by-30-centimeter) rectangle—large enough to wrap the roast without stretching the dough.

7 Discard one of the egg yolks and beat the other in a bowl with 1½ teaspoons water. Sprinkle the roast with 1 teaspoon thyme leaves and lay it on the rolled-out dough. Wrap it completely in the dough, pressing the seams closed with your fingers. Make sure they are quite well sealed. Place the wrapped roast on the parchment paper–lined sheet pan or baking dish and carefully brush its doughy top with the egg yolk mixture. Be careful not to drip yolk on the parchment paper. If you do drip, wipe it up with a paper towel.

continued on p. 220

EDITOR'S NOTE

Even though this recipe contains a pound of salt, the meat does not get overly salty; most of the salt remains in the crust, which is removed before serving. Just enough penetrates to perfectly season the roast.

8 Bake the roast on the middle rack of the oven for 30 minutes if you want it to be rare. When you remove the roast from the oven, place it on the prepared oven rack and allow it to rest for at least 20 minutes. The roast will stay hot, so you can wait even longer, but not more than 1 hour.

9 Warm your serving platter in the oven, which should still be hot even though it is off. To serve, make a vertical cut in the salt crust at one end and pull the roast out. Throw the crust away. Season the meat with pepper and slice it thickly on the bias, arranging the slices on the hot serving platter.

Robuchon calls for bringing the chicken cooking liquid to a "shiver" just below the boiling point—such a clear, if unorthodox, instruction. This recipe represents French home cooking at its best.

CHICKEN *with* MUSHROOMS *and* TARRAGON

SERVES 4

PREPARATION 15 minutes

COOKING 35 minutes

- ¾ pound (350 grams) small white button mushrooms, stem ends trimmed, caps rinsed clean, and drained; quarter them if they are on the large side
- 2 tablespoons butter
- 1 free-range chicken, about 3½ pounds (1.8 kilograms), cut into 8 pieces

Salt

Pepper

- 1 tablespoon olive oil
- ⅓ cup (8 centiliters) dry white wine
- 1 bouquet garni (2 sprigs fresh thyme, 1 bay leaf, and 4 stems parsley, wrapped and tied in a green leek leaf if possible)
- 2 cloves garlic, peeled, degermed, and minced
- 5 shallots, peeled and minced
- 4 medium tomatoes, peeled, seeded, and diced
- 2 tablespoons minced tarragon

1 Put the mushrooms in a saucepan with 3 tablespoons water and 1 scant tablespoon butter. Cover, bring to a boil, and boil for 3 minutes. Remove the mushrooms and save their cooking liquid.

2 Season each piece of chicken with a good pinch of salt and a dash of pepper. In a Dutch oven just large enough to hold the chicken pieces in a single layer, heat 1 tablespoon olive oil and then 1 tablespoon butter. When the butter foams, turn the heat to low and add the pieces of chicken, nestled against each other. Cook over medium heat for 5 minutes to brown, turning to color evenly. Add the wine, bouquet garni, garlic, and shallots. Scatter the diced tomatoes and sprinkle 1 tablespoon tarragon. Add the mushroom cooking juice and bring the liquid to a "shiver" just below the boiling point. Cover and simmer for 30 minutes.

3 At the end of cooking, add the mushrooms to the pot just long enough to warm them. Sprinkle the chicken with the rest of the tarragon and taste for salt and pepper.

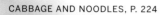
CABBAGE AND NOODLES, P. 224

ARTHUR SCHWARTZ'S JEWISH HOME COOKING

by ARTHUR SCHWARTZ

Cooking teacher and author Arthur Schwartz worries that the assimilation of Jews in America could lead to the demise of Jewish home cooking—a cuisine he loves. In his fifth book, he aims to preserve Jewish food traditions by giving readers a thorough collection of recipes, some updated to suit modern tastes. "A little makeover never hurt anyone," he says, explaining why his recipes might go lighter on the schmaltz (chicken fat) than an old-fashioned Eastern European recipe, or why he might change a cooking method here or there. When he makes his Cabbage and Noodles, for instance, he doesn't boil the cabbage—the usual (and stinky) method. Instead, he caramelizes the shredded cabbage in butter before tossing it with noodles, poppy seeds and sour cream.

Published by Ten Speed Press, $35

Schwartz says to use anywhere from 2 to 8 tablespoons of butter in this divine dish; go for the max to get the best results. The poppy seeds and sour cream only make the recipe more heavenly.

CABBAGE *and* NOODLES

SERVES 4 TO 8,
DEPENDING ON HOW IT IS SERVED

- 1 (2½- to 3-pound) cabbage
- 2 to 8 tablespoons butter, or ¼ cup schmaltz (see Editor's Note) or peanut, corn, or canola oil
- 1 medium onion, thinly sliced or chopped (optional)
- 1 teaspoon salt, or more to taste
- 1 pound (or less) egg noodles (wide, medium, bow ties, any shape but fine)

Freshly ground black pepper
About ¼ cup poppy seed, for garnish (optional)
Sour cream or cottage cheese, for garnish (optional)

In the brutal climate of Eastern Europe, easily storable cabbage was one of the few vegetables Jews could eat most of the year. According to Claudia Roden in The Book of Jewish Food, *"Every shtetl smelled immensely of cabbage." As late as the 1960s, it wasn't much different in the apartment houses of Flatbush (Brooklyn), Forest Hills (Queens), Washington Heights (Manhattan), or the Grand Concourse ("duh" Bronx).*

Long cooking is supposedly what causes cabbage to smell bad, but I find that only long boiling does it. Smothering it in a covered pot with only its own moisture and some fat—butter, schmaltz, or vegetable oil, depending on how you intend to serve it—doesn't produce the bad odor. And it is delicious at every stage of cooking, from just wilted, still pale green, through golden tender shreds, then brown, sweetly caramelized tendrils of amazingly intense flavor.

Marion Gold, a Hungarian cook and the late mother of cookbook writer Rozanne Gold, taught me to first salt the cabbage, then leave it for 24 hours to leach out excess moisture before cooking it slowly in a whole stick of butter until it becomes deeply caramelized. Only then did Marion toss the cabbage with egg noodles, either wide ones or bow ties. Gilding the lily, I like mine with a big spoon of sour cream, too, which makes it a main course. Sometimes, I'll use cottage cheese instead, which also makes it substantial enough to eat for its own sake. And some Hungarians add poppy seed toward the end of the cooking.

The caramelized cabbage is also used as a filling for a savory strudel. Just wrap the cooked cabbage in several layers of phyllo pastry, each sheet brushed with melted butter and lightly sprinkled with dry bread crumbs, and bake.

Unless you are buying just-picked cabbage, however (what old recipes call "new cabbage"), salting is unnecessary. I find that most supermarket cabbage does not have much moisture. Without salting, the cabbage just takes about 20 minutes longer to get deep brown, and it is just as delicious. You might add a sliced onion to the cabbage, as Marion said she used to do until she realized it didn't make much of a difference.

Core the cabbage, shred it finely and wash well, then dry in a clean kitchen towel or salad spinner. In a large pot, melt the butter over medium heat. (A whole stick of butter is what Marion Gold used, and it does make the cabbage divine.) Add the cabbage, onion, and salt. Toss the cabbage in the melted fat. Cover the pot and let steam until well wilted, about 10 minutes.

Toss again. Cover the pot, decrease the heat to medium-low, and cook for 1½ hours longer, tossing the cabbage every 20 minutes or so. If the juices have not evaporated after the first hour, increase the heat.

After about 2 hours, the cabbage will have begun to brown. Raise the heat and continue to cook, uncovered, tossing more often, until the cabbage is a deep brown.

As the cabbage is delicious at any point, you can toss it with egg noodles or serve it alone as a vegetable, in either case seasoned with freshly ground black pepper and, if necessary, more salt. Garnish with poppy seed and sour cream.

Despite the name, this tzimmes is more like a beef stew with carrots than a carrot side dish. Schwartz slow-cooks inexpensive short ribs with lots of carrots and prunes until the meat is incredibly tender.

CARROT TZIMMES

SERVES 6 TO 8

1½ to 2 pounds flanken (see Editor's Note) or chuck stew meat, cut into large chunks

1 medium onion, coarsely chopped

2 pounds carrots, peeled and sliced ⅓ inch thick

1 teaspoon salt

½ teaspoon freshly ground black pepper

½ pound large prunes, preferably sour prunes, preferably not pitted

In Yiddish, the word tzimmes *means "a fuss," an unduly long procedure, a complicated mess. Few recipes for carrot tzimmes live up to the name. They may contain many ingredients, but they are throw-everything-in-the-pot-and-let-it-cook dishes.*

For several reasons, carrot tzimmes has special meaning as a dish for Rosh Hashanah, aside from the rest of the year when we eat it because we like it. First, the word for carrots (plural) in Yiddish is mehren, *which is also the word for "be fruitful and multiply." In essence, eating carrots is asking for that blessing. To add meaning on top of superstitious meaning, we cut the carrots in rounds to resemble golden coins. In addition, tzimmes is a sweet dish—indeed, a sweetened dish—and eating sweet foods on the New Year is supposed to bring sweetness the rest of the year.*

Preheat the oven to 250°F.

In a large stovetop casserole, over medium-high heat, sear the meat a few pieces at a time. When browned, remove and set aside on a platter. When all the meat has been browned, add the onion to the pan and sauté for about 3 minutes, scraping up the brown residue on the bottom with a wooden spoon. In the casserole on top of the onion, layer half the carrots, then half the meat, then the remaining carrots, and the remaining meat, seasoning each layer with salt and pepper. Add just enough water to barely cover everything. Bring to a simmer.

EDITOR'S NOTE

Short ribs are usually cut parallel to the bones, but flanken are cut across the ribs. Ask your butcher for flanken, or use regular short ribs or any cut from the round, flank or chuck; all are perfect for braising.

Cover and transfer to the oven. Cook for 1 hour. Add the prunes, pushing some to near the bottom of the pot. Return to the oven for another hour. Uncover the pot, and continue baking in the oven for 1 more hour.

It is best to let the tzimmes cool, then reheat it, even a day or two later. If made ahead and refrigerated, you can easily skim the fat from the top of the casserole.

Variations

Many families like their tzimmes sweeter than this one. After cooking the prunes for 1 hour, taste, and stir as much as ½ cup of honey or firmly packed brown sugar into the liquid.

For sweet potato and prune tzimmes, follow the recipe for Carrot Tzimmes, but substitute 2 pounds of sweet potatoes, peeled and cut into very large pieces (each 8-ounce potato can be cut into quarters), for the carrots. In addition to the prunes, you may want to add as much as ½ pound of dried apricots.

Some cooks make a combination tzimmes using both carrots and sweet potatoes. You can divide the poundage of vegetables evenly or unevenly between the two vegetables.

Schwartz butterflies chicken before roasting it, ensuring supercrispy skin and evenly cooked meat. He also rubs the bird with fresh garlic-paprika paste instead of the traditional garlic powder.

GARLIC *and* PAPRIKA RUBBED ROAST CHICKEN

SERVES 2 TO 4

- 6 large cloves garlic, crushed or pressed
- 1 tablespoon sweet Hungarian paprika
- 1 teaspoon salt
- ½ teaspoon freshly ground black pepper
- 1½ tablespoons corn, canola, or peanut oil
- 1 (3- to 4-pound) whole chicken

Long before contemporary chefs used rubs to season food, Jewish mothers were massaging chickens with garlic, paprika, salt, and pepper. The later-day American version of this seasoning may have included garlic powder, or onion salt, or may have been based on Lawry's steak seasoning or another supermarket-bought mix that contains mainly salt and MSG, but it was an early-day rub, nevertheless.

Since I abhor garlic powder, I use crushed garlic. I add good imported Hungarian paprika, salt, and freshly ground pepper. This blend, made into a paste with the addition of some vegetable oil, I not only rub onto the skin, but also tuck under the skin. It makes such a Yiddish aroma as it cooks. Using a modern high-temperature, butterfly roasting method, my roasted chickens come out with juicy white meat and crisp skin. As I much prefer dark meat to white, I also use the same rub and high temperature for roasting thighs and drumsticks alone. Obviously, it works for breasts alone, too.

Preheat the oven to 450°F.

In a small bowl, blend together the garlic, paprika, salt, pepper, and oil.

On a cutting board, cut the chicken in half alongside the backbone. Cut out the backbone. (I like to roast the backbone alongside the chicken, allowing myself the pleasure of eating

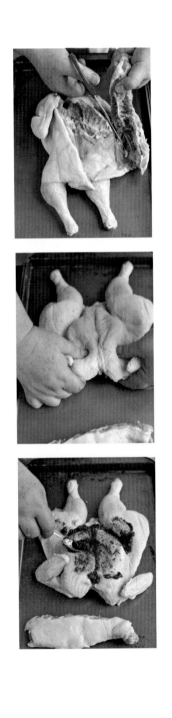

it—the cook's share.) Place the chicken skin-side up, and press the butterflied chicken down to flatten it. Massage the chicken on both sides with the garlic-paprika paste, pushing some of it under the skin. Place the chicken, skin-side up, on a jellyroll-type baking sheet. Roast for 45 minutes.

Remove from the oven and let rest for 5 minutes before cutting it into serving pieces.

EDITOR'S NOTE
Use sturdy kitchen shears if you're butterflying a chicken; a knife can get slippery, and cutting through bones will dull or even nick the blade. You can also have your butcher butterfly the chicken, or simply roast bone-in parts instead (they are done when the internal temperature is 165°F).

Both options for the dough here are fantastic; the Standard Pastry and the Sour Cream Pastry each yield buttery, flaky cookies.

RUGELACH

MAKES 4 DOZEN

STANDARD PASTRY

- 1 cup (2 sticks) unsalted butter, at room temperature
- 1 (8-ounce) package cream cheese, at room temperature
- 2 cups bleached all-purpose flour
- ¼ teaspoon salt

SOUR CREAM PASTRY

- ½ cup (1 stick) unsalted butter, at room temperature
- 4 ounces cream cheese, at room temperature
- ½ cup sour cream
- 1 egg
- 2¾ cups bleached all-purpose flour
- ¼ teaspoon salt

APRICOT-WALNUT FILLING

- ⅔ cup apricot preserves
- 1 cup finely chopped walnuts
- ½ cup sugar mixed with 1 tablespoon ground cinnamon
- ½ cup raisins

- 1 egg, beaten, for egg wash
- 1 tablespoon sugar mixed with ⅛ teaspoon ground cinnamon, for sprinkling

In the kosher bakeries of New York City—we're mainly talking Brooklyn here—there are three kinds of rugelach being sold these days. There is the cream cheese and butter pastry type that used to be made only at home. To their credit, the bakeries have maintained the haphazard, balabatish *look of these. There are yeast rugelach, a Danish-pastry style with a layered dough, similar to the old days but now shaped into larger crescents that are more precisely coiled. The third type is made with what used to be called "frozen dough," a form of puff pastry, fatty and crunchy.*

Like babka, rugelach is another ethnic food that has gone through the "immigrant experience," during which Old Country foods get richer and bigger. These days in metro New York City, you can find rugelach the size of Danish at stores the likes of Dean & DeLuca. And chocolate, not traditional walnut and cinnamon—maybe with a dab of apricot preserves—is the most popular flavor.

Not so long ago, rugelach were dainty crescents, one of the more elegant Yiddish sweets. Indeed, the word ruggle *means "royal."* Ach *makes it plural.*

Philadelphia cream cheese is international now, and so are rugelach. I will never forget eating a wonderful little pastry in Solopaca, a wine market town in the province of Benevento, north of Naples—in any case, an out-of-the-way place. When I asked how these pastries were made, the bakery clerk said it was a secret. When pressed, she said cheese was the secret. Cheese? Of course, it dawned on me, Philadelphia! We were eating rugelach on a hill town in southern Italy.

EDITOR'S NOTE
Feel free to fill the rugelach with your favorite preserves in place of the apricot—we particularly like raspberry and black currant—or use a few different flavors of jam for variety.

The Standard Pastry recipe here is the one most frequently published and used, although some versions add an egg yolk or perhaps a spoonful or two of sour cream in addition to the cream cheese. However, I find the second, Sour Cream Pastry, a slightly more tender and appealing version. Tom Halik of Just Rugulach (as with many Yiddish words, there are many English spellings), a Brooklyn-based baker who sells his very delicious and popular pastries at various New York City Greenmarkets (our farmers' markets) and through mail order, uses a version of the Standard Pastry, but he rolls it out very thin, and instead of making small crescents, he uses an easier and more contemporary way of forming rugelach, shaping a strudel-like roll and cutting it into approximately 1-inch-wide slices. Directions for both doughs and shapes follow.

To make the Standard Pastry, in a stand mixer fitted with the paddle, cream together the butter and cream cheese on medium speed. Stop beating, add the flour and salt all at once, then continue to beat on low speed until the dough holds together around the paddle.

To make the Sour Cream Pastry, in a stand mixer fitted with the paddle, cream together the butter and cream cheese on medium speed. Add the sour cream and egg to the creamed butter mixture and continue beating on medium speed until the mixture is smooth. Stop beating, add the flour and salt all at once, then continue to beat on low speed until the dough holds together around the paddle.

If making crescent pastries, divide the dough evenly into 4 balls. Wrap each ball in plastic wrap. If making into loaves to slice, divide the dough evenly into fourths, and shape each piece into a log about 2 inches in diameter, using a piece of wax paper to help form the sticky dough, then wrap it in plastic.

continued on p. 232

Chill the dough for at least 4 hours. The dough can be held in the refrigerator for up to a week, or in the freezer for up to several months.

When ready to bake, let the dough come to cool room temperature before rolling it out. It should be pliable but not soft.

Position a rack in the center of the oven. Preheat the oven to 350°F.

To make the crescents, on a lightly floured board, roll out 1 dough ball into an approximately 9-inch circle. To make rugelach slices, roll out 1 log of dough into an approximately 6- by 12-inch rectangle.

To make the filling, warm the apricot preserves (in the microwave or by submersing the jar in a hot water bath—both good techniques for this step). Brush about 2 tablespoons of preserves over each dough circle or rectangle, brushing to the edges. Evenly sprinkle each piece of dough with about 2 tablespoons of nuts, then 1 tablespoon of cinnamon sugar, then 2 tablespoons of raisins.

To make crescents, cut each circle into 8 wedges. Roll each wedge from the outside into the point. As each crescent is formed, place it on an ungreased baking sheet. If making strudel-style pastries, roll up the rectangle from a long side. Either way, don't make the rolls tight.

Brush the rolled-up doughs with beaten egg and sprinkle with an additional 1 tablespoon cinnamon sugar. (Some sugar will inevitably end up on the board. Don't worry about it.) Slice the strudel-style pastries into ¾- to 1-inch pieces. Transfer the pieces to an ungreased baking sheet. Repeat with the remaining balls of dough.

Bake for 25 minutes, until well browned. As soon as the rugelach come from the oven, transfer with a metal spatula to a serving plate. Cool completely before serving. They are actually better the day after they are baked. The rugelach may be stored in an airtight container for a little over 1 week.

BEST OF THE BEST EXCLUSIVE

In addition to being an expert on Jewish cooking, Schwartz leads culinary vacations in Italy. His classic take on veal Marsala has a delicate sauce made with sliced mushrooms, broth and butter.

VEAL MARSALA

SERVES 4

2 tablespoons unsalted butter
3 tablespoons extra-virgin olive oil
½ pound cremini mushrooms, thinly sliced
Kosher salt and freshly ground pepper
1 tablespoon coarsely chopped flat-leaf parsley
8 veal cutlets (about 1 pound)
¼ cup all-purpose flour
½ cup Marsala
2 tablespoons low-sodium chicken broth

1 In a medium skillet, melt 1 tablespoon of the butter in 1 tablespoon of the olive oil. Add the mushrooms and cook over moderately high heat until beginning to brown, about 5 minutes. Season with salt and pepper, remove from the heat and stir in the parsley. Keep warm.

2 Season the veal cutlets with salt and pepper and lightly dredge them in flour, tapping off the excess. In a large skillet, melt the remaining 1 tablespoon of butter in the remaining 2 tablespoons of olive oil. Sauté the veal (in batches if necessary) over high heat until just cooked through, about 30 seconds per side. Transfer to plates and keep warm.

3 Wipe out the skillet. Add the Marsala and bring to a boil, scraping up the browned bits from the bottom of the skillet. Add the chicken broth and simmer until the sauce lightly coats the back of a spoon, about 1 minute. Season with salt and pepper. Pour the sauce over the veal, top with the mushrooms and serve.

CAULIFLOWER CROSTINI, P. 236

FRANK STITT'S BOTTEGA FAVORITA

by FRANK STITT *with* KATHERINE COBBS

birmingham meets Bologna in chef Frank Stitt's second cookbook, which is based on recipes from his wonderful Alabama restaurant Bottega. It's a greatest-hits compilation, with over 200 dishes that have been served at Bottega since it opened in 1988. Recipes combine ingredients and influences from the American South and all over Italy—a novel concept that Stitt makes work magnificently. He tosses ravioli with crawfish, treats grits like polenta and suggests topping pizza with barbecue sauce. And his fabulous tortelloni with crabmeat, ricotta and nutty brown butter is even better with a hit of Tabasco.

Published by Artisan, $40

This recipe is an ingenious use of cauliflower: Transformed into a smooth, garlicky puree, it's spread on toast and then topped with thin slices of raw florets, sun-dried tomatoes and capers.

CAULIFLOWER CROSTINI

MAKES 8 CROSTINI

8 slices (about ½ inch thick by 2 inches long) focaccia, baguette, or other crusty bread

About 5 tablespoons extra-virgin olive oil

½ head cauliflower

2 cloves roasted garlic (see Roasting Garlic)

Kosher salt and freshly ground white pepper

Dash of Tabasco or other hot sauce

4 sun-dried tomatoes, reconstituted in 1 cup hot water, drained, and finely julienned

2 tablespoons capers, rinsed

Tiny flat-leaf parsley sprigs

Agrumato lemon oil (optional; see Editor's Note)

Preheat the oven to 450°F.

Brush the slices of bread with about 1 tablespoon of the olive oil. Arrange on a baking sheet and toast in the oven until crisp, 8 to 10 minutes. Set aside.

Trim the cauliflower and separate it into large florets. Slice one-quarter of the florets into thin slices and set aside.

Steam the remaining florets in a steamer basket over boiling water until soft, 12 to 15 minutes.

Transfer the steamed cauliflower to a food processor, add the roasted garlic and salt and pepper to taste, and puree until smooth. With the processor running, pour in the remaining ¼ cup olive oil. Add a dash or two of hot pepper sauce, then taste and adjust the seasonings.

Spoon a layer of the cauliflower puree on each toast. Top with the sun-dried tomatoes, capers, and raw cauliflower slices. Garnish with tiny parsley sprigs and drizzle with a little agrumato lemon oil or extra-virgin olive oil.

Roasting Garlic

To prepare roasted garlic cloves, cut off the top ¼ inch of one or more bulbs of garlic, and place each one on a sheet of aluminum foil. Season with salt and pepper, a few thyme sprigs, and a teaspoon of extra-virgin olive oil. Wrap tightly in the foil and roast in a 325°F oven for about 45 minutes, or until the cloves are soft but not mushy. Let cool, then squeeze out the soft pulp.

TO DRINK A crisp, light white wine, such as Bianco di Custoza

EDITOR'S NOTE

Citrus agrumato is a wonderfully fragrant olive oil infused with the flavor of fresh fruit. It's made by pressing whole lemons or oranges along with olives. Manicaretti imports a good agrumato; it's available at specialty stores and zingermans.com.

This luscious sauce—which includes capers, green olives, parsley and toasted pine nuts as well as walnuts—would be great with any lean fish, but it's particularly good with meaty tuna steaks.

TUNA *with* LIGURIAN WALNUT SAUCE

SERVES 4

Four 6- to 7-ounce tuna steaks
Maldon sea salt and freshly ground
　　black pepper
　1　shallot, thinly sliced
　2　tablespoons red wine vinegar
　⅓　cup delicate extra-virgin olive oil,
　　　plus oil for the grill or skillet
　2　tablespoons walnut oil
　¾　cup walnut halves, toasted
　　　(see Editor's Note on p. 240)
　¼　cup pine nuts, toasted
　2　tablespoons capers, rinsed
　¼　cup coarsely chopped flat-leaf
　　　parsley
　¼　cup pitted Picholine or Niçoise
　　　olives, coarsely chopped
Yolks from 2 hard-boiled eggs,
　　chopped (optional)

I find great pleasure in this rather quirky sauce of walnuts. Its earthy nuttiness is enhanced further with walnut oil, making it a wonderfully full-flavored embellishment for a hearty fish like tuna and a rich and slightly exotic sauce for pasta. The sauce is best if the vinegar mixture is combined with the nuts at the last second.

Season the tuna with sea salt and pepper and set aside.

Prepare a hot fire in a grill. (If you wish to cook the tuna on the stovetop, see below.) While the grill is heating, combine the shallot and vinegar with sea salt and pepper in a medium bowl. Set aside to macerate for 10 minutes.

Rub the grill grate with an olive-oil-soaked cloth (or heat 1 tablespoon olive oil in a large skillet over medium-high heat). Put the fish on the grill (or in the hot pan) and cook until the edges begin to turn opaque, about 2 minutes. Turn and cook for about 2 minutes more for medium-rare. Transfer the fish to a rack and tent with foil to keep warm.

Whisk the olive and walnut oils into the shallot-vinegar mixture. Add the walnuts, pine nuts, capers, parsley, and olives and toss thoroughly to combine.

Place the fish on warm plates and serve with a heaping spoonful of the walnut sauce. Top with the chopped egg yolk, if desired.

TO DRINK Cinque Terre or other simple, light, young white wine

For anyone who likes picking off the crispy pieces on top of baked pasta, this is the ideal dish. The shells aren't swimming in sauce and cheese, so their edges get nice and crunchy in the oven.

BAKED SHELLS *with* RICOTTA *and* FENNEL SAUSAGE

SERVES 4

- 1 pound large pasta shells
- 1 tablespoon olive oil
- ¾ pound Italian sausage with fennel, removed from casings
- 2 cups Marinara Sauce (recipe follows)
- 1 cup ricotta

Kosher salt and freshly ground black pepper

- ½ cup freshly grated Parmigiano-Reggiano

Baked pasta dishes—aromatic and bubbly, with golden brown edges—can be assembled ahead of time and then popped onto the top shelf of a hot oven to heat through. Once the prep is done, it's smooth sailing. All you have to do is make a salad to round out the meal.

Preheat the oven to 475°F.

Bring a large pot of generously salted water to a boil over high heat. Add the shells, stir, and cook until al dente. Drain.

While the pasta cooks, heat the olive oil in a large skillet over medium-high heat. Add the sausage and cook, stirring to break up any clumps of meat, until browned, about 8 minutes. Drain the pan of excess fat. Add the Marinara Sauce and cook for 2 minutes. Add the ricotta, stir to combine, and season with salt and pepper. Remove the pan from the heat.

Spread a few spoonfuls of the marinara mixture over the bottom of a gratin or baking dish large enough to hold the shells in a single layer. Stuff the shells with more of the mixture and arrange them in the dish. Spoon the remaining sauce over the top and sprinkle with the Parmigiano.

Bake for 15 minutes, then run under the broiler until browned and bubbling hot.

TO DRINK Chianti or Rosso di Montalcino

MARINARA SAUCE

MAKES 4 CUPS

¼ cup olive oil
1 large white onion, cut into
 1-inch dice
3 garlic cloves, finely chopped
2 carrots, peeled and cut into
 1-inch dice
2 celery stalks, cut into 1-inch dice
2 cups dry white wine
One 28-ounce can San Marzano
 tomatoes, with their juice
Bouquet garni: 4 or 5 sprigs each
 thyme, basil, and parsley; 4 bay
 leaves; 2 dried red chiles; and
 optional Parmesan rind wrapped
 in cheesecloth
1 tablespoon dried oregano
Pinch of red pepper flakes
Kosher salt and freshly ground
 black pepper

This is our standard tomato sauce, the base for most of our pizzas and a staple we always have on hand. Use it for baked feta as well as for pasta.

Pour the oil into a large saucepan and heat over high heat. When the oil begins to shimmer, add the onion, garlic, carrots, and celery and sauté, stirring frequently, until the vegetables have softened considerably, about 15 minutes.

Add the white wine, bring to a simmer, and simmer until reduced by half. Pour in the tomatoes with their juice and stir well. Push the bouquet garni down into the middle of the mixture. Reduce the heat to medium and simmer until the vegetables break apart when pressed gently against the side of the pan with a spoon, about 30 minutes.

Remove the bouquet garni and add the oregano and pepper flakes. Blend with a handheld immersion blender, or in a food processor or regular blender, until smooth. Taste the sauce and season with salt and pepper to your liking. This keeps for several days in the refrigerator and freezes well.

EDITOR'S NOTE
Frugal cooks don't throw out Parmesan rinds; instead, they store them in a bag in the freezer, then simmer them in soups or sauces to add a savory, nutty flavor. A rind is included in the bouquet garni here, but you can also just put one in the pot, then remove it before serving.

This pasta salad is a hodgepodge that, against all expectations, turns out to be a terrific all-in-one meal. It's perfect for a picnic.

TORTELLINI SALAD *with* CHICKEN, PINE NUTS, SULTANAS *and* BALSAMIC

SERVES 4

- ¼ cup Homemade Mayonnaise (recipe follows) or high-quality commercial mayonnaise
- ¼ cup Balsamic Vinaigrette (recipe follows)
- 2 small heads romaine lettuce, sliced into 1-inch-wide strips
- 4 cups (about 1 pound) cooked store-bought fresh cheese tortellini

Four 6-ounce skinless, boneless chicken breasts, grilled and cut into large cubes

- 1 heaping tablespoon pine nuts, toasted (see Editor's Note)
- ¼ cup sultanas (golden raisins)
- ½ cup cherry tomatoes, halved, or quartered if large
- 1 scant tablespoon chopped flat-leaf parsley

Kosher salt and freshly ground black pepper

The few times we've dared to replace this dish on the Bottega Café menu, our regular crowd screamed in protest. It's deliciously simple once you've assembled all the components, and very satisfying. I have been known to snack on this on those many afternoons when lunch has passed me by.

Whisk the mayonnaise and vinaigrette together in a small bowl.

Toss the romaine leaves with half of the dressing in a large bowl and divide among four plates. Add the tortellini, chicken, pine nuts, sultanas, half of the tomatoes, and the parsley to the bowl and toss to coat with the remaining dressing. Season with salt and pepper and toss again. Arrange on top of the lettuce leaves, garnish with the remaining cherry tomatoes, and serve.

TO DRINK Pinot Grigio (Livio Felluga)

continued on p. 242

EDITOR'S NOTE

To toast nuts, spread them on a sheet pan and bake in a 325°F oven, tossing every few minutes, until golden and fragrant. Alternatively, spread the nuts on a microwave-safe plate and cook at high power, stirring every minute, until golden and fragrant.

HOMEMADE MAYONNAISE

MAKES 1¾ CUPS

1 large egg
1 egg yolk
½ teaspoon salt, or to taste
Juice of ½ lemon
1 teaspoon Dijon mustard
Pinch of cayenne
1½ cups canola or grapeseed oil
1 to 2 tablespoons warm water,
    if needed

Homemade mayonnaise is one of the most versatile sauces there is. During my first book tour, a Southern grande dame exclaimed, "Southern ladies do not serve store-bought mayonnaise!" At the restaurant, we make mayo by hand with a balloon whisk and elbow grease, but the food processor does a good job. In a pinch, good store-bought mayonnaise (I like Hellman's, called Best Foods out West) is a fine stand-in.

Combine the egg, egg yolk, and salt in a food processor and process for 30 seconds. Add the lemon juice, mustard, and cayenne and process for 15 seconds. With the machine running, slowly pour the oil through the feed tube until the mayonnaise is thick and emulsified. If the mixture becomes too dense, stop pouring in the oil and add warm water, a little at a time, until the mayonnaise loosens, then slowly incorporate the remaining oil. Taste and adjust the seasoning. The mayonnaise can be stored, covered, in the refrigerator for up to 1 week.

BALSAMIC VINAIGRETTE

MAKES A GENEROUS 1 CUP

1 medium shallot, finely
    minced
⅓ cup balsamic vinegar
½ teaspoon chopped thyme
Kosher salt and freshly ground
    black pepper
¾ cup extra-virgin olive oil

Balsamic vinegar has become a victim of its own success. True artisanal balsamic vinegar is one of Italy's treasures, but there are many more imitation balsamics than the authentic variety, aceto balsamico di Modena, which is aged in wood barrels of decreasing size as it matures and concentrates. As with most ingredients, you get what you pay for. An excellent value is condimento balsamico di Modena. It captures balsamic's true spirit—the fruitiness of ripe grapes transformed and matured— and is good for most purposes.

Letting the shallot macerate in the vinegar tames its bite while infusing the vinegar with its flavor.

Combine the shallot, vinegar, thyme, and salt and pepper in a small bowl. Set aside to macerate for about 10 minutes.

Whisk in the olive oil and taste and adjust the seasonings. The vinaigrette will keep for several days in a jar in the refrigerator.

BEST OF THE BEST EXCLUSIVE

Stitt loves the tenderness of lamb steaks cut from the leg. He always asks the butcher for the sirloin portion, which is the best part.

LAMB STEAKS *with* TURNIP GRATIN

SERVES 4

2 pounds turnips, peeled and coarsely shredded
Kosher salt
1 tablespoon unsalted butter
2 garlic cloves, halved
1 cup heavy cream
1 large egg
3 ounces Gruyère cheese, coarsely shredded (1 cup)
Pinch of fresh, finely grated nutmeg
Freshly ground pepper
Four 6-ounce boneless leg of lamb steaks (see Editor's Note)
2 tablespoons extra-virgin olive oil
4 thyme sprigs

EDITOR'S NOTE
Leg of lamb steaks are boneless, quick-cooking and less expensive than chops. They're not typically available prepackaged, though, so ask for them at the butcher counter. You can also use 4 lamb chops in this recipe instead.

1 Preheat the oven to 400°F. In a large-mesh strainer, toss the shredded turnips with 1 teaspoon of salt and let stand for 30 minutes.

2 Squeeze out as much water as possible from the turnips. In a large skillet, melt the butter. Add the turnips and cook over high heat, stirring occasionally, until browned in spots, about 4 minutes.

3 Rub an 8-by-11½-inch glass or ceramic baking dish with the cut side of one of the garlic cloves. In a large bowl, whisk the cream with the egg. Add the Gruyère, nutmeg, ¼ teaspoon of pepper and 1 teaspoon of kosher salt. Stir in the turnips. Scrape the turnip mixture into the baking dish and bake for about 30 minutes, until bubbling and browned on top. Let cool for 5 minutes.

4 Meanwhile, season the lamb steaks with salt and pepper. In a large skillet, heat the olive oil until shimmering. Add the lamb and cook until browned, about 3 minutes. Turn the lamb, add the garlic halves and thyme to the skillet and cook until the meat is medium-rare, about 3 minutes longer. Transfer to a cutting board and let rest for 5 minutes. Slice the lamb steaks, transfer to plates and serve with the turnip gratin.

SERVE WITH Sautéed escarole or collard greens.

MAKE AHEAD The turnip gratin can be baked up to 3 hours in advance. Reheat before serving.

ROASTED ZUCCHINI AND MINT SALAD, P. 246

OSTERIA

by RICK TRAMONTO *with* MARY GOODBODY

many haute American chefs today also have casual places. Rick Tramonto of Chicago's elegant Tru restaurant, for one, used to own Osteria di Tramonto, where he served the hearty food of his childhood. While not always simple, many of those Italian recipes naturally translate well to home kitchens—which is why this cookbook, Tramonto's sixth, works so well. There's a range of terrific Italian dishes, from a Roman-style omelet with fresh Italian sausage to short ribs with garlic mashed potatoes, and lots of detailed wine-pairing suggestions: Food served in *osterias* (taverns) is intrinsically wine-friendly. Anyone who enjoys food and wine together will find much to love here.

Published by Broadway Books, $35

When zucchini is in season, any new ideas for using it—like this eye-catching, fresh-tasting salad—are always welcome.

ROASTED ZUCCHINI *and* MINT SALAD

SERVES 4

8 zucchini, halved
    lengthwise
4 sprigs fresh mint
About ⅔ cup croutons
About ½ cup toasted almonds
½ cup extra-virgin olive oil
Juice of 3 lemons
Kosher salt and freshly
    ground black pepper
Fresh mint leaves

This summer salad is light and refreshing with the crunch of almonds and croutons and the brightness of mint and lemon juice. Try it—you'll love it as much as our customers do. It's a perfect antipasto, but also can be a side salad. Your choice.

1 Preheat the oven to 500°F.

2 Lay the zucchini on a baking sheet, skin side up, and bake for about 8 minutes, or until the zucchini are golden brown on the flat, fleshy side. Let the zucchini cool slightly and then slice into half-moons.

3 In a bowl, mix the zucchini, mint sprigs, croutons, and almonds. Drizzle with olive oil and lemon juice, toss, and then season to taste with salt and pepper.

4 Arrange on a serving platter and garnish with fresh mint leaves.

The tomatoey sauce for this homey lasagna is made with hot Italian sausage and plenty of crushed red pepper, so it's good and spicy.

GLORIA'S LASAGNA

SERVES 8; MAKES 1 LASAGNA

MEAT SAUCE
- 3 tablespoons olive oil
- ½ large yellow onion, finely diced
- 2 tablespoons minced garlic
- 1 pound ground spicy Italian sausage
- 1 pound ground beef
- ½ cup white wine
- Two 14-ounce cans plum tomatoes
- 1 tablespoon ground fennel seeds
- 2 teaspoons crushed red pepper flakes
- 1 tablespoon chopped fresh basil
- 1 teaspoon chopped fresh oregano

CHEESE FILLING
- 1 pound ricotta cheese
- 1 large egg
- ½ cup freshly grated Parmigiano-Reggiano cheese
- Kosher salt and freshly ground black pepper

LASAGNA
- 1 pound lasagna sheets
- Olive oil
- 1 cup freshly grated Parmigiano-Reggiano cheese

Because my mom made a big pan of this lasagna at least once a week when I was growing up, it's near and dear to my heart. There is nothing fancy or "restauranty" about the recipe; instead it's about as down-to-earth and satisfying a dish as you will ever find. My mother insisted on high-quality ricotta cheese and always mixed Italian sausage with ground beef. I remember eating it for breakfast the next day.

1 Preheat the oven to 400°F.

2 To prepare the meat sauce, heat the olive oil in a large sauté pan over medium-high heat. Add the onion and garlic and cook for 3 to 4 minutes, or until softened but not colored. Add the sausage and beef and cook, stirring, for 10 to 12 minutes, or until cooked through and no pink beef remains. Using a slotted spoon, remove the meat and vegetables from the pan. Drain and discard the fat left in the pan.

3 Add the wine and cook over medium-high heat, stirring with a wooden spoon and scraping up any browned bits. Let the wine simmer briskly for about 2 minutes, or until the pan is dry. Add the tomatoes, fennel seeds, and red pepper to the pan along with the meat mixture. Cook over medium heat until hot. Stir in the basil and oregano, remove from the heat, and set aside until needed.

4 To make the cheese filling, in a large mixing bowl, stir the ricotta, the egg, and ½ cup of Parmigiano-Reggiano. Season to taste with salt and pepper.

continued on p. 248

5 Using a handheld mixer, beat the cheese mixture for about 4 minutes, or until smooth. Set aside until needed.

6 To prepare the lasagna, bring about 1½ gallons of salted water to a boil in a large pot over high heat. Add the lasagna sheets one by one, stirring the water as each one enters the pot. Cook for about 8 minutes, or until the lasagna sheets are cooked about three-quarters of the way through. They should be tender, but not ready to fall apart.

7 Drain the lasagna sheets and toss lightly with a touch of olive oil so they do not stick together. Lay them out on a kitchen towel until you are ready to assemble the lasagna. (This can be done 24 hours in advance.)

8 To assemble the lasagna, ladle about ½ cup of the meat sauce into the bottom of a rectangular baking dish measuring about 9x13x2 inches. Spread the sauce over the bottom of the pan.

9 Lay pasta sheets on top of the sauce and then top with half of the cheese filling, spreading it evenly over the pasta. Spoon a third of the remaining sauce over the cheese and top with a third of the Parmigiano-Reggiano.

10 Add more sheets of pasta and repeat the layering. Finally, finish with pasta and the remaining ingredients, ending with the Parmigiano-Reggiano.

11 Bake for about 1 hour, or until heated through and bubbling around the edges. Let the lasagna sit for 15 minutes before cutting into squares for serving.

THE SOMMELIER RECOMMENDS The spicy Italian sausage in this rendition of lasagna gears it up for a red wine with some spunk. A simple, straightforward Barbera from Castello del Poggio or the Barbera and Pinot Nero blend "Le Grive" from Forteto della Luja will add a nice dash of bright red fruit.

This pasta with butter and Parmesan cheese sauce (thickened with pasta cooking water) is like a sophisticated mac and cheese.

PENNETTE *with* PANCETTA *and* PEAS

SERVES 4

- 6 ounces pancetta, diced (about 1 cup)
- ¼ cup diced yellow onion
- 2 cups frozen peas
- 1¼ cups chicken stock
- 1 pound dried pennette pasta
- 6 tablespoons unsalted butter
- ¾ cup freshly grated Parmigiano-Reggiano cheese
- Kosher salt and freshly ground black pepper
- ¼ cup extra-virgin olive oil

Pennette is small penne, or tubular pasta. I like it here because the peas and small pieces of pancetta in the simple sauce cling to the little noodles when the final dish is enriched with a generous dose of butter and grated cheese. This is easy pasta cooking at its best.

1 In a small saucepan, cook the pancetta over low heat until crispy and the fat is rendered. Add the onion and cook for about 6 minutes, or until the onion softens and is slightly caramelized.

2 Add the peas and stock to the pan, stir, raise the heat to medium, and continue to cook gently.

3 Meanwhile, cook the pasta according to the package instructions until nearly al dente. Drain, reserving about ¼ cup of the pasta water.

4 Add the pasta to the sauce and cook for about 2 minutes, or until the pasta is al dente. Add a little pasta water, if needed, to thin or loosen the sauce.

5 Add the butter to the pasta and stir until the butter is incorporated. Stir the cheese into the pasta and season to taste with salt and pepper. Finish with a drizzle of olive oil.

THE SOMMELIER RECOMMENDS This is a pasta dish for white wine lovers. The flavor components to consider here are salty Parmigiano, green tones from the peas, and the smoky pancetta. Try a ripe, round Inzolia from Sicily produced by Baglio di Pianetto. The grape varietal is indigenous to the island and was originally primarily used to make Marsala.

EDITOR'S NOTE
Pancetta is an unsmoked Italian bacon that adds savory richness to sauces, soups and beans. It can be stored for months in the freezer and is actually easiest to dice while still frozen.

A classic chicken piccata involves sautéing thin cutlets in a pan. Tramonto's roasted version, with its lemony white wine sauce seasoned with capers and parsley, is easier but no less delicious.

ROAST CHICKEN PICCATA-STYLE

SERVES 4

Two 3-pound whole chickens
Kosher salt and freshly ground
     black pepper
½ cup clarified butter
     (see Editor's Note on p. 252)
     or vegetable oil
2 lemons, sliced about
     ¼ inch thick
2 cups dry white wine
½ cup unsalted butter
3 tablespoons drained capers
Juice of 2 lemons
2 tablespoons chopped fresh
     flat-leaf parsley

Roast chicken is one of life's simpler pleasures, and because I am so enamored with it, I am always on the lookout for new and interesting ways to cook it. Piccata usually refers to thin cutlets served with a lemony sauce, but for this I use partially boned chickens—and boning the birds is the only difficult part of the recipe. But you can have your butcher do it. Everything else is straightforward. I love the flavors of lemon, capers, and a good confetti of parsley with the roast chicken—a simple pleasure made even more gratifying when cooked this way.

1 Split the chickens in half and remove the breast section of one half with the wing attached. Leave the skin between the breast and the leg attached, cracking the thigh joint of the chicken and cutting through to separate the leg from the body while it remains attached to the breast by a thin strip of skin. Remove the drumstick completely, trying to leave as much skin from the leg intact as possible. Make an incision in the thigh along the thigh bone and remove the thigh bone. Repeat on the other side and with both chickens. Ask your butcher to do this for you, if you like. (Reserve the drumsticks and carcass for stocks.)

2 Preheat the oven to 400°F.

3 Season the chicken with salt and pepper.

4 Heat 2 large ovenproof sauté pans over medium-high heat. Put ¼ cup of clarified butter or oil in each pan and cook the chicken halves, skin side down, for about 4 minutes. Transfer

continued on p. 252

the pans to the oven and cook for about 12 minutes, or until the chicken is cooked through. Remove the chickens from the pans and let them rest for about 5 minutes.

5 Put the lemon slices in the pans and let them cook over high heat for about 1 minute so that they caramelize. Add the wine and cook, stirring with a wooden spoon and scraping up any browned bits, for 2 to 3 minutes, until reduced by half.

6 Add the unsalted butter and capers and stir the sauce to emulsify the butter with the pan juices. Squeeze the lemon juice into the sauce, remove from the heat, and continue stirring until blended. Stir in the parsley.

7 Put a chicken half on each serving plate, skin side up, and spoon equal amounts of sauce over each. Serve immediately.

THE SOMMELIER RECOMMENDS Lemon, butter, and capers are the ultimate white wine accoutrements, and the rule is not excepted here. Choose a fuller-bodied style of wine, enveloped in oak, and your meal will be perfectly matched. Chardonnay is the obvious grape to choose, but these days winemakers are doing Chardonnay-like things to other grapes. Vie di Romans in Friuli makes an oak-aged Pinot Grigio called "Dessimis."

BEST OF THE BEST EXCLUSIVE

Preparing farro (whole-grain wheat) like risotto is a brilliant idea: You cook the grain in a small amount of broth, stirring and adding more broth as it's absorbed, until the dish becomes thick and creamy.

FARRO RISOTTO
with SUMMER VEGETABLES

SERVES 4

4 cups low-sodium chicken broth
2 tablespoons extra-virgin olive oil
1 small onion, finely diced
1 cup farro (see Editor's Note on p. 89)
Kosher salt and freshly ground pepper
12 pearl onions
3 garlic cloves, thinly sliced
½ small fennel bulb, finely diced
1 small zucchini, finely diced
⅓ cup fresh or frozen corn kernels (from 1 ear of corn)
16 grape tomatoes, halved
¼ cup pitted kalamata olives, quartered
¼ cup thinly sliced basil
½ cup freshly grated Parmigiano-Reggiano cheese
2 tablespoons unsalted butter
1 tablespoon sherry vinegar
2 tablespoons heavy cream
1 tablespoon chopped flat-leaf parsley

1 In a small saucepan, bring the broth to a simmer; keep warm. In a medium saucepan, heat 1 tablespoon of the olive oil. Add the onion and cook over moderately high heat until softened, about 3 minutes. Add the farro and cook until lightly toasted, about 2 minutes. Add 1 cup of the warm broth and cook over moderate heat, stirring occasionally, until nearly absorbed. Continue adding the broth 1 cup at a time and stirring constantly until it is nearly absorbed between additions. The farro is done when the grains are tender and most of the broth has been absorbed, about 25 minutes. Season with salt and pepper, remove from the heat and keep warm.

2 Meanwhile, in a small pot of boiling water, blanch the pearl onions until tender, about 3 minutes. Drain and peel them.

3 In a large skillet, heat the remaining 1 tablespoon of olive oil. Add the garlic and cook over moderately high heat until fragrant, about 30 seconds. Add the pearl onions, fennel, zucchini and corn and cook until the vegetables are browned in spots, about 4 minutes. Add the tomatoes, olives and basil and cook until warmed through, about 1 minute. Season with salt and pepper. Stir the vegetables into the farro. Add the Parmigiano-Reggiano, butter and vinegar and stir until the butter is melted. Stir in the cream. Spoon the farro into bowls, sprinkle with the parsley and serve.

GRILLED BEEF TENDERLOIN WITH ASPARAGUS
AND ROASTED RED ONION VINAIGRETTE, P. 256

HOME COOKING WITH CHARLIE TROTTER

by CHARLIE TROTTER

Charlie Trotter is known for the outrageously complex food he prepares at his eponymous Chicago restaurant—and his previous 14 cookbooks reflect this. His new book, however, is geared to cooks looking for amped-up home recipes, not to cooks trying to re-create the acclaimed chef's elaborate restaurant dishes. These recipes may require confidence in the kitchen, but not superhuman effort. As Trotter writes, "Great food doesn't have to entail frantic foraging for ingredients and performing Herculean feats." He knows when to make clever, time-saving substitutions—by swapping smoked salmon for fresh in an elegant faux tartare, for instance—and how to elevate simple ingredients like pork and potatoes with a bacon-sherry vinaigrette.

Published by Ten Speed Press, $25

Whisking roasted onion with balsamic vinegar creates a spectacular vinaigrette that turns beef and asparagus into an elegant meal.

GRILLED BEEF TENDERLOIN *with* ASPARAGUS *and* ROASTED RED ONION VINAIGRETTE

SERVES 4

VINAIGRETTE
- 1 small red onion
- ¾ cup extra-virgin olive oil
- 3 tablespoons balsamic vinegar (see Author's Note)
- 2 tablespoons chopped fresh chives

Salt and freshly ground black pepper

- 1½ pounds beef tenderloin
- 2 tablespoons extra-virgin olive oil

Salt and freshly ground black pepper
- 1 pound asparagus spears, trimmed
- 1 teaspoon red amaranth sprouts (see Editor's Note)

EDITOR'S NOTE
Red amaranth sprouts are a flavorful, eye-catching garnish for this dish. Order them from sproutliving.com, or substitute a sprinkle of chopped chives or whole flat-leaf parsley leaves.

To prepare the vinaigrette

Preheat the oven to 350°F. Place the onion and olive oil in a small ovenproof pan and cover tightly. Roast for 50 to 60 minutes, or until the onion is soft. Let the onion cool in the olive oil, and then remove the onion, reserving the oil. Julienne the onion and place in a medium bowl. Add the balsamic vinegar and slowly whisk in the reserved olive oil. Add the chives and season to taste with salt and pepper.

To prepare the beef

Prepare a medium-hot grill. Rub the beef with the olive oil and season to taste with salt and pepper. Grill for 4 to 5 minutes on each side, or until medium-rare or cooked to the desired doneness. Remove the beef from the grill, let rest for 5 minutes, and cut into ¼-inch-thick slices.

To prepare the asparagus

Bring a medium pot of salted water to a boil. Add the asparagus and cook for 5 minutes, or until tender.

Fan the asparagus on each plate, with the stem ends in the center. Layer the beef slices in an overlapping pattern over the stem ends of the asparagus and spoon the vinaigrette over the asparagus and beef. Garnish with amaranth sprouts.

AUTHOR'S NOTE Balsamic vinegars are aged for varying lengths of time, and their virtues increase with age. The longer it is aged, the smoother and more syrupy the vinegar will be. It is worth the money to buy, at minimum, the 12-year-old variety. It will make an enormous difference in the final flavor of any dish.

Trotter adores warm dressings. In this recipe, he uses a warm bacon vinaigrette to add flavor to roasted pork and Yukon Gold potatoes.

HERB-CRUSTED PORK *with* ROASTED POTATOES *and* BACON-SHERRY VINAIGRETTE

SERVES 4

VINAIGRETTE
- 4 ounces bacon, julienned
- ½ cup olive oil
- ¼ cup sherry wine vinegar
- 1 small shallot, finely diced
- Salt and freshly ground black pepper

- 1½ pounds pork tenderloin
- 6 tablespoons extra-virgin olive oil
- Salt and freshly ground black pepper
- ¼ cup chopped fresh thyme
- ¼ cup chopped fresh rosemary
- ½ cup chopped fresh flat-leaf parsley
- 2 tablespoons canola oil
- 2 pounds small Yukon Gold potatoes, quartered

To prepare the vinaigrette

Cook the bacon in a small sauté pan over medium heat for 8 to 10 minutes, or until crispy. Place the bacon and ¼ cup of the rendered bacon fat in a small bowl. Whisk in the olive oil, vinegar, and shallot and season to taste with salt and pepper.

To prepare the pork

Preheat the oven to 375°F. Rub the pork with 3 tablespoons of the olive oil and season with salt and pepper. Coat the pork with the thyme, rosemary, and ¼ cup of the parsley. Place in a hot sauté pan with the canola oil and sear for 5 minutes on each side. Roast in the oven for 25 to 30 minutes, or until the internal temperature reaches 155°F on a meat thermometer.

Meanwhile, prepare the potatoes

Place the potatoes on a baking sheet and toss with the remaining 3 tablespoons olive oil. Sprinkle the remaining ¼ cup parsley over the potatoes, season with salt and pepper, and roast alongside the tenderloin for 20 minutes, or until tender.

Remove the tenderloin from the oven, let it rest for 10 minutes, and then cut the meat into ¼-inch-thick slices. Spoon some of the potatoes on one side of each plate and layer the pork slices in an overlapping pattern next to the potatoes. Drizzle the vinaigrette over the meat and potatoes and top with freshly ground pepper.

Instead of fussing with fresh salmon, Trotter combines smoked salmon with capers and shallots in this simple starter.

SMOKED SALMON TARTARE
with HORSERADISH CREAM

SERVES 4

- 3 tablespoons olive oil
- 12 thin 2-inch-diameter circles sourdough bread (see Author's Note)
- ¼ cup heavy cream
- 1 tablespoon plus 1 teaspoon finely grated fresh horseradish
- 2 teaspoons finely chopped fresh chives
- Salt and freshly ground black pepper
- ¾ cup finely diced smoked salmon
- 3 tablespoons chopped fresh chervil
- 1½ tablespoons chopped capers
- 1½ tablespoons chopped shallots
- 1 teaspoon fresh fennel bulb top (thin green part only)

To prepare the bread

Preheat the oven to 350°F. Using 2 tablespoons of the olive oil, brush each side of the bread circles with oil and place on a baking sheet. Toast in the oven for 10 minutes, or until golden brown. Remove from the oven and set aside.

To prepare the cream

Place the cream in a small bowl and whip with a whisk for 2 minutes, or until soft peaks just begin to form. Stir in the 1 tablespoon horseradish and the chives and season to taste with salt and pepper.

To prepare the salmon

Place the salmon, chervil, capers, shallots, and the remaining 1 tablespoon olive oil in a small bowl and mix thoroughly. Season to taste with pepper.

Place 3 pieces of the toasted sourdough in the center of each plate and top with a small spoonful of the horseradish cream. Spoon some of the smoked salmon tartare over the cream, top with freshly ground black pepper, and garnish with the fennel tops and the 1 teaspoon grated horseradish. Serve immediately.

AUTHOR'S NOTE If you prefer to pass these appetizers rather than serve them on a plate, use 24 circles of bread only 1 inch in diameter and proceed as directed.

The snapper here is great, but it's the creamy white grits that stand out. Trotter folds them with caramelized onion, chopped chives and fresh lemon juice, creating the ultimate side dish.

SAUTÉED SNAPPER *with* CARAMELIZED ONION– STREWN GRITS *and* RED WINE PAN SAUCE

SERVES 4

GRITS
1½ cups water
  2 teaspoons salt
  ½ cup white grits
  1 red onion, julienned
  1 tablespoon unsalted butter
  2 tablespoons chopped
     fresh chives
  1 tablespoon freshly squeezed
     lemon juice
Salt and freshly ground
     black pepper

  4 (5-ounce) snapper fillets, skin on
Salt and freshly ground
     black pepper
  2 tablespoons canola oil
  1 shallot, diced
  1 cup red wine
  ½ cup extra-virgin olive oil
  1 tablespoon cider vinegar
  1 tablespoon chopped
     fresh chives

EDITOR'S NOTE
For the crispest skin, pat the fish completely dry before frying so that moisture doesn't create steam in the pan. And use a large nonstick skillet to help keep the crispy skin from clinging and tearing.

To prepare the grits

Place the water and salt in a medium saucepan and bring to a boil. Stir in the grits, decrease the heat to low, and simmer for 25 to 30 minutes, or until soft.

Cook the red onion and butter in a small sauté pan over medium heat for 10 to 12 minutes, or until golden brown and caramelized. Fold the onion, chives, and lemon juice into the cooked grits, season to taste with salt and pepper, and keep warm.

To prepare the snapper

Season the snapper with salt and pepper and score the skin side with a sharp knife or razor blade. Heat the canola oil in a large sauté pan over medium-high heat. Cook the snapper, skin side down first, for 2 minutes on each side, or until golden brown. Remove from the pan, cover, and keep warm.

To prepare the sauce

Cook the shallot in the same pan over medium heat for 2 to 3 minutes, or until translucent. Add the wine and cook over medium-high heat for 10 minutes, or until reduced to ¼ cup. Add the olive oil, vinegar, and chives and stir well. Season with salt and pepper.

Spoon some of the grits in the center of each plate and top with a piece of snapper. Drizzle the pan sauce over the snapper and around the plate.

While these sweet-tart little cakes bake, they separate into a soft pudding layer on the bottom and a more cakelike layer on top. If Key limes aren't available, substitute regular limes or even lemons.

KEY LIME PUDDING CAKES

SERVES 8

- 2 tablespoons unsalted butter, at room temperature
- ½ cup plus 1 tablespoon sugar
- 1½ tablespoons finely grated Key lime zest (from about 6 limes)

Pinch of salt

- 3 large eggs, separated, plus 1 large egg white
- 3 tablespoons all-purpose flour
- ¼ cup plus 2 tablespoons fresh Key lime juice (from about 12 limes)
- ¾ cup whole milk

Fresh raspberries, for serving

1 Preheat the oven to 325°F. Lightly spray eight 6-ounce ramekins with vegetable oil cooking spray and set the ramekins in a large roasting pan. In a large bowl, using a handheld electric mixer, cream the butter with the sugar, lime zest and salt. Add the 3 egg yolks one at a time, beating well between additions. Beat in the flour, then add the lime juice and milk; beat until incorporated.

2 In a medium bowl, using clean beaters, beat the 4 egg whites to stiff peaks. Fold the egg whites into the batter until no streaks remain. Pour the batter into the prepared ramekins and set the roasting pan in the oven. Add enough boiling water to the roasting pan to reach halfway up the sides of the ramekins. Bake for about 35 minutes, until the cakes are set and the tops are lightly browned.

3 Using tongs, transfer the pudding cakes to a rack to cool, about 30 minutes. Serve the cakes in the ramekins, or run a paring knife around the edges and invert them onto plates. Garnish with fresh raspberries and serve warm or chilled.

MAKE AHEAD The pudding cakes can be refrigerated, covered, for up to 1 day.

Chanterelles, the prized wild mushrooms that inspired the restaurant's name.

CHANTERELLE

by DAVID WALTUCK *and* ANDREW FRIEDMAN

We wanted diners to find everything beautiful to look at and intense and unforgettable to eat," writes chef David Waltuck about opening Manhattan's Chanterelle in 1979 with his wife, Karen. The couple succeeded in creating a remarkable restaurant that is now a culinary landmark, an "idiosyncratic take on a three-star French restaurant." This book is a glorious tribute to Chanterelle and to Waltuck's cooking, which combines exacting French technique with an irreverent American sensibility. Recipes vary in difficulty but are all fantastic, making *Chanterelle* a must-have for anyone who wants a peek inside the mind of this pioneering New York chef.

Published by The Taunton Press, $50

You might think putting crabmeat in gazpacho is a mistake—
the sweet, mild seafood could easily be overwhelmed by such a
vibrant soup—but the balance of flavors here is perfect.

GREEN GAZPACHO *with* CRABMEAT

SERVES 4

   8 ounces fresh lump crabmeat
  ½ cup plus 1 tablespoon olive oil
2½ tablespoons freshly squeezed
     lemon juice, plus more to taste
Kosher salt
Black pepper from a mill
  2 cups loosely packed fresh chives
     cut into 2-inch segments
  1 cup loosely packed fresh
     dill fronds
  2 cups loosely packed fresh sorrel
     leaves, with the center ribs
     removed
  2 cups loosely packed fresh
     flat-leaf parsley leaves
  2 cups loosely packed watercress,
     with stems
  1 tablespoon coarsely chopped
     fresh serrano chile
  1 large English (hothouse)
     cucumber
  ¾ cup seedless green grapes
  ½ cup cold water
1 to 2 teaspoons American black
     caviar, such as paddlefish
     (optional)

One of the great culinary resources of New York City is the Union Square Greenmarket. I was walking the market one morning when the summer harvest was at its great, green peak: Everywhere I looked there were lush bunches of herbs, piles of cucumbers, and baskets piled high with green peppers. I wanted to gather up all that green goodness and go back to my kitchen and make something. I remembered hearing of a green gazpacho—to this day, I don't know where—and decided to try that. Back at Chanterelle, I processed vegetables along with some serrano pepper for heat and a variety of herbs to give it a potent garden aroma. I finished the soup with olive oil and lemon juice, and rounded it out with crabmeat. Then I decided to make the crab the co-star of the dish, with the gazpacho acting almost like a sauce.

Put the crabmeat in a medium bowl and squeeze out any excess water. Gently pick through it to remove any bits of shell or cartilage, taking care to not break up the pieces any more than necessary. Add 1 tablespoon of the oil, ½ tablespoon of the lemon juice, ½ teaspoon of the salt, and 1 grind of black pepper and toss gently to combine. Taste and adjust the seasoning with more salt, pepper, and lemon juice, if necessary. Cover with plastic wrap and refrigerate for up to 2 hours.

Bring a large pot of water to a boil. Fill a large bowl halfway with ice water. Blanch the chives, dill, sorrel, parsley, and watercress for 10 seconds, then quickly transfer them to the ice bath to stop the cooking and set the color. Drain and squeeze out any excess water, then coarsely chop the herbs.

EDITOR'S NOTE
Sorrel is a leafy spring green
that resembles spinach but has a
lemony tartness. Look for it at
farmers' markets and specialty
stores. If it's not available, substitute
arugula in this recipe, or use
baby spinach and add a teaspoon
of grated lemon zest.

Put the chopped herbs, chile, cucumber, grapes, water, and the remaining ½ cup oil and 2 tablespoons lemon juice in a blender and process until smooth. Transfer the soup to a bowl, cover with plastic wrap, and refrigerate for up to 2 hours.

To serve, set a 2- or 3-inch ring mold in the center of a wide, shallow bowl and fill it with one-quarter of the crabmeat salad, pressing down firmly. Gently lift the ring away from the salad and repeat with the remaining 3 bowls. (Alternatively, you can simply mound one-quarter of the salad in the center of each bowl.) Ladle equal amounts of the chilled gazpacho around the crabmeat in each bowl. Garnish with the caviar, if desired, and serve.

Prep Talk: Blanching Leafy Herbs

Blanching fresh herbs brightens and sets their green color and softens their flavor. The easiest way I know to blanch parsley and other leafy herbs such as tarragon and cilantro is to tie them in cheesecloth before submerging them in the boiling water. This facilitates removing the herb from both the hot water and the ice water in which it's shocked.

The intense sauce for this chicken calls for dozens of whole garlic cloves, which become tender, golden and sweet in the oven. You'll want to pop them in your mouth between bites of chicken.

CHICKEN *with* VERJUS *and* GARLIC CLOVES

SERVES 4

4 large boneless chicken breast halves, skin on, preferably "frenched" (first wing joint still attached)
Kosher salt
Black pepper from a mill
¼ cup canola or other neutral oil
1½ cups garlic cloves, peeled
2 cups verjus
2½ cups Chicken Stock (recipe follows)
3 tablespoons cold unsalted butter, cut into ½-inch cubes
Freshly squeezed lemon juice, if necessary
3 tablespoons coarsely chopped fresh flat-leaf parsley

A variation on the classic chicken with forty cloves of garlic, this recipe makes great use of verjus. Once known almost exclusively to chefs, verjus—an acidic juice made from unripe wine grapes—has grown in popularity among home cooks in recent years. Here, it's the perfect complement to the garlic and chicken; the combination is so complete that very little technique is called for: the chicken is browned and finished in the oven and the sauce is made by lightly browning the garlic, deglazing with verjus, and finishing with butter.

I like to use California verjus in this and other dishes (my preferred brand is Fusion) because it has a more complex sweet-and-sour quality than French verjus, which is overwhelmingly sour.

Preheat the oven to 425°F.

Heat a large heavy-bottomed sauté pan over medium-high heat. Season the chicken on both sides with salt and pepper. Pour the oil into the hot pan. When it begins to smoke, add the chicken, skin side down, and cook until the skin is well browned, 7 to 8 minutes. Turn and cook the other side for 3 minutes. Transfer the breasts to a baking sheet, skin side up.

Pour all but 2 tablespoons of oil out of the pan. Reduce the heat to medium, add the garlic, and cook, stirring a few times, until the cloves are golden brown but no darker, about 5 minutes. Add the verjus, raise the heat to high, and scrape up any browned bits stuck to the bottom of the pan. Cook until the liquid is syrupy and slightly caramelized, about 5 minutes, but take care not to burn the sugars in the verjus. Pour in the stock, bring to a boil, and reduce by two-thirds, 10 to

EDITOR'S NOTE
Winemakers sometimes press unripe grapes into verjus. This pleasantly tart juice can be used in place of wine or vinegar. Buy it at specialty stores or from terrasonoma.com, or substitute dry white wine here.

15 minutes. Reduce the heat to medium-low and swirl in the butter, one cube at a time, to thicken and enrich the sauce.

Place the chicken breasts in the oven to finish cooking them and recrisp their skin, 4 to 5 minutes.

Meanwhile, taste the sauce and adjust the seasoning with salt and pepper. It should be sweet and sour, but more tart than sweet. Adjust with a few drops of lemon juice if necessary. Swirl in the parsley.

Place a chicken breast on each of 4 dinner plates. Top with a spoonful of sauce and serve immediately.

CHICKEN STOCK

This is probably the most called-upon stock in any restaurant kitchen. My version is fairly streamlined, with no peppercorns, herbs, or celery to distract from the essence of the chicken.

MAKES ABOUT 6 QUARTS

5 pounds raw chicken carcasses, necks, backs, and trim (I usually include chicken wings, which add a lot of flavor and gelatin)

2 large carrots, unpeeled, cut into 1-inch chunks

1 medium onion, unpeeled, cut into 1-inch chunks

1 garlic head, in its skin, cut in half horizontally

32 cups (2 gallons) cold water

Put the chicken, carrots, onion, garlic, and water in a large heavy-bottomed stockpot over medium heat. Bring to a boil and skim the surface with a spoon to remove any scum that rises to the top. Reduce the heat so the liquid is simmering and cook, skimming the surface periodically to remove any scum, until the stock tastes unmistakably of chicken, about 4 hours. (If the water drops below the top of the solids during that time, add a few more cups.)

Use tongs or a slotted spoon to discard as many of the solids (especially the bones) as possible from the pot. Carefully strain the stock through a cheesecloth-lined strainer set over a stainless steel bowl. If not using right away, cool the stock. To do this, fill a very large bowl with ice, then set the bowl of stock in it, encouraging the hot liquid to cool quickly. Skim off the fat that rises to the surface. The stock can be refrigerated in an airtight container for up to 3 days or frozen for up to 2 months.

by DAVID WALTUCK *and* ANDREW FRIEDMAN

This recipe involves a basic chef technique—reducing wine and stock in a pan—that every serious home cook should master in order to create dishes with incredible depth of flavor.

PORK CHOPS *with* GINGER, SAUTERNES *and* COARSE MUSTARD

SERVES 4

- ¼ cup peeled and coarsely chopped fresh ginger
- 2 cups Sauternes or Muscat
- 2 cups Chicken Stock (recipe on p. 267) or high-quality low-sodium store-bought chicken stock
- Four 10-ounce bone-in center-cut pork chops, trimmed of fat
- Kosher salt
- Black pepper from a mill
- ¼ cup canola or other neutral oil
- 1 tablespoon freshly squeezed lemon juice
- 3 tablespoons grainy mustard
- ¼ cup (½ stick) cold unsalted butter

This dish takes a number of pork-friendly condiments and fuses them together into a powerful sauce reminiscent of honey mustard—it's sweet and hot, with a peppery undercurrent thanks to an infusion of ginger. There are not many ingredients here, but each one contributes a distinct and forceful flavor.

Put the ginger and Sauternes in a medium heavy-bottomed saucepan, bring to a boil, reduce the heat to medium, and reduce, swirling, until it becomes caramelized and syrupy, about 15 minutes. Strain through a fine-mesh strainer set over a bowl and discard the ginger. Return the reduction to the pan and pour in the stock. Bring to a boil and reduce the sauce to 1 cup, about 30 minutes. Remove from the heat. (The sauce can be refrigerated in an airtight container for up to 24 hours.)

Preheat the oven to 400°F.

Heat a large, heavy-bottomed, ovenproof sauté pan over high heat until very hot. Season the pork chops generously with salt and pepper. Pour the oil into the hot pan, let it get hot, and add the chops. Brown the meat well, about 4 minutes per side. Drain and discard the oil, then place the pan in the oven for 5 to 7 minutes. Transfer the chops to a plate or platter and keep covered and warm while you finish the sauce.

Use a paper towel to carefully wipe any excess oil out of the sauté pan. Return the pan to high heat, pour in the Sauternes reduction, and bring to a boil. Add the lemon juice and mustard, then whisk in the butter, 1 tablespoon at a time.

Put a chop on each of 4 dinner plates and divide the sauce among the servings, covering the chops. Serve immediately.

BEST OF THE BEST EXCLUSIVE

Waltuck completely remakes this bistro classic by swapping in mild, crisp-skinned snapper for the traditional poached salmon. The lean fish is a divine match for the sweet port and shallot sauce.

PAN-SEARED SNAPPER *with* LENTILS *and* RED WINE–SHALLOT SAUCE

SERVES 4

- 3 tablespoons extra-virgin olive oil
- ½ small onion, finely chopped
- 2 garlic cloves, minced
- 1¾ cups low-sodium chicken broth
- 1 cup French green lentils, picked over
- 1½ sticks (6 ounces) cold unsalted butter, cut into ½-inch dice
- 3 tablespoons red wine vinegar
- 3 tablespoons coarsely chopped flat-leaf parsley

Kosher salt and freshly ground pepper

- 2 cups dry red wine
- 5 large shallots, thinly sliced
- 2 tablespoons ruby port
- 4 thyme sprigs
- 1 bay leaf

Four 6-ounce red snapper fillets

- 2 tablespoons canola oil

1 In a medium saucepan, heat the olive oil. Add the onion and garlic and cook over moderate heat until softened, about 5 minutes. Add the chicken broth and lentils and bring to a simmer. Cover and cook over low heat until the lentils are tender and the broth has been absorbed, about 35 minutes. Remove from the heat. Stir in one-third of the butter, 2 tablespoons of the vinegar and the parsley and season with salt and pepper.

2 Meanwhile, in another medium saucepan, combine the red wine with the shallots, port, thyme sprigs, bay leaf and the remaining 1 tablespoon of red wine vinegar. Bring to a boil and cook over high heat until the liquid is reduced to 3 tablespoons, about 15 minutes; discard the thyme sprigs and bay leaf. Gradually whisk in the remaining butter over low heat, a few cubes at a time, until a glossy sauce forms. Remove from the heat and season with salt and pepper. Keep warm.

3 Season the snapper with salt and pepper. In a large nonstick skillet, heat the canola oil until shimmering. Cook the snapper skin side down over high heat until crisp, about 6 minutes. Turn the fillets and cook until white throughout, about 2 minutes longer.

4 Spoon the lentils into shallow bowls and top with the fish. Spoon the red wine–shallot sauce on top and serve.

MAKE AHEAD The cooked lentils can be refrigerated for up to 3 days. Reheat before serving.

CREDITS

ON THE COVER
"Silhouette" dining table by Brocade Home, brocadehome.com. "Herrick" lattice wallpaper by Osborne & Little, osborneandlittle.com.

A16: FOOD + WINE
Reprinted with permission from *A16: Food + Wine* by Nate Appleman and Shelley Lindgren with Kate Leahy. Copyright © 2008 by D.O.C. Restaurant Group, LLC. Photography copyright © 2008 by Ed Anderson. Ten Speed Press, Berkeley, CA. www.tenspeed.com.

ITALIAN GRILL
Four recipes and book cover image from *Italian Grill* by Mario Batali and Judith Sutton. Copyright © 2008 by Mario Batali. Photography copyright © 2008 by Beatriz da Costa. Reprinted by permission of HarperCollins Publishers.

CUISINE À LATINA
Fresh Tastes and a World of Flavors from Michy's Miami Kitchen
Copyright © 2008 by Michelle Bernstein. Photographs copyright © 2008 by John Kernick. Published by Houghton Mifflin Company.

BAKING FOR ALL OCCASIONS
A Treasury of Recipes for Everyday Celebrations
From *Baking for All Occasions*.

Text copyright © 2008 by Flo Braker. Photographs copyright © 2008 by Scott Peterson. Used with permission of Chronicle Books LLC, San Francisco. Visit ChronicleBooks.com.

HEIRLOOM COOKING WITH THE BRASS SISTERS
Recipes You Remember and Love
From *Heirloom Cooking with the Brass Sisters*. Copyright © 2008 Marilynn Brass and Sheila Brass. Photographs copyright © 2008 Andy Ryan. Published by Black Dog & Leventhal Publishers, Inc.

URBAN ITALIAN
Simple Recipes and True Stories From a Life in Food
By Andrew Carmellini and Gwen Hyman. Copyright © 2008 by Andrew Carmellini and Gwen Hyman. Photographs by Quentin Bacon. Published by Bloomsbury USA.

GIADA'S KITCHEN
New Italian Favorites
From *Giada's Kitchen: New Italian Favorites* by Giada De Laurentiis. Photographs by Tina Rupp. Copyright © 2008 by Giada De Laurentiis. Used by permission of Clarkson Potter/Publishers, an imprint of the Crown Publishing Group, a division of Random House, Inc.

BOBBY FLAY'S GRILL IT!
From Bobby Flay's Grill It! by Bobby Flay with Stephanie Banyas and Sally Jackson.

Copyright © 2008 by Boy Meets Grill, Inc. Photographs copyright © 2008 by Ben Fink. Used by permission of Random House Inc.

SCREEN DOORS AND SWEET TEA
Recipes and Tales from a Southern Cook
From *Screen Doors and Sweet Tea: Recipes and Tales from a Southern Cook* by Martha Hall Foose. Copyright © 2008 by Martha Foose. Photographs copyright © 2008 by Ben Fink. Used by permission of Random House, Inc.

MEDITERRANEAN FRESH
A Compendium of One-Plate Salad Meals and Mix-and-Match Dressings
From *Mediterranean Fresh* by Joyce Goldstein. Copyright © 2008 by Joyce Goldstein. Photographs by Andre Baranowski. Copyright © 2008 by Andre Baranowski. Used by permission of W. W. Norton & Company, Inc.

THE BOOK OF NEW ISRAELI FOOD
A Culinary Journey
From *The Book of New Israeli Food* by Janna Gur with photographs by Eilon Paz. Copyright © 2007 by Al Hashulchan Gastronomic Media Ltd. All rights reserved. Published in the United States by Schocken Books, a division of Random House, Inc.

660 CURRIES

From *660 Curries* by Raghavan Iyer. Copyright © 2008 by Raghavan Iyer. Food photography by Ben Fink. Published by Workman Publishing Company, Inc.

OLIVES AND ORANGES

Recipes and Flavor Secrets from Italy, Spain, Cyprus and Beyond

By Sara Jenkins and Mindy Fox. Text copyright © 2008 by Sara Jenkins and Mindy Fox. Photographs copyright © 2008 by Alan Richardson. Published by Houghton Mifflin Company.

BAKED

New Frontiers in Baking

By Matt Lewis and Renato Poliafito. Text copyright © 2008 by Matt Lewis and Renato Poliafito. Photographs copyright © 2008 by Tina Rupp. Published in 2008 by Stewart, Tabori & Chang, an imprint of Harry N. Abrams, Inc.

BIG NIGHT IN

More Than 100 Wonderful Recipes for Feeding Family and Friends Italian-Style

From *Big Night In.* Text copyright © 2008 by Domenica Marchetti. Photographs copyright © 2008 by Susie Cushner. Used with permission of Chronicle Books LLC, San Francisco. Visit ChronicleBooks.com.

THE ART AND SOUL OF BAKING

From *The Art and Soul of Baking* by Sur la Table with Cindy Mushet. © 2008 by Sur La Table, Inc. Photographs by Maren Caruso. Published by Andrews McMeel Publishing, LLC.

SECRETS OF THE RED LANTERN

Stories and Vietnamese Recipes from the Heart

First published in 2007 by Murdoch Books. Text copyright © 2007 by Pauline Nguyen. Recipes © 2007 by Luke Nguyen and Mark Jensen. Design and photography copyright © 2007 by Murdoch Books Pty Limited. This edition published in 2008 by Andrews McMeel Publishing, LLC.

SWEET!

From Agave to Turbinado, Home Baking with Every Kind of Natural Sugar and Sweetener

From *Sweet!* by Mani Niall. Copyright © 2008 by Mani Niall. Photographs copyright © 2008 by Sheri Giblin. Reprinted by permission of Da Capo/Marlowe & Co., a member of Perseus Books Group.

THE BEST CASSEROLE COOKBOOK EVER

With More Than 500 Recipes!

From *The Best Casserole Cookbook Ever.* Text copyright © 2008 by Beatrice Ojakangas. Photographs copyright © 2008 by Susie Cushner. Used with permission of Chronicle Books LLC, San Francisco. Visit ChronicleBooks.com.

THE COMPLETE ROBUCHON

From *The Complete Robuchon* by Joël Robuchon. Translated from the French by Robin H. R. Bellinger. Translation copyright © 2008 by Alfred A. Knopf, a division of Random House, Inc.

ARTHUR SCHWARTZ'S JEWISH HOME COOKING

Yiddish Recipes Revisited

Reprinted with permission from *Arthur Schwartz's Jewish Home Cooking* by Arthur Schwartz. Copyright © 2008 by Arthur Schwartz. Photography copyright © 2008 by Ben Fink. Ten Speed Press, Berkeley, CA. www.tenspeed.com.

FRANK STITT'S BOTTEGA FAVORITA

A Southern Chef's Love Affair with Italian Food

Excerpted from *Bottega Favorita.* Copyright © 2008 by Frank Stitt. Used by permission of Artisan, a division of Workman Publishing Co., Inc., New York. All rights reserved. Photographs © 2008 by Christopher Hirsheimer.

OSTERIA

Hearty Italian Fare from Rick Tramonto's Kitchen

Jacket cover and recipes from *Osteria: Hearty Italian Fare from Rick Tramonto's Kitchen* by Rick Tramonto and Mary Goodbody. Photographs by Tim Turner. Copyright © 2008 by Rick Tramonto. Used by permission of Broadway Books, a division of Random House, Inc.

HOME COOKING WITH CHARLIE TROTTER

Reprinted with permission from *Home Cooking with Charlie Trotter* by Charlie Trotter. Copyright © 2000, 2008 by Charlie Trotter. Photography copyright © 2008 by Kipling Swehla. Ten Speed Press, Berkeley, CA. www.tenspeed.com.

CHANTERELLE

The Story and Recipes of a Restaurant Classic

From *Chanterelle* by David Waltuck and Andrew Friedman. Text © 2008 by David Waltuck. Photography © 2008 by Maria Robledo. Published by The Taunton Press.

INDEX

Page numbers in **bold** indicate photographs.

Page numbers in **bold** indicate photographs.

Page numbers in **bold** indicate photographs.

Page numbers in **bold** indicate photographs.

FOOD&WINE
BOOKS

More books from
FOOD & WINE

Annual Cookbook 2009
Over 700 recipes from the world's best cooks—
from chefs like Mario Batali and Thomas Keller to
the talented staff of the F&W Test Kitchen.

Cocktails '09
More than 150 amazing drink and snack recipes
from America's most acclaimed mixologists and chefs,
plus an indispensable guide to cocktail basics and
the country's best nightspots.

Wine Guide 2009
The most up-to-date guide, with almost 1,000
recommendations and an easy-to-use food
pairing tip sheet.

Available wherever books are sold, or call 1-800-284-4145
or log on to foodandwine.com/books